Praise for
The Good News About Bad Behavior

"An engaging, conversational writer, Lewis intersperses the neurological deep-dive with fly-on-the-wall reporting on families in action and examples from her parent-training group. . . . Lewis provides a reassuring road map forward. And a little more help with the laundry won't hurt, either."

—*Seattle Times*

"Household jobs can build a child's capability, helping them practice independence and autonomy, foster connection with the family, and help them become capable adults, according to *The Good News About Bad Behavior*, an insightful new book."

—*San Francisco Chronicle*

"At a time when families are feeling pressed for time and stressed by the demands of modern living, Katherine Reynolds Lewis makes an urgent case for connection, communication, and giving children space to develop their own capability. With compelling stories and research, Lewis's book is a welcome guide through the land mines of modern parenting."

—Brigid Schulte, award-winning journalist, director of
The Better Life Lab at New America, and author of the
New York Times bestseller *Overwhelmed*

"If you hate disciplining your kids with time-outs and punishments, you're in for a treat. Instead of trying to control children, this timely book shows how you can teach them to control themselves."

—Adam Grant, *New York Times* bestselling author of *Give
and Take*, *Originals*, and *Option B* with Sheryl Sandberg

"Katherine Reynolds Lewis, armed with the latest behavioral science research and her eye-opening journalistic inquiry, introduces a new discipline model. . . . An absolute must-read for anyone raising or teaching 'difficult' children, and insightful to anyone eager to teach kids how to regulate their own behavior and ultimately thrive in society on their own."

—Julie Lythcott-Haims, *New York Times* bestselling author
of *How to Raise an Adult* and *Real American*

"Katherine Reynolds Lewis has written a smart, compassionate book for the twenty-first-century parent. Forget the carrot-and-stick approach to redirecting children's behavior. We can help our kids develop their inner motivation for behaving well—while simultaneously forging lasting family bonds—by following the wise guidance in *The Good News About Bad Behavior*."

—Daniel H. Pink, *New York Times* bestselling author of
When and *Drive*

"Katherine Lewis has written an important book that will give hope and support to mothers and fathers who want both understanding and answers. With a parent's compassion and a journalist's rigor, she offers advice from the trenches while providing a realistic roadmap towards a better family life. Blending solid science and highly readable storytelling, *The Good News About Bad Behavior* is sure to become a parent must-read."

—Judith Warner, author of *Perfect Madness* and
We've Got Issues

"A book that is both incredibly fascinating AND insanely helpful? That's what you're holding in your hands. A great book! It is both reassuring and fantastic to know that there's a way out of bad behavior, and a very rational reason for why it exists in the first place!"

—Lenore Skenazy, president of Let Grow and author of
Free-Range Kids

"The definitive book on raising children to cope with the distractions and temptations of the modern world. A must read for parents and educators looking to do things differently than in the past."

—Laura Vanderkam, author of *I Know How She Does It:
How Successful Women Make the Most of Their Time*

"*The Good News About Bad Behavior* is the book parents and teachers need in order to understand the link between empathy and genuine, human connection to positive behavioral outcomes. Lewis explains how children's lack of self-regulation and resilience is at the root of so many modern parenting dilemmas and gives practical, useful advice for how to do better for our kids. *The Good News About Bad Behavior* is an important addition to my parenting and education library."

—Jessica Lahey, *New York Times* bestselling author of
The Gift of Failure

The Good News About
Bad Behavior

The Good News About Bad Behavior

Why Kids Are Less Disciplined Than Ever—
And What to Do About It

Katherine Reynolds Lewis

PublicAffairs
New York

PublicAffairs
Hachette Book Group
1290 Avenue of the Americas, New York, NY 10104
www.publicaffairsbooks.com
@Public_Affairs

Printed in the United States of America

Originally published in hardcover and ebook by PublicAffairs in 2018
First Trade Paperback Edition: April 2019

Published by PublicAffairs, an imprint of Perseus Books, LLC, a subsidiary of Hachette Book Group, Inc. The PublicAffairs name and logo is a trademark of the Hachette Book Group.

The poem "Sacred Words from a Great-Grandfather" in Chapter 6 is reprinted by permission. © 1975 Ronald F. Ferguson.

The publisher is not responsible for websites (or their content) that are not owned by the publisher.

Print book interior design by Amy Quinn.

The Library of Congress has cataloged the hardcover edition as follows:
Names: Lewis, Katherine Reynolds, author.
Title: The good news about bad behavior : why kids are less disciplined than
    ever—and what to do about it / Katherine Reynolds Lewis.
Description: First edition. | New York : PublicAffairs, [2018] | Includes
    bibliographical references and index.
Identifiers: LCCN 2017040079 (print) | LCCN 2017047603 (ebook) | ISBN
    9781610398398 (ebook) | ISBN 9781610398381 (hardcover)
Subjects: LCSH: Discipline of children. | Parent and child. | Parenting.
Classification: LCC HQ770.4 (ebook) | LCC HQ770.4 .L49 2018 (print) | DDC
    649/.64—dc23
LC record available at https://lccn.loc.gov/2017040079

ISBNs: 978-1-61039-838-1 (hardcover), 978-1-61039-839-8 (ebook),
978-1-5417-7406-3 (paperback)

LSC-C

10 9 8 7 6 5 4 3 2 1

For Samantha, Maddie, Ava, and my love, Brian

Contents

Author's Note

THIS BOOK CONTAINS BOTH SCENES I observed and scenes that I re-created through interviews with people who were present and documentary evidence, when available. I am present in some way in the scenes I reported in person. Whenever someone's emotion is described, I interviewed that person after the fact to ask what they were feeling at the moment.

I am immensely grateful to the educators, parents, and children who welcomed me into their classrooms and homes to observe and learn. I have changed some names and identifying details.

The Good News About Bad Behavior

Part 1

The Problem

1

Introduction

CAMILA CULLEN'S EVENINGS WERE BEGINNING to feel like torture. Like an endless game of whack-a-mole.

She tried to ignore the muffled thumps as she read a book in bed. Then a door burst open. She looked up. Through the open door of her bedroom, she saw a slight figure dash out of the room across the hall and run upstairs.

Mariana. Probably headed to the attic playroom to grab some toys.

Camila checked her watch. 10:00 p.m. She sighed.

I wonder what time she will fall asleep. How many nights can she keep this up?

Mariana, age seven, and her younger brother, four-year-old Alejandro, had been "partying at bedtime," as they called it, for days. The pair seemed to be in open revolt, and Camila, forty-one, finally got tired of fighting it. She and her husband, Colin, forty-two, had tried everything they could think of to bring peace to the family's evenings. They played soft music. They lay down beside their offspring. They threatened and pleaded. Nothing worked consistently to get the children to sleep.

Testy from sleep deprivation, Camila and Colin had squabbled with each other over how to handle bedtime. Defeated, the parents decided to stop nagging, threatening, or wheedling—just for a week—to see what would happen.

Bedtime became chaos. Mariana and Alejandro would rile each other up, laughing and running around like crazy. After each late night, the mornings dragged out later and later. The family twice

3

pulled into their Washington, DC, public charter school noticeably tardy. The tired-out kids simply couldn't get out the door on time.

Camila felt hopeless. She wondered if they should put the children in separate bedrooms. Alejandro went to sleep more willingly. He was always the first to say he was tired of the party and climb into bed. But Mariana could play with toys, build structures, or just dance around the room until 11:00 p.m. some nights. It was the fall of 2015, and the school year stretched ahead of the family ominously.

With them in the same room, no sooner had Camila kissed and tucked in one child than the other popped out of bed to get water or a stuffed animal or with some other excuse.

"I'm exhausted," she told me in a phone interview. "I cannot do anything because I'm spending all my time putting them to bed."

~~~

THE CULLENS ARE TWO OF the parents you'll meet in this book, but they are far from alone. In fact, stories like theirs are so common that they have effectively redefined normal. Parents increasingly struggle with kids who can't seem to control their behavior or emotional response. Government data confirm this. A sweeping study by the National Institute of Mental Health revealed that one in two children will develop a mood or behavioral disorder or a substance addiction before age eighteen. Extensive research I present in Chapter 2 shows that this represents an actual change in children, not just a rise in diagnosis.

So if you look around and see misbehaving, undisciplined children everywhere, it's not your imagination. Children today are fundamentally different from past generations. They truly have less self-control.

Simply put, we face a crisis of self-regulation.

I hope the cutting-edge research and stories of real families in this book will transform your view of discipline—and give you examples of both what to do and what not to do. By the conclusion, you'll see how the Cullens pushed through their bedtime frustration with persistence that paid off. After they absorbed and implemented the key principles in this book, they turned bedtime into a peaceful family ritual.

This book makes the case that when adults crack down on bad behavior, they undermine the development of the very traits that children need to become self-disciplined and productive members of society. Tactics such as time-outs and rewards for behavior you want may seem to help in the short run. But I'll show how they actually hold children back by undermining their self-regulation, one of the bedrock skills for success in school, in college, in the workplace, and beyond.

It's entirely understandable that when children misbehave, adults feel an urge to squash the unwanted behavior. We should resist that impulse. It's exactly the opposite of what's needed.

Instead, pay attention. View the child's actions as a clue to a puzzle that can only be solved with the child's engaged cooperation and as an opportunity to help that child develop an important skill. It's easy to forget that just as children need practice to learn how to ride a bike, tie their shoes, and do math, they must try and fail and try again when it comes to managing their own behavior.

Can you imagine sending your child to time-out because they couldn't ride their bike all the way to the stop sign and back? Of course not. First, it simply doesn't work. It's not as though a time-out is going to improve their balance or coordination. Second, you'd be throwing away a prime opportunity to engage your child in a constructive moment, a teaching moment. When you factor in what you might call the opportunity cost of punishment, it's not just that traditional discipline really doesn't work—it moves you away from the goal.

There's another way. A growing number of parents, educators, and psychologists are finding success with research-backed models of discipline that share three common threads: connection, communication, and capability. They are restoring order to turbulent families, giving disruptive children control over themselves, and even eliminating symptoms of attention and anxiety disorders in some kids.

This book tells the stories of this nascent movement, the champions of which aren't even fully aware of the shared building blocks in their methods or of the growing body of science that supports their results. The first part, chapters 1 to 4, explains why we face a crisis of self-regulation and lays out the scientific discoveries that underpin this assertion. The second part, chapters 5 to 9, describes the three key steps shared by all the successful discipline models I've studied and takes readers inside four of these models as adults teach children to self-regulate. The conclusion, chapters 10 and 11, gives practical advice for adopting these techniques and changing old habits.

You will learn facts that may surprise you. You'll discover how social media and family schedules have contributed to children failing to launch. You'll learn that there is zero association between the time moms and dads spend with their school-age children and the kids' behavior or academic performance. You'll meet parents who achieved domestic harmony by treating their home as a learning lab, not a shrine to perfection.

By the end of the book, I hope you will respond to unwanted behavior in a child not with alarm but with eagerness. Rather than seeing misbehavior as a problem, my goal is for you to see it as an expected and totally normal part of how modern kids develop—and a chance to practice the tools I'll explain in the pages ahead.

~~~

I FIRST STARTED PUZZLING OVER the question of how contemporary kids respond to discipline when my middle child entered kindergarten in 2009.

One warm, early fall day, I volunteered for recess duty at the school. From my post near the blacktop, I saw some older boys playing wildly, sending kickballs flying around the playground and narrowly missing a group of little kindergartners at play. I warned them to take the rough play away from the younger children. They paused and looked over at me. I walked closer to repeat my instructions while making direct eye contact.

They simply ignored me. They resumed their dangerous rough play.

I live in a solidly middle-class community in a quiet, leafy Maryland suburb of Washington, DC—similar to the upstate New York area where I was raised. Back then, kids in the schoolyard would never have ignored a parent's instructions. As I compared notes with other parents, I heard similar stories in all walks of life. Children ignoring lifeguards at the neighborhood pool. New kindergarteners unable to sit still or keep their hands to themselves. Something seemed to have changed dramatically without our even realizing it. As fascinating as it is to ask why children have changed, the first thing I needed to know was: *What now? How can I get these boys to play safely?* I needed discipline strategies different from the ones my parents and teachers used.

The experience my husband and I had with our children confirmed this insight. As a child, I was a typical good girl, eager to excel in school and please adults, often found reading quietly in my bedroom. Our oldest daughter, Samantha, now twenty-five, shares a similar temperament. Our two younger kids are entirely different creatures. Natural extroverts, they burst into a room with the barely contained energy of a pair of puppy dogs. I could understand them being wiggly at mealtimes when they were two or three. But even at age eight or nine, they'd sit still at dinner for just a few minutes before jumping out of their seats to play with our dog or come to me for a hug.

My journal notes from when my youngest daughter was three and a half are full of frustration at her refusal to dress after a bath, brush her teeth, go to bed on time, or even put on her shoes to walk out the door for school. My middle child, now fourteen, has often flatly refused to attend religious school or another scheduled activity. When my similarly high-energy and headstrong husband was young, a raised hand or stern look from his mother got him back in line. Some critics argue that parents today have gone soft; the solution, they say, is to be strict and in charge. But the command-and-control method of discipline never resonated with me, and I'll show in this book why it isn't best for today's children.

When my kids' defiance first cropped up, I used time-outs, counting to three, sticker charts, and whatever methods I could find in the parenting books in a vain attempt to get them to do what I wanted. One new technique might extinguish bad behavior for a few weeks, but before long a fresh problem would crop up. At one point, I endured a stretch when every single day ended with me or a child in tears over bedtime.

As a mother, I needed a better way—something that would honor my desire to respect my kids as individuals but keep the family from descending into total chaos. As a journalist with two decades' experience gathering facts and analyzing problems, I burned to understand why so many parents were having the same difficulties. None of the responses to misbehavior I saw around me—whether squelching, "tiger" parenting, or bubble-wrapping children—seemed to reliably produce capable, confident adults. I wondered why parenting seems so much harder nowadays, even though parents of my generation devote more time and energy to our children than at any point in modern history, according to time use researchers.

I called on my early training as a physics undergraduate at Harvard to examine, with a critical eye, hundreds of research studies on what the latest science could tell us about this broad societal problem. I started interviewing parents and educators about what seemed to work. Then, in July 2015, *Mother Jones* magazine published my first round of reporting about new discipline techniques. Within days of appearing on MotherJones.com, the article became the site's most-read story ever, with more than 4 million views, 790,000 Facebook shares, 6,000 tweets, and 980 comments.

To my shock, I seemed to have struck a raw cultural nerve. I realized that millions of people were facing the same fears, confronting the same problems, and also looking for solutions. Parents and teachers around the world told me that the piece changed their approach with children. It made its way into conference sessions and university curricula and attracted interest in Sweden and Germany.

Galvanized by this response, I embarked on a cross-country quest, shadowing families and classroom teachers in ten different states. I visited homes in Vermont where children were cheerfully taking responsibility for household chores. In Maine, I observed a revolutionary new model for rehabilitating the most troubled kids in homes, schools, psychiatric wards, and even youth prisons that reduced discipline problems by 70 percent or more. I learned about brain function from leading neuroscientists and agreed to let them test my connection to my daughter with a magnetic resonance imaging (MRI) machine. I watched Santa Fe meditation teachers offer mindfulness tools to anxious children. I traveled to inner-city classrooms in Baltimore and Columbus where the rowdiest children quieted the instant they heard a harmonica.

I sought out the real-life stories behind the rising rates of youth anxiety, depression, behavioral disorders, and substance abuse. I looked for experts to challenge my growing conviction that kids today are simply unable to manage their behavior, thoughts, or emotions the way they could in generations past. Traveling everywhere from Texas and Wisconsin to Massachusetts, I spoke with hundreds of parents, educators, psychologists, and other professionals who care about kids to learn what helps children thrive. I took parenting education classes and tested their recommendations on my own children, eventually becoming a certified parent educator.

As I interviewed parent after parent who only wanted the very best for their children, the most common question I heard was, "How do we get the kids to do what we want?" It took five years of research for me to understand that, somewhat tragically, we all are asking the wrong question. The right question is, "Why *can't* the kids do what we want?"

The following chapter explains why.

2

An Epidemic of Misbehavior

ON A CHILLY WINTER DAY in 2003, two Russian psychologists, Elena Smirnova and Olga Gudareva, opened the doors to a Moscow kindergarten. They greeted the teachers and walked to the play area of the building. Then they began work on a simple experiment. They pulled one child aside and told them to stand perfectly still, timing how long they could maintain the pose. Next, they asked them to play a role—to pretend to be a sentry guarding a palace—and timed the child again.

The study replicated a famous experiment from 1948 in which the Russian psychologist Z. V. Manuilenko demonstrated that children can control themselves better when they're playing pretend. Over many months, Smirnova and Gudareva repeated the process with all the children and also observed the kids' play unfolding naturally. Back at their lab, they crunched the numbers, breaking down the data according to age, from four to seven years old. They discovered that they had succeeded in replicating the results of their predecessor. In each age group, the average length of time children could keep the pose increased when they were standing still as part of a game.

But their second finding was more interesting: the children they observed were less mature than the ones in the 1948 study—or, at least, their play habits were. For example, only a few of the kids were assigning specific roles and interacting with their classmates in an imaginary scenario—behaviors that Manuilenko had observed as common six decades earlier. "Contemporary preschoolers mostly demonstrated an immature ability to pretend play," Smirnova told me in an email interview. She knows about play. She's director of Moscow State University's Toy and Game Center and the author of twenty books, including a textbook on child psychology.

And the third finding of the research stopped Smirnova in her tracks. She found a dramatic drop in self-control from fifty-five years earlier. While pretending to be sentries, the modern four- to five-year-olds could hold the pose for only one-third of the time their counterparts did in 1948. The six- to seven-year-old group could stand still for three minutes on average, compared with twelve minutes for the children observed in the 1940s.

That means that first- and second-graders of the early Cold War era could stay still four times as long as modern kids.

It may seem trivial to be concerned about child's play. Aren't there more pressing dangers confronting modern children?

But play isn't minor at all. For decades, child development researchers have amassed evidence that play is a crucial building block in children's growth, helping them develop abstract thought, self-control, social cooperation, and other essential skills. For example, kids begin to move beyond a concrete mind-set when they play pretend. When a child holds up a forked stick and declares, pretending it's a gun, "Bang bang! You're dead!" that's abstract thought.

Games also help kids develop self-regulation. Both the inherent fun and the social pressure to keep a game going give children strong incentives to control their actions. If a child pushes and shoves, their peers may refuse to play with them again, or they may hit back. This reaction gives the disruptive child a powerful reason to override the urge to lash out—stronger motivation than if an adult intervened. By practicing self-control in play, they gain greater impulse control in other areas of life.

These are the reasons that the changes Smirnova observed in how kindergarten kids were playing in 2003 caused her deep concern. You may wonder whether these developments represented a side effect of communism, or perhaps a sign of the unraveling Soviet society. Yet in the United States as well, researchers have documented an erosion in children's ability to self-regulate.

Jean Twenge first grew interested in whether we're better off emotionally than previous generations during her graduate studies at the University of Michigan in the 1990s. A tomboy as a child, she'd started out researching gender roles, which were (and still are) changing dramatically. She became fascinated by mental illness in women. One day she was in Professor Susan Nolen-Hoeksema's office discussing her quest for a dissertation topic. Nolen-Hoeksema suggested looking at change in depression over time.

"I have this memory of her pulling these articles out of her drawer, saying, 'There's all this good evidence on depression going up,'" recalled Twenge, who decided to focus her thesis on anxiety and neuroticism. "And sure enough, that's what I found." She published a paper showing that college students and children in 1993 reported substantially more anxiety and neuroticism than the same groups in 1952.

But wait. Couldn't it be that modern doctors are just more aware of mental health and better able to screen and diagnose for anxiety and depression?

Twenge had to verify that her results were real. To do this, she compared answers to the questions that related to impulsivity, depression, anxiety, and attention problems on four psychological surveys given to a total of 6.9 million high school and college-aged Americans in the 1980s, and to the same age group again two decades later. Since she was looking at symptoms, not the prevalence of disorders, her results couldn't be skewed by different diagnostic practices or better awareness.

The results troubled her: there had been dramatic increases in depressive symptoms and distractibility over the past twenty years. For example, in one study she found that three times as many teens had trouble sleeping and thinking clearly in the period 2012–2014 as compared to 1982–1984. She also found a steady increase in college students' rebelliousness. Now a psychology professor at San Diego State University, Twenge continues to rack up evidence that something has changed dramatically in our culture and is making young people today significantly more anxious, depressed, neurotic, and narcissistic than their counterparts three or four decades earlier.

Why is this societal shift happening? It's impossible to know for sure, but Twenge shared some well-supported theories, notably in her book *iGen*.

"We can't ever prove that one thing causes it, or anything causes it. You can't randomly assign people to grow up in different generations," she said. "We know that focusing on money, fame, and image is correlated with anxiety and depression."

Mass media, reality television, and celebrity culture became more pervasive over the same time period in which she found depression and anxiety rising. These cultural influences all drive young people to focus externally when figuring out their goals and desires, instead of looking inside themselves to ask: *Who am I? What fills me with passion? What feeds my curiosity and desire to learn?* People who focus externally—who are "extrinsically motivated," in psychology lingo—tend to have lower levels of happiness and life satisfaction. It's better to be intrinsically motivated, to follow your own internal drives and interests.

More recently, the advent of social media is a likely culprit behind rising mental illness, as studies emerge connecting personal electronics use to social disconnection and blunted empathy. One experiment found that when preteens participated in an outdoor education program without access to screens for just five days, they scored higher on emotional intelligence. Multiple studies have found that the more time people spend on Facebook, Instagram, and the like, the more likely they are to feel depressed.

~~~

CELIA DURRANT, FORTY-SEVEN, SEEMED ALL blond curls and Southern drawl as she described her befuddlement with her teen daughters' peer group and social media use. She has observed the full spectrum of online adolescence in the upscale Dallas suburb where she lives with her children Kaya, sixteen, Alex, fourteen, and Olivia, twelve, and her husband, Bobby Ahern. His children, London, fourteen, Violet, twelve, and Edison, ten, divide their time between Dallas and their mother's home in Houston. I followed Durrant home from work on a sunny spring day, and we walked together up the driveway to her five-bedroom Craftsman home, set in a lush landscape of trees, bushes, and a private pool.

"The two older girls are quite popular, and I think that adds to anxiety, that they are scared to death they are missing out on something if they don't have the phone with them," Durrant said, noting that both Kaya and London see therapists for anxiety. "I'm a very laid-back mom. I'm pretty open. All of our kids just do their stuff. I don't ever have to get on them about homework. It's not an environment of stress. I truly believe it has to do with this social media, never unplugging, the stress of the social part of it."

Over a recent spring break, her girls noticed "snaps" coming daily from the accounts of their friends who were traveling in Europe—but the snaps weren't photos of European scenes. In an act of adolescent friendship peculiar to the social media age, the traveling teens had given their friends their Snapchat logins and asked them to blast out a picture each day to all their contacts so that they wouldn't lose their Snapchat streaks while on vacation. Snapchat creates a "streak" when two friends have sent each other snaps for at least three consecutive days.

Durrant introduced me to Kaya, Olivia, London, and London's friend Dvora, who was visiting Dallas for a weekend sleepover. Three poodle-mix dogs barked excitedly at our feet. Durrant pointed out the family chickens through the glass door, all named after famous women: Marilyn, Rosie, and Eleanor. A fourth chicken, Beyoncé, had recently died. The older girls and I walked to the kitchen, taking seats around a heavy wooden table with ten chairs.

Looking at their Snapchat accounts, I saw long columns of names, many labeled with a number next to a flame emoji. The number tells how many days in a row the account holder and the listed person have exchanged snaps.

"If you have a streak with someone, even someone you barely know at your school, you have to open it and close it every day. They may have a hundred on there that they have to open and close," Durrant said. "It's like a job."

The girls didn't seem burdened by the work. Kaya showed me the screen on Snapchat displaying her friends' "stories," a collection of recent videos and photos they had posted. The screen was divided between updated stories that she hadn't viewed yet and stories she'd already seen. Kaya selected about a dozen names.

"Basically, you can tap all these and that means you're going to watch them consecutively. It plays them, you tap until you go through them," she said. As the updates began to play, she tapped them quickly, forcing each one to advance before the preset time of five seconds— too fast to look at any of the images.

"I don't like looking at these people because I don't care about them. I need to unfollow these people," she said. "Basically, you just tap and you can look at them or, like me, just don't."

I watched the blur of faces and settings. Then a flash of skin. "Was that a topless photo?" I asked.

"She's a fitness guru, and she's always talking about her fitness routine," Kaya said. She pulled up the account to show me a trim young woman in a sports bra and leggings, reclining on a lounge chair. "She's really annoying. She's always boasting about her body."

"Why don't you drop her?" Durrant asked.

"I need to unfriend her, but I keep forgetting," said Kaya, explaining that perhaps 40 percent of her Snapchat friends are people she follows but doesn't know, either celebrities like Kim Kardashian or social media celebs like this woman.

I turned to London's phone. The screen was slightly cracked. She began tapping through a similar row of names, opening snaps from her friends as quickly as a telegraph operator. "I am too lazy to answer people, so I'll click on all of them and open all of them," she explained.

But then a photo of a boy and girl kissing caught her eye. She quickly switched to the camera, snapped a selfie, and typed a caption over the image: "Awee cute couple."

Then she backspaced. Created a new caption: "Awee y'all are cute." Sent.

Why had she paused the onslaught of snaps? It was a personal snap the boy sent just to her, she explained. He knew she was friends with the girl and wanted her to see their joint selfie.

The conversation switched to Instagram. London spends more time on "Insta," as they call the social network, scrolling through profiles or watching food videos. Kaya likes the cute animal videos. They both use the "explore" feature to discover accounts that are similar to the ones they already follow.

"It's such a waste of time, but I like watching these food videos," London said. "It's like eating it, but not. It's like, insane."

I asked about the rules associated with each social media platform. On Instagram, they post once a week or even less often, and only when they "look pretty"—they've put on makeup and fixed their hair for going out. The day I visited, Kaya and London wore T-shirts and shorts with their faces scrubbed clean. Kaya's hair hung in waves past her shoulders, still damp from a post-school shower.

When we had spoken by phone before my visit, they explained that many kids create "Finsta" accounts. That's teenage shorthand for Fake Instagram, which is a second account that parents don't know about. Teens post sexier images or ask about parties and drugs on Finsta accounts.

London's thumbs worked her phone sideways, up and down, faster than I could follow. She reminded me of a blackjack dealer. I asked whether social media influenced their self-images.

"I definitely think when you follow a bunch of famous people, you see their pictures and you compare yourself to them," Kaya said. "You see it all the time, it's constantly in your face. In reality, only 10 percent of the world looks like that, but it doesn't seem like it when it's always in your face."

"I have bad body issues because of Instagram," London said. "You think you look pretty, and then you see a photo and you're like, 'Nope.'"

"Why do you keep looking?" Durrant asked.

"You're always going to see it," said Kaya, her voice rising in pitch. "Why are you interrupting?"

"I'm sorry, I'm just interested."

"It's not like a choice. It's there, always. You don't even follow them, you're always going to see them," Kaya said.

"You're always going to see them, it doesn't matter," London agreed.

Olivia appeared in the doorway. Flat-ironed hair. Face fully made up. A lacey blue blouse over white pedal pushers. She was waiting for a ride to her friend's birthday party. In the meantime, she plopped down at the table, cuddling the dog. She listened intently to the older girls.

The discussion picked up pace. The four girls switched off speaking and listening as quickly as they were flipping through their phones. My gaze moved from one girl to the next like the camera in a Quentin Tarantino movie.

People in Olivia's grade (seventh) send nudes via Snapchat. A sixteen-year-old boy in the community is currently being prosecuted for child pornography because he recorded friends having sex and shared the video. Kaya knows a guy who had to switch schools because of sexting. London knows a girl who sent nude photos to a guy and his mom saw them. Dvora knows a girl who sent nudes over iMessage and the boy's mom saw them. The mom forced him to break up with the girl.

Guys, not girls, they said, ask for nudes. Guys may randomly send nudes, something even Olivia agreed happens. When a girl sends nudes without being asked, that's just desperate and dumb, the girls said. They expressed shock at the stupidity of the kids in these stories, or sympathy. They would never send nudes themselves, they said.

"There are weird things going on. Things have been changing quickly," London said. "When we were in sixth grade, we never did that stuff. But when we were in seventh grade, the sixth-graders were crazy bad."

"In high school, since everyone does it, sending nudes, it's never really talked about. It's never talked about unless a girl sends it to a guy and they're not even dating," Kaya said. "The guys have gotten smarter about sending them around because they know the consequences."

"That is not true in Houston. The guys have gotten worse. There are so many group chats of guys that literally all they do is send nudes," London said. "The guys are so pushy. One of my friends, the only reason she sent nudes is he kept asking her over and over. She was young, so she just—it was too much."

When one girl had the floor, the others took the opportunity to peek at their phones. Dvora stuck her tongue out one inch to snap a coy selfie for posting. The conversation turned for a while to the behavior of boys in Dallas versus Houston, and then I asked how their use of social media had evolved over time.

"As a teenage girl, I think everyone uses it to post cute pictures of themselves, in high school for sure. It's definitely changed from sixth grade, when it was pretty innocent," Kaya said. "You think: *That's cute, I'm going to share that with everyone so they can see it and validate it.*"

London shared the thought process behind what to post on Instagram: making sure the photo is high-quality, the setting looks good, and the caption is clever, funny, or even just straightforward. "I want to get as many likes as possible, so I'm not going to post just random things. I want my feed to look good," she said.

The girls explained the unwritten rules. No random photos. Selfies only—no flowers or scenery. You can post a bikini picture, but only from the front, not from behind. (None of them posted bikini shots, though.) No weird or long captions. Don't post a picture with a guy who isn't your boyfriend, or people will think it's an announcement of coupledom. Stay positive. If you decline an invitation with a lie, don't subsequently post something on social media that shows you're doing something other than what you said. Use Twitter to wish friends a happy birthday.

For boys—"guys"—there are only three types of posts, London said. "A picture with their friends chilling, big group photos. Guys post a lot of group photos. Or one of them holding a fish. We live in the South; that's the only type of guy around. Or them with their family. A guy wouldn't post a solo photo of themselves."

Social media morphs from an innocent curiosity in middle school to a tool for older teenagers to define themselves. "When you're younger, you use it because you're surrounded by it constantly. You're wondering about it. As you grow older, it's your page, you're trying to show what you're about. In high school, you compare yourself a lot, you're constantly looking at other people's posts. At first, it's fun, and then it turns into a competition almost. That's a big part of it," Kaya said. "I definitely think it causes anxiety for a lot of people, and I'm sure depression too, when you're always looking at models on there. I definitely think they're related."

~~~

RESEARCH SUPPORTS KAYA'S SUSPICION. ONE experiment led by the University of Michigan psychologist Ethan Kross found that college students were more likely to feel lonely, worried, or sad the more often they used social media. In addition, the heaviest social media users felt less overall satisfaction with their lives.

Psychologists believe that's because of a phenomenon called "social comparison." All of us instinctively compare ourselves to those around us, in order to gauge our well-being. Social media not only gives us a bigger pool of people with whom to compare but also presents a distorted picture. People most often put up posts that show themselves in a positive light—looking attractive, on vacation, happy—so it's natural to feel inferior by contrast. And because children's brains are still developing, social comparison has a greater impact on them than on adults. Follow-up research suggests that passive social media use—idly scrolling through a feed—harms mental health more than active use—going onto Facebook with a plan to post something or connect with a specific person.

Kross's team wanted to test whether they might simply be observing a correlation between heavy social media use and those people who were already depressed. A statistical analysis showed that, indeed, people who felt lonely were more likely to use social media. However, when the researchers controlled for the loneliness variable, they found that social media use predicted less life satisfaction, even taking into account that lonely people turn to social networks in search of connection.

The growth of social media adds a new dimension to the question of how technology use shapes young brains. Researchers began work in this area by looking at the impact of television and video games amid ominous links to attention deficit hyperactivity disorder (ADHD), which has doubled since the 1970s.

In 1998, the pediatrician Dimitri Christakis took paternity leave with his two-month-old. He noticed that his son became mesmerized by the flashing screen whenever the television was on. Christakis knew that his son's brain wasn't developed enough to decipher the language and meaning of TV programs. This experience sparked his two-decade-long interest in the impact of technology on early learning, attention span, and risk-taking. He's now director of the Center for Child Health, Behavior, and Development at Seattle Children's Research Institute.

It's undeniable that kids today spend more time on screens. In 1970, children were four years old before they regularly started watching TV. Nowadays, the average age is four months. By age five, the typical kid is on a screen for four and a half hours a day, which is 40 percent of their waking hours.

Kids' time is more structured and sedentary than ten or twenty years ago, both inside and outside school. They spend more time sitting behind desks and less time being physically active. The in-school hours children spend in physical education or at recess have plummeted even as the academic demands have climbed. When children are bored, they're now more likely to pick up a television remote or iPad than to play outside. The explosion of media and portable electronics increases distractibility and anxiety for both parents and children. Screen use raises two concerns: a device's impact on a child's development, and its replacement of healthier activities, like exploratory play or interaction with a caregiver, peer, or sibling.

Scientists have drawn a direct line between children spending more hours in front of television and their growing attention problems, like ADHD. Christakis led a team that looked at more than

1,200 children's habits, as reported to the National Longitudinal Survey of Youth (NLSY). For every weekly hour of TV children watched before age three, they were 10 percent more likely to develop an attention problem by age seven, controlling for race, gender, mother's education, and similar factors. On the other hand, when parents stimulated kids' brains by doing things like reading to them, singing, and taking them to museums, each hour a week reduced the odds of the children developing attention problems by 30 percent, according to Christakis. (With these studies, as with Kross's research, researchers can't prove causality through prospective experiments, so they use statistical analyses to isolate the variables of interest.)

Researchers have found similar results when looking at all electronic media. Kids exposed to more screen time tend to have more emotional difficulties, poorer family functioning, and attention problems. One caveat: young people who feel isolated in their real-life communities often find valuable social support via the Internet. For tweens or teens beginning to explore an LGBTQ+ identity, for example, social media can be a healthy lifeline.

As Christakis continued his research, he developed a hunch that prolonged exposure to a rapidly changing screen during that critical early stage of brain growth would precondition children's minds to expect high levels of stimulation, leading to inattention later on when real life turned out to be more boring.

To test this, he developed television for mice.

His lab overstimulated baby mice with sounds from animated shows and flashing lights, exposing them to this stimulation six hours a day for their entire childhood. Then the researchers subjected the mice to several well-established tests of normal behavior to see how they differed from typical mice. The previous use of the tests in rodent studies examining the impact of enriched environments on development gave the scientists a historical basis for comparison.

First was the open field test. By nature, mice stick to the edge of a space, such as a grassy field, in order to avoid being spotted and eaten by predators. They do sometimes forage for food toward the center of the space, but only rarely. Mice show this predilection in a laboratory box by running around the edges and making few forays into the center. When Christakis put the overstimulated mice in a box, they ran around like crazy, entering the center more often and spending more time there than normal mice. This is risk-taking behavior in a mouse. In humans, it might look like driving recklessly or testing limits with drugs and sex.

Next, Christakis presented the mice with an unfamiliar object and a familiar one, a common test of working memory and learning that researchers also use in primates and human babies. Giving new objects more attention stems from the mammalian instinct to forage for food. Once mice, chimps, or infants have sussed out an object, they'll spend less time on it in the future—a sign to scientists that they've learned about it.

Typical mice spent 75 percent of their time exploring the new object. But the overstimulated mice spent the same amount of time on each object, either because they couldn't distinguish familiar from unfamiliar or because they didn't care. Either the mice had poor short-term memory or they couldn't learn.

A final test took mice through a complex maze and found that the overstimulated mice actually were faster initially at finding the exit, because they explored more fearlessly, but then they failed to remember the escape route. By the fourth day of the maze, the typical mice were finding the path more quickly and easily.

In sum: extreme electronics exposure led to risk-taking, hyperactive mice with poor learning abilities. Of course, it's not guaranteed that human brains work just like mouse brains. But still, these findings don't seem to be good news for the future of our screen-loving species.

"Our brains evolved over millennia to process things that happened in real time. Until the advent of media, everything by definition happened in real time, because we didn't have the capacity," Christakis explained in an interview. "We've shown in previous studies that block play promotes language development and attention. . . . [Children are] cognitively more engaged in that activity than they are in passively viewing a video."

One way to understand the impact of screens on development is through a phenomenon known as "joint attention." "A person will direct a child's attention to something and they will turn, look at what they're pointing out, and instinctively turn to the caregiver, asking, essentially, 'What is this?'" Christakis said. "This happens hundreds of times a day. It's incredibly important to the children's development and the architecture of the brain."

Some children's brains are wired differently. Kids with autism, for instance, early on show weakness in their ability to engage in joint attention. They're less likely to make eye contact, to follow a caregiver's gaze, and therefore to begin to understand language and another person's intentions. Even before kids receive an official diagnosis of autism, researchers like Christakis can spot the signs by evaluating their capacity for joint attention.

"We know that screens, because of the way they command children's attention, diminish opportunities for joint attention," he said. Children ages eight to eighteen use electronics an average of seven and a half hours a day, according to a Kaiser Family Foundation study. Except for sleeping, that's more time than we give to any other activity.

~~~

MY INTERVIEWS WITH SMIRNOVA, TWENGE, and Cristakis alarmed me. I wondered if it's possible to reverse these seemingly profound changes to the minds of children. Then a visit with a researcher at the National Institute of Mental Health (NIMH) convinced me that children have fundamentally changed but that we must forge ahead, because there is no turning back.

A team led by NIMH's Kathleen Merikangas became the first to analyze a nationally representative sample of teenagers for mental illness. As I mentioned in the previous chapter, the findings were shocking: one in two children will develop a mood or behavioral disorder or a substance addiction by age eighteen. This point is worth underscoring: every other child in your kid's preschool classroom will have something going on before high school graduation.

This stunning statistic holds the potential to be incredibly discouraging.

But I refuse to feel despair. I believe that this number—one in two—can ultimately free us all. There's no need for parents to feel ashamed or isolated by a child's diagnosis—they are not alone. Indeed, any parents struggling with kids' misbehavior have company, diagnosis or not.

Of those children with a diagnosis, Merikangas's team found that nearly 40 percent experienced two or more disorders. Anxiety starts appearing first, by age six for half of kids who will be diagnosed, then behavioral disorders by age eleven, followed by mood disorders around thirteen and substance use by age fifteen. These figures refer to the median age for each diagnosis; half will develop these conditions later.

When you encounter a child acting out, consider whether one of these diagnoses might lie at the root of their behavior. Take a child who refuses to speak in class. Or the kid who throws a temper tantrum when it's time to get in the car for the soccer game. Their stubbornness may arise from fear and anxiety, even if they can't articulate it.

Anxiety also can lead to social disruption. Sometimes the kids who tease and bully are motivated by their own deep-seated anxiety. The kind of power plays often found in middle school may also be traced to an anxious perpetrator. For example, the girl in a clique who's pushing to exclude another girl may be driven by her own anxiety about fitting in. Nearly one-third of adolescents—32 percent—receive an anxiety diagnosis, according to the NIMH study.

Next most common are behavioral disorders, such as ADHD, which affect 19 percent of children; mood disorders (14 percent); and substance use disorders (11 percent).

All these conditions boil down to self-regulation: being able to manage your own impulses, moods, thoughts, and behavior. And anecdotal evidence suggests that even children without an official diagnosis are less likely to automatically obey adults' orders or to fall in line the way children did in previous generations. That's why it's so hard to get kids to do what you want. That's why the boys on the elementary school playground ignored my instructions.

One simple fact reinforces that it's not just better screening or diagnosis: more children are dying from suicide. Gregory Plemmons, associate professor of pediatrics at the Monroe Carell Jr. Children's Hospital at Vanderbilt University, led a team that found that the number of kids admitted to US children's hospitals owing to suicidal thoughts or self-harm had doubled from 2008 to 2015. The suicide rate doubled for children ten to fourteen years old and rose 41 percent for teens fifteen to nineteen years old, between 2006 and 2016, according to figures from the Centers for Disease Control and Prevention.

"The fastest-growing group does seem to be the youngest age group kids, the ten- to fourteen-year-olds," Plemmons told me. "It's alarming. Twenty years ago, I never saw eight- or nine-year-old kids that are having these thoughts."

What's driving these changes, aside from the rise in media use, as cited by Christakis and Twenge? Merikangas blames pressure to achieve in academics and extracurriculars. When she served as a fellow at Yale University, undergraduate students would cry on her shoulder about receiving Bs. "The kids would come to me; they didn't want to tell their parents their grades," she recalled. "There's a dramatic increase in the stress we are putting on these children from the age of three and four, when they compete to get into nursery school. There's much more competitiveness to get into university."

This isn't to say that helicopter parenting caused the crisis in self-regulation. Children are each born with a unique set of skills and challenges owing to genetics and environmental factors beyond parents' control. However, supportive, research-informed parenting can certainly help manage a disorder—and potentially ameliorate its impacts or symptoms.

Modern middle-class parents see their children as budding talents to be cultivated rather than as workers vital to the household, farm, or family business. But this perspective sends kids the subconscious message that their worth is based on their achievement in all these areas— which, by the way, are extremely difficult to master. When 15,000 kids in your county play in the soccer league, how can you ever be the best? If the click of a mouse shows you a seven-year-old piano virtuoso on YouTube, what's the use of stumbling through your scales? There will always be someone smarter, faster, and more talented, unless you're the rare true prodigy.

Seen another way, children are unemployed. So often their days are full of homework, music, sports, and extracurricular obligations, but no true responsibilities to the family or community. Nobody depends on them to care for a younger sibling, to clean the house, or to put dinner on the table. Adults think they're helping children by doing these tasks themselves, or outsourcing them. In fact, not giving them simple household chores deprives kids of the chance to build skills and be useful. Just think about how disorienting and demoralizing it is for adults to find themselves jobless—is it any surprise that children without any real responsibilities are increasingly anxious and depressed? Moreover, parents miss the opportunity to connect with kids while teaching them cleaning, laundry, cooking, bike repair, lawn work, and other necessary tasks.

This all undermines children's motivation and well-being. In psychology, self-determination theory holds that humans' ability to thrive is based on autonomy, competence, and connection to other people. But children today often have little control over their schedule and are given few opportunities to develop life skills or contribute to the smooth running of the household.

~~~

I MET JENNIFER WANG AT her home in Great Falls, Virginia, just before 5:00 p.m., when her son John usually returns home from his magnet school for the gifted and talented. He leaves the house at 8:22 a.m. every day for the hourlong bus ride, but after he comes home, "that's when his real day starts," said his mom, fifty-three.

She showed me around the French country-style mansion while we waited. It was stunning: nine bedrooms, a four-car garage, an in-law suite, and a hot tub, sauna, and pool, on an immaculately kept 1¾-acre lot. The interior resembled a tastefully decorated luxury hotel, without a stray belonging on the floors, counters, or furniture.

We were chatting outside on the back patio, overlooking the pool and gardens, when we heard noise from inside. In the kitchen, John's father, Gilbert, fifty-three, was quickly unpacking Styrofoam Chinese food containers. Jennifer joined him to get dinner on the table. Jennifer, John, and I sat down to eat at 5:15 p.m., while Gilbert retreated to his office. He works from home as a trader, so he usually does most of the after-school driving with John.

The dinner felt pressured. Jennifer was eager for John to squeeze in his required hour of piano practice before we left at 6:30 for swim practice. After just seven minutes, she asked: "Are you done?"

But John seemed in no hurry to get to the piano. He wandered to the fridge to get a cheese stick, then demanded cake. She counted out the five remaining pieces of beef in his dish and promised cake if he finished them all. He agreed.

"Okay, hurry up then," she said. It was 5:29 p.m. The clock was ticking.

John asked for cut-up strips of cheese. Jennifer bustled to the fridge and offered him a selection of sliced cheeses. He chose yellow. All the yellow ones. She cut them up.

At 5:35 p.m., John had only two more pieces of beef to eat. Somehow he managed to stretch out the rest of the dinner, including cake and an Icee Pop, until 5:52 p.m., despite his mother's repeated injunctions—thirteen by my count—to hurry.

He sat down at the piano, after minimal dawdling, and played several beautiful pieces before we hurried into the car at 6:31 p.m. Once at the pool, he swam backstroke for ninety minutes straight, only stopping when the kids ahead of him in the lane slowed his progress. Then he kickboarded for a half-hour, nearly mowing down the girl in front of him—she was five years older, but he kicked fast.

On Tuesdays, John goes straight from school to an advanced math class, then to swimming. On Thursdays he has lessons with an elite piano instructor, Barbara Wilson. Years earlier, Jennifer had wanted John to study with Barbara, but the teacher thought he was too young. She referred him to another piano studio. The previous year, John had finally aced the audition and won a spot with Barbara.

"We told him Barbara has very high standards, she only accepts the best. Then he will make that extra effort," Jennifer explained. Barbara Wilson teaches only students who commit to her daily minimum practice sessions, which they log on a time sheet. The expected practice time climbs as the children grow older. Typically, her students gain acceptance to the country's competitive music conservatories as well as the most selective liberal arts colleges.

On the weekends, John swims for four hours each day—more if there's a meet—and makes up any practice time he owes his piano teacher because of the Tuesday math class.

All told, John's weekdays run to eleven hours of activities. His weekends are crammed with practice and competition. That's a lot for a nine-year-old who weighs just over seventy pounds soaking wet.

High-achieving children like John fire up the competitive and anxious impulses in my brain. I start to worry: Should I be pushing my own kids more? What if I had introduced sports and music earlier—would they be top performers now?

John's older sister Lily played varsity tennis, excelled at painting, and graduated from an elite Northern Virginia high school as well as an Ivy League college. She just signed on with a private equity firm. "I told her, you are only rich if you spend less than you're earning," said Jennifer, who had only $300 when she came from China to the United States in 1991 for graduate school. "I try to teach her, in addition to being successful in your career, you also have to be wise."

Jennifer said that John enjoys his activities and usually completes his tasks on time. But the one thing that falls off John's schedule is playtime. There's no chance to roam the neighborhood backyards or play a pickup game of catch. "Occasionally we'll have playdates, but not a lot because his schedule is kind of busy," she said. "When he goes to swim every day, he has some friends there. He will chat with them, socialize with them, and 'do business' with them, he calls it, with the Pokémon cards."

This keeps my inner tiger mom at bay.

We know that play is important by looking at the animal kingdom. From dolphins to ravens and dogs, animals instinctively play with objects and with each other as part of their healthy development. Indeed, when not eating or sleeping, young mammals are most likely found playing.

Rats and monkeys deprived of play become more aggressive and fearful than their peers. Research with monkeys suggests that young monkeys raised without peer play opportunities can't interpret other monkeys' emotional signals and experience difficulty in social situations. By contrast, playful rats show higher levels of a protein that is key to developing neural plasticity—in other words, the ability to learn.

When it comes to young humans, play is just as important—if not more, given how complex our social interactions are. Through play, children learn how to make decisions, solve problems, and control their emotions.

"Young human beings are designed to develop through play. You can list all the aspects—physical, intellectual, emotional—play promotes all of that," said Peter Gray, professor emeritus at Boston College and the author of *Free to Learn: Why Unleashing the Instinct to Play Will Make Our Children Happier, More Self-Reliant, and Better Students for Life.* "We in our modern society have destroyed the culture of childhood. Children are more or less constantly directed, supervised, and protected by adults. They're not learning how to plan their own activities. They're not learning to negotiate with their playmates about rules, because there's always an adult there to do it for them."

Gray points to a barrage of evidence that children who have more autonomy and more unsupervised playtime develop better learning skills, more creativity, and a greater sense of responsibility for their own actions. In a 2014 paper, researchers at the University of Colorado at Boulder reported that children with more unstructured time displayed better executive function, which is the ability to control their thoughts and behavior to achieve a goal. This is an especially important finding because children with better executive function are more likely to succeed in school and career—and even to become healthier adults—according to decades of longitudinal studies.

Remarkably, executive function is a more important predictor of academic success than intelligence.

The third-graders at Ohio Avenue Elementary School in Columbus love to play "Mrs. Davies Says." They quickly copy their teacher's movements as she calls out:

"Mrs. Davies says put your hands on your head!"

"Mrs. Davies says touch your toes!"

"Mrs. Davies says hop on one leg!"

"Keep hopping."

They sigh, good-naturedly, when they miss a cue and have to sit down. Then they watch with bright eyes, enjoying their classmates' attempts to resist Mrs. Davies's trickery.

They don't realize that this simple game—a rebranded Simon Says—is helping them develop self-control. They must check their impulse to copy their teacher's visual movements until their brains process her words to determine whether she said, "Mrs. Davies says . . . " before the command. The more they practice this self-control in play, the better they get at controlling their impulses in other contexts, such as jostling in line or competing for favorite toys at recess.

"The very best prediction of how a child will do in school is whether they can sit still and get along with others," said Kathy Hirsh-Pasek, a Temple University professor and the coauthor of *Becoming Brilliant: What Science Tells Us About Raising Successful Children*. "They may look like they're playing, but really they're developing those skills."

Another simple way to develop executive function is a drum circle or rhythm game. Children must look at each other and listen to the rhythm, adjusting their own beat to stay in sync with the other players.

"All of these games share that they're asking you to regulate, to think, to stop before you act. If I can get you to think and stop before you act, I've created social regulation," Hirsh-Pasek said.

Make-believe games involve several important social skills that build children's self-control. They first must plan their play, by deciding who will be the doggy, the robber, or the teacher. Then they must control their impulses and follow the rules of whatever scenario they've devised. The patient in a game of doctor, for instance, must resist the urge to try on the stethoscope. That's the doctor's role. Finally, pretend play encourages the development of perspective-taking—the ability to see someone else's point of view—as children try on different roles. This ability is key to nurturing empathy and guarding against narcissism.

"When I look at play, I don't see what other people see," Hirsh-Pasek said. "I put on a different kind of glasses, and those lead me to a suite of skills that are very important for children's success."

Sadly, a focus on academics and testing has pushed recess and play out of the school day. From 1981 to 2003, the amount of time school-age children spent playing fell by one-third. The overload of academic work doesn't end when the school bell rings: children as young as three years old are enrolled in after-school tutoring programs like Junior Kumon and Kaplan, part of a $4 billion tutoring industry.

Many parents have a secret desire to raise superstars like John and Lily Wang, who excel at sports, music, and school and eventually will land top jobs in corporate America. But the research on play and executive function reminds me that these prodigies can't be created on demand through rigid training schedules—these are children who are naturally gifted and competitive and already inclined to excel early in life. Children develop on their own schedule, and pushing them young risks burning them out. Ultimately, I will measure the success of my own parenting, not by the medals and awards my children win, but by their character, work ethic, and independence.

~~~

WHEN CHILDREN SHUTTLE FROM PLAYDATE to soccer practice to home without much say in the daily schedule, they miss out on unstructured, kid-directed play. They rarely get to negotiate with playmates, work out problems, and control their own emotions and responses in order to stay in the game. These are all crucial skills for success in school and life, but kids are hampered from practicing them because there's always an adult watching, ready to intervene.

My own children attended full-time day care from the time they were five months old until they started kindergarten. They played with other kids in a supervised way, with a teacher always nearby to interrupt rising conflict. By the time they were in first and third grades, they were attending an organized after-school activity every day, partly as enrichment and partly as convenient child care. Around that time, I learned about some of the benefits of unstructured play.

So I decided to scale back. Soon my kids had just one or two commitments after school. On other days, they sought out their neighborhood friends, playing in each other's yards or roaming through our shared backyard woods. Many times they were gone for hours, building forts, or kicking a soccer ball around together. Occasionally a child would return early, upset over a fight with a friend. One time my daughter burst through the door complaining of a torn shirt—the neighbor boy had been too rough tackling her in soccer. She refused to play with him for several days—and I'm guessing he learned a lesson about the importance of self-control while missing his former playmate.

The self-regulation crisis isn't just an issue for middle- and upper-middle-class families. On the other end of the socioeconomic spectrum, children also face rising rates of ADHD and anxiety and other disorders associated with surviving trauma and living in an uncertain environment. Many don't even have access to a safe playground where they'd develop those important peer interaction and self-regulatory skills. In either setting, children lack opportunities for the exploratory play that develops self-control or the parent-supervised household chores that can give them a real sense of contributing to the family.

Physical trauma, such as abuse, and emotional trauma, such as living with a drug-addicted parent, make children more likely to develop anxiety, depression, and substance abuse in adulthood. Emotionally neglected children are more socially withdrawn, inattentive, and academically underachieving in their elementary school years. In a sense, the United States protects children less than any other major country—corporal punishment is legal, and the United States is the only country that hasn't ratified the United Nations' "Convention on the Rights of the Child."

Is it any wonder that there's an explosion of teen mental illness and failure to launch among adult children in their midtwenties?

Take nine-year-old Elyse David of Rumson, New Jersey. Since kindergarten, she's been on the go nonstop. The skinny, brown-haired ball of energy plays soccer, dances, takes gymnastics, acts in plays, takes singing lessons, and participates in Girl Scouts. Her weekly schedule is a checkerboard full of activities and out-of-school commitments.

By third grade, Elyse had been diagnosed with ADHD and anxiety. Her mother, Susan David, felt exhausted just trying to keep up with the tween's changing moods and perfectionism. Elyse acted as if her life were a precariously balanced stack, and if one thing went wrong—if she missed a step in dance or misplaced her soccer uniform—it would all come tumbling down.

"When she thinks something is going to be too hard, she will avoid it because she doesn't want to fail," said David, a self-employed caterer and single mom. "She's frustrated and sad a lot of the time because she feels she's letting herself and everybody down. It's hard to watch your kid be like that."

But David doesn't see much of an alternative to her daughter's packed schedule. Elyse's classmates and the other kids in the neighborhood are similarly busy with after-school pursuits, so even if Elyse had more free time, she'd have trouble finding playmates.

You can never say conclusively that a child's anxiety is caused by overscheduling or competitive parenting. Mental and behavioral illnesses develop because of a combination of genetic vulnerability and the environmental conditions the child experiences. That's one reason siblings raised in the same home can turn out so differently. But the conditions of modern middle-class life can push susceptible children over the edge into a disorder, whereas a few decades ago, they would've grown up without any problems. It's clear the pressure doesn't help.

By allowing their kids to follow their drive to play, parents may help protect them against developing the kind of anxiety that besets kids like Elyse, Kaya, and London.

Beginning in the early twentieth century, psychologists believed that phobias develop from previous traumatic experiences, perhaps even ones that are poorly remembered. They relied on Ivan Pavlov's observations of dogs becoming conditioned to associate a ringing bell with receiving food and John B. Watson's controversial experiments on a child who grew fearful of a white rat once the researchers associated the animal with a loud noise. In the mid-1990s, however, some scientists, including Richie Poulton, a New Zealand clinical psychologist, seriously challenged this conditioning hypothesis.

Poulton directs the Dunedin longitudinal study, one of the most comprehensive and long-running collections of data on individuals' physical and behavioral health over the life span. The study follows more than 1,000 people born in 1972 and 1973 in Queen Mary Maternity Centre in the Otago region in southeastern New Zealand. Scientists gather answers from individuals (or their parents) at ages three, five, seven, nine, eleven, thirteen, fifteen, eighteen, twenty-one, twenty-six, thirty-two, and thirty-eight. The study is known for its low dropout rate, compared to other longitudinal studies. Poulton and his team work to minimize the inconvenience for participants of being assessed by helping them travel to the university and giving them breaks between the sessions of questions and physiological assessments.

After several researchers found no relationship between early traumas and children's phobias through parent questionnaires, Poulton grew interested in whether he could ask the question more rigorously through the Dunedin data set. Studies that analyze people's answers given at the time they are experiencing events are typically more reliable than retrospective studies, in which researchers ask people to recall past episodes.

Poulton started digging through his databases. He began with falls, which are the most common accident for young children, whether from playground equipment, a ladder, or another structure. He looked at children who had experienced a fall between ages three and nine that was serious enough to require medical attention. Then he pulled up the list of simple fears at age eleven and again at age eighteen to see whether there was any pattern connecting the children who had a fall with those who developed a phobia about heights.

He discovered a pattern, but not the one that Pavlov and Watson would have predicted. Rather than *causing* children to become scared of heights later in life, an early fall seemed instead to have *protected* them from developing such a phobia. The children without a fear of heights were actually more likely to have experienced a fall at an earlier age.

How could this be?

He repeated the study with children who had a water phobia, looking for traumatic experiences with water earlier in life. No relationship. Then he looked at separation anxiety. Again, he found that those children who had experienced separations from their parents early in life were *less* likely to have separation anxiety at ages eleven or eighteen.

The impulse to shield children from early injuries and scares, rather than exposing them to these experiences, appears to actually contribute to their fears, anxieties, and phobias later in life. Poulton's research suggests that, within reason, we should let kids naturally experience the consequences of risky play and exploration. That's how they learn their own limits and develop confidence in themselves.

Unfortunately, over the last sixty years, children's unsupervised and outdoor playtime has fallen sharply. One report found that the area where children are allowed to roam unsupervised has shrunk by 90 percent since the 1970s. This shift arises not only from over-scheduling of academics and extracurriculars but also from parental fears that kids roaming unsupervised might be hurt or even abducted. More significantly, as women flooded into the workforce and divorce rates climbed, the model of a breadwinner father and a stay-at-home mother disintegrated. Now, in the vast majority of households raising children, every adult works for pay. There's no parent home after school when kids might be playing in the backyard or down the street. Instead, kids go to after-care or day care.

As a working mother myself, I'm not recommending a return to the 1960s model, if such a thing were even possible. But it's important to recognize the impact of these broad societal changes on our children and to compensate in the ways we can. That's why the writer Lenore Skenazy created the "free-range kids" movement to support parents in letting their children walk or bike to school, play unsupervised, and take small steps to becoming more independent. Skenazy burst into the national spotlight when a column about her nine-year-old riding the New York City subway alone came under intense criticism.

When I first started interviewing play researchers and reading up on the benefits of downtime, I got a sinking feeling in my stomach. Perhaps I'd ruined my children. After all, they'd been in day care since before they could walk, constantly under the eye of a responsible adult. No wonder they lost sweatshirts and homework sheets! How could they possibly have developed adequate executive function? They had experienced all three of the factors that researchers blame for children's loss of the ability to self-regulate: the growth of media and technology; a focus on academics and abilities instead of contribution and character; and the decline in both unstructured play and outdoor time.

Faced with the evidence of all the rising maladies and dysfunctions of our modern society, it's tempting to throw up our hands and despair. But since we can't go back in time, we must find our way forward. We must accept that the world has been transformed. We no longer live in villages where aunts and grandmothers lend a hand to new parents, or where all kids can roam from house to house safely.

Children's response to discipline has fundamentally changed—forever. We can't just give up on the tens of millions of kids who misbehave or have anxiety, ADHD, or depression. Obedience is no longer our goal. We must tackle the defining challenge of our era: teaching our children how to self-regulate.

As I learned about the dramatic increases in disorders related to a lack of self-regulation, my kids' short fuses and uncooperative behavior made more sense. I vowed to rebuild their self-control. But where to start? I needed to understand more about how the brain works, both in a developing child and in the moment when self-control is needed. Next stop: a neuroscience laboratory.

3

The Brain and Discipline

A MIDDLE-AGED MAN LAY FLAT on his back on the bed of a magnetic resonance imaging (MRI) machine. He waited to hear his mother's critical comments so scientists could study his brain's reaction.

His gray socks pointed up toward the ceiling, and a white blanket covered his body from ankle to neck. His head poked inside a giant white cylinder containing the MRI's high-powered magnet—a combination of four coiled wires that together would create a web of magnetic fields as a current passed through the wire. At eight and a half feet, the chunky plastic body of the MRI took up nearly one-third of the room.

Three scientists bustled around the man with cords, explaining what they were doing as they hooked up equipment. The man's gaze followed them. His head rested in a plastic cage with a camera at eye level. A wire running through the cage would help form a magnetic field around his head when the machine was turned on. The MRI imaging technologist would control which wires received a current, depending on the angle required to capture the desired image.

Before entering the room, the scientists used a wand like the ones used in airport security to identify any metal on their bodies or the study participant's body. The machine generates a 3 Tesla magnetic field, about sixty times as strong as a refrigerator magnet, so any overlooked metallic object could become a dangerous projectile near the MRI. Even something as small as a forgotten hairpin could be ripped out and sent flying into the magnet.

I watched this scene from the room next door, looking through a giant observation window while seated at a row of tables that held computer monitors, phones, a tangle of cords, and a few ancient-looking pieces of equipment. Since starting the research that became this book, I'd wanted to observe an fMRI (functional MRI) experiment. It was finally about to happen, in the basement of the New York State Psychiatric Institute at Columbia University Medical Center.

The experiment, a collaboration between the New School for Social Research professor Wendy D'Andrea and the University of Pittsburgh, aimed to examine the impact of criticism on the brains of people with a history of depression, mood disorders, borderline personality, anxiety, or trauma. The goal was to understand how people with mental illness disassociate in the moment of stress, what helps them self-regulate, and also how and why they often fail to connect their symptoms with trauma in their past. This study provided me with a glimpse of affective neuroscience at work—a field devoted to understanding how our emotions, behavior, motivations, and relationships connect to the physical structures of our brain.

Nadia Nieves, manager of the New School's Trauma and Affective Psychophysiology Lab, had already spent three days with the study participant, putting him through a barrage of psychological tasks and questionnaires. He had experienced deep depression for many years but was a candidate for the experiment because he was presently stable.

Nieves asked him to think of an important person in his life, such as his mother, and then to imagine that he overheard her making critical comments about him. She asked him to write down the words she used. Those phrases would be what psychologists call "scripts," because they unfold the same way every time, like lines in a play. They're at the center of an entire body of research into criticism and self-regulation.

The scientists walked out of the MRI room and took seats beside me. Nieves adjusted some dials on the equipment in front of her, and I heard the burst of a female voice.

"He's a perfectionist and expects perfection from those working—"

The sound cut off. Nieves had accidentally played the scripts out loud.

She typed some words on her screen to see if the study participant could read them. She adjusted the sound levels and checked the monitors that showed his heartbeat and breath patterns, key signs of the body's response to stress and emotions. Then she and the technologist, Natacha Gordon, started calibrating the scanner.

It was on.

I heard a loud mechanical whirring noise and then three buzzes, a rhythm that repeated. Then a long, higher-pitched beep. Another beep. It was like a 1960s vision of a starship control room.

On the other side of my chair, Gordon pulled up a cross-sectional image of the man's brain. It looked sort of like an X-ray, but with more detail and different structures in white. Three more images appeared, each at a different angle. An even louder series of beeps began.

"It's too loud," the participant said. His voice came through a speaker on the desk in front of Nieves. She looked over at Gordon.

The truth is that it's noisy inside a magnetic resonance imaging scanner. You hear a constant loud whirr and occasional knocking of parts as the machine shifts position. The side of the scanner is just inches from your face. It would be claustrophobic even if you hadn't been instructed to stay perfectly still to avoid blurring the image. Many study participants couldn't tolerate the experience.

"I don't think we can do anything about the sound of the scanner," Gordon told Nieves. "We can try to give him more padding, but I mean, you saw the padding he got."

"Do you want me to stop the scan?" Nieves asked the participant through a thin microphone poking out from the equipment in front of her.

"Yeah, just for now."

Gordon clicked on her keyboard. The room quieted. I crossed my fingers.

"Hey, are you okay?" Nieves asked through the microphone.

"Yeah, I'll be fine. I just want to get this over with."

"If the scanner is too loud, though, it's going to be like that for the rest of the time," she told him.

"Okay, that's fine, let's just do it."

Gordon clicked. The loud beeping—the sound the scanner made when it was collecting data—resumed. After the scan ended, the participant told me that the calibration experience was the hardest—just lying still surrounded by noise. He had to use reframing techniques that Nieves taught him. That helped manage the stress. He imagined he was lying in his bed at home, watching TV. Once the tasks started, focusing on completing them helped him feel less uncomfortable.

Over the next ninety minutes, Gordon and Nieves guided him through a series of exercises, such as asking whether certain words were relevant to him and telling him to guess heads or tails on a coin flip. He responded verbally or through a plastic device in his hand and a computer mouse taped to his leg. He rated his mood before and after each set of tasks.

Then Nieves played the negative comments, which her lab calls Hooleys, after the scientist who devised the method. The participant's toes wiggled a bit, but he didn't seem overly disturbed by hearing his mother's criticism flowing out of a speaker while scientists watched his brain response. I felt surprise at how mundane the scene looked, knowing what must have been roiling inside his head.

~~~

NEUROSCIENTISTS HAVE BEEN STUDYING THE inner workings of the brain for decades. They've figured out the general purpose of each physical structure. The prefrontal cortex governs higher-order tasks like thinking, emotion regulation, planning, and problem-solving. The amygdala, sometimes thought of as the survival brain, controls physiological responses to emotions such as fear or excitement. Researchers examine still pictures of the brain's structures in MRI machines and analyze real-time changes in the brain via fMRI studies, like the one I observed, in order to see which neurons activate while people are watching a video, recalling a memory, or experiencing an emotion. In rats, they may inject a stimulant to see how the brain regions change.

Over the years scientists have discovered that learning and repeated experiences actually alter the physical structure of the brain, creating new neuronal pathways. This is especially important in children, whose brains are more plastic.

Humans are unique among mammals in having an extended juvenile phase of life, with brains that do not fully mature until our midtwenties. Neuroscientists believe that this quarter-century of development gives humans a giant advantage by providing extra time in which the brain can be shaped to be creative, solve problems, navigate social situations, and respond to any number of new circumstances. It also gives parents a crucial role in creating an environment in which children can learn, develop, and grow. Our genes and inborn temperament are just the starting point for the person we will become. (A child's in-born temperament also may influence the parenting they receive. Some research has shown that the most challenging kids elicit strong-arm parenting from both their own parents and unrelated adults.)

We know parents are important. It's an obvious point, and it's backed by decades of research on human behavior. But as neuroscience has matured, people like D'Andrea are now beginning to link behaviors to brain circuits—to connect the two fields. It is becoming increasingly clear that people's emotions and social behaviors have neural signatures. Scientists are starting to map the mind onto the physical structures of the brain.

In particular, researchers want to understand exactly how the parent-child relationship influences the development of the brain's ability to self-regulate. They're asking questions such as: How does physical contact or proximity with a parent change the brain response? What about parental empathy? What are the differences in children's brains when parents nag them versus when they are verbally abusive? How does a mother's encouragement nourish the brain? What happens inside children's brains during a defiant moment? Or when they experience discipline?

The events of childhood sculpt the brain in ways that can stay with a person for life. For instance, children raised in orphanages often experience lasting brain changes because, even though their physical needs are met, they're unable to form a secure emotional attachment to a caregiver and they experience chronic stress. Studies of the brains of children raised in Romanian orphanages with ten-to-one infant-adult ratios found abnormalities in the prefrontal cortex and amygdala. As a result, the children were more impulsive and had deficits in attention and intellect.

Does this mean that experiencing any stress at all is bad for children?

Not at all. It's important for babies and young children to learn to tolerate moderate amounts of stress, and then to experience relief. For example, when infants cry to be fed and are nursed by a responsive mother, their brains release a flood of endorphins into their nervous systems. These are the "feel-good" hormones we experience after exercise. This arousal-relief cycle actually helps tone infants' brains by developing self-regulatory neural patterns and building trust that their needs will be met.

Similarly, when children separate from their parents to go to preschool, they may be upset and cry. If comforted by loving caregivers—and reunited with the parents later, as promised—they learn confidence and are better protected from developing anxiety in the future. Repeated separation or feelings of anxiety, followed by reassurance and calming, is actually protective. Children who never face stress are more likely to respond with anxiety or overreaction because it's so unfamiliar.

The brain consists of nearly 90 billion neurons—individual nerve cells that learn from repeated experience, constantly forming new patterns and connections. The more you cycle through getting ramped up and self-regulating, the stronger those neural networks become. In other words, the better your brain gets at self-regulation.

The problems arise when children experience neglect or abuse. If they never attach to a responsive caregiver, their self-regulatory systems don't develop the ability to distinguish real threats from imagined ones, and they tend to overreact. In laboratories, stressful situations cause a spike in neural response in the brains of insecurely attached adults, and they recover less quickly than people with secure attachment. This heightened neural response can lead to aggressive and risky behavior. Indeed, decades of research by psychologists and social workers show that early childhood trauma can cause long-term damage to mental and physical health. It's not inevitable—human brains are remarkably resilient and morph dramatically throughout adolescence—but early trauma puts you at risk for a number of poor outcomes.

Scientists began to understand the long tail of trauma in the mid-1990s. A team from the Centers for Disease Control and Prevention (CDC) and Kaiser Permanente looked at 17,000 mostly white, middle-class, college-educated adults. They asked how many of those people in their childhood had experienced one or more traumas of ten different types: psychological, physical, or sexual abuse; emotional or physical neglect; living with someone who abused substances, was mentally ill, or had been to prison; parental divorce or separation; or witnessing their mother being abused.

They found that two-thirds of the population had experienced at least one of these adverse childhood events (ACEs) and that one in eight people had experienced four or more. By cross-tabulating ACE scores with health outcomes, they discovered that high ACE scores increased the risk for seven of the ten leading causes of death in the United States. They also found higher risk for depression, unemployment, substance addiction, suicide, and troubled relationships. Since that time, further research has reinforced the broad health impacts of these childhood experiences.

When it comes to discipline, children who experience corporal punishment, including spanking, are more likely to be aggressive, criminal, and abusive as adults. In addition, psychologists are beginning to find evidence linking harsh verbal abuse to conduct problems and depression, much in the way they've linked these problems with physical abuse.

The University of Pittsburgh psychology professor Ming-Te Wang led a study of harsh verbal discipline—defined as yelling, cursing, or insulting children after misbehavior—in nearly 1,000 families with teenage children. In a 2014 paper, he reported that nearly half of the parents used harsh verbal discipline, but that it wasn't effective in stopping misconduct. Actually, the children who had been disciplined harshly were more likely to act out or show symptoms of depression when questioned the following year. The same effects were seen with parents who generally had a warm relationship with their children, showing that parental warmth didn't lessen the negative impact of yelling at or insulting children.

Bottom line: when adults scream at or insult children, the impact is similar to hitting. Harsh verbal discipline or abuse puts kids into a fight-or-flight state in which they can't access the higher-order parts of their brain to reason or learn from the experience. Since the parent is the source of stress, they can't also serve that important calming role. This leaves the child in a persistent state of arousal.

So what's left as a discipline technique? Connection and empathy. Increasingly, scientists believe that when children receive empathy or comfort from a parent or trusted adult, they are better able to self-regulate to the point where they can begin learning how to consciously control their behavior. The more they self-calm, the more deeply the experience carves grooves in their brains—in other words, the better they get at self-regulation.

~~~

THE PSYCHOLOGIST JIM COAN DEVISED an unusual experiment to test the importance of empathy in helping us regulate our emotions. One by one, he put sixteen women in an MRI scanner and watched their brains as either a blue O or a red X appeared in front of their faces. The red X meant that they had a 20 percent chance of getting shocked. The blue O meant that they were safe. Coan repeated these steps under three scenarios: lying there alone, holding a stranger's hand, and holding a spouse's hand.

While waiting for the O or X to appear, "your brain lights up like a Christmas tree," said Coan, who performed the experiment during a postdoctoral fellowship at the University of Wisconsin and is now a professor at the University of Virginia. Your amygdala triggers your body's reaction to threat—which includes physiological responses such as sweat, a faster heartbeat, and quicker breaths—as your body reallocates energy to the muscles that may be called upon to run or do battle. Meanwhile, your prefrontal cortex strains to keep you still and control your desire to scream, "Get me out of here!"

The prefrontal cortex is the top, outer layer of brain located beneath your forehead. It wraps around the part of the brain known as the limbic system, which includes the hypothalamus and amygdala. Think of the amygdala and hypothalamus as the short-term survival parts of your brain that are ready for action. Meanwhile, the prefrontal cortex governs higher-level functions.

As Coan collected data, he discovered some striking patterns. In the first scenario, when the women were alone, their brains responded the way brains typically do in response to threat, as just described. In the second scenario, when they were holding a stranger's hand, there was less activity in the regions of the brain associated with the physiological response, the fight-or-flight reaction, showing that support from another person calmed them. And in the third scenario, their brains were dramatically quieter and less reactive to the threat when they were holding their partner's hand, both on the physiological level and in the higher functions of the brain. For instance, the hypothala-mus, which controls the release of cortisol—the hormone that regulates stress—showed closer-to-normal levels of activity in this last scenario.

In short: holding a spouse's hand actually helped the study partic-ipants regulate their emotions, and scientists could see it happening inside their brains on the neurobiological level. This is important be-cause when you can regulate yourself during a stressful or trying mo-ment, scientists believe, you are better able to access the rational parts of your brain and problem-solve, instead of going into an emotional downward spiral.

"The more emotionally aroused you are, oftentimes the harder it is for you to think. It becomes a really important thing to be able to down-regulate your emotional feelings if you're having a rough time," Coan told me the first time I interviewed him about his research. The spouse empathy experiment has been cited hundreds of times since he conducted it, an important signal that other scientists find the research groundbreaking. Coan has replicated his findings with broader and more representative samples of people.

Coan's interest in spouses and self-regulation dates to when he was the lab coordinator for John Gottman, possibly the most famous researcher on healthy and damaged marriages. There Coan saw how couples in strong marriages would support one another even in the middle of a conflict, often through an affectionate touch or a message that diffused growing tension.

Those observations came back to him while he was earning a PhD in clinical psychology at the University of Arizona and treating World War II–era veterans suffering from post-traumatic stress dis-order (PTSD). One patient refused even to begin trying preliminary treatment, such as talking about his wartime experiences.

"I couldn't get him to do simple relaxation techniques. Anything we worked on made him too afraid," Coan said.

On the third visit, the man mentioned that he wanted his wife to attend future sessions. Coan readily agreed. At the next appointment, he guided the man through progressive muscle relaxation, which in-volved tightening and flexing each set of muscles and then relaxing them. The man's wife offered to do the exercises with him.

As soon as she clasped his hand, the man's demeanor changed completely. Suddenly, he was mentally present and ready to work with

Coan. The power of holding hands extended throughout the process. Whenever the man ran into a stumbling block, his wife would take him by the hand and he would relax.

"I couldn't get him to talk at all unless he was holding his wife's hand. It was like a magic switch," Coan said. "He would be nervous, fidgeting, wouldn't make eye contact, and she would reach over and grab his hand and I had him. He wasn't off in some other space managing some thoughts and feelings that I didn't have access to. That really left an impression."

～～

To truly understand the research on the impact of our close relationships on our mental health and self-regulation, let's go back to the late 1950s in England. Specifically, Camberwell, a district in southeast London, where a British sociologist named George Brown led a team that followed male patients who had been in a mental hospital for more than two years. They wanted to better understand why long-term psychiatric patients in hospitals rarely successfully reentered society. Some of the patients in their sample had returned home to a spouse or parent, while others had had to find paid lodging in boardinghouses.

To Brown's surprise, patients with schizophrenia who were discharged to the care of loved ones actually fared worse than those living with strangers. They were more likely to relapse in the environment that we might assume would have been more socially supportive.

How could that be? Brown lacked any body of research to help him understand this finding. No British scientists had investigated the environment in which schizophrenia patients were living as a potential factor in their mental health.

Intrigued, the team created a research study to explore the role of family relationships in recovery from schizophrenia. As they interviewed patients and their families, they began to see patterns in the emotional climate of their lives. When patients lived with critical, hostile, and overly involved family members—typically a parent or spouse—they fared worse at follow-up. Those who lived in boardinghouses experienced no such stressors.

Through this research, Brown and his colleagues developed a concept called "expressed emotion," which has proven over the past six decades to be a significant factor in mental health. Expressed emotion (EE) refers specifically to when a key relative of the psychiatric patient speaks about that person in critical, hostile, or emotionally overinvolved ways. The team worked up a set of questions called the Camberwell Family Interview, which took one to two hours to complete. The conversation was recorded, and a trained coder counted up comments made by the family member in order to gauge the level of EE.

Comments deemed critical could be something negative about the family member or they could simply be comments delivered in a critical tone of voice. Hostile remarks could be aspersions on the patient ("She's very selfish and self-involved") or rejection and expression of dislike ("I can't stand to be around him anymore"). Emotional overinvolvement included dramatic or overprotective attitudes about the patient ("We can't be apart—it would kill me").

In a series of papers, Brown's team demonstrated that schizophrenia patients with family members high in expressed emotion were more likely to relapse. The scientific community followed up on this research. One discovery was that when a family member with high EE entered the room, a patient's blood pressure spiked. By contrast, if a low-EE relative came in, their presence helped the patient self-regulate.

Over the decades that followed, study after study connected high EE with worse outcomes among patients with depression, bipolar disorder, anxiety, post-traumatic stress disorder, eating disorders, and substance abuse. Indeed, the connection in depression appears to be stronger than in schizophrenia—at even lower levels of family members' expressed emotion, there's a higher likelihood of relapse.

This breakthrough helped doctors predict which patients might need more support during their recovery, because of high-EE relatives. They could offer these families additional counseling, treatment, and help in building communication skills. But the process of assessing EE took hours: first the one- to two-hour family interview, then two to four hours of coding by an individual trained to detect the voice changes that indicated criticism. The training itself took two weeks or more and could be hard to obtain. It was simply impractical for most busy doctors' offices.

So researchers started looking for a shortcut.

Enter Jill Hooley, a psychology professor at Harvard University, and her colleague John Teasdale of the Medical Research Council in Cambridge, England. The pair tried simply asking psychiatric patients about their most important relationship, how critical that person was on a scale of 1 to 10, how critical the patient was of that person, how upset the patient felt when criticized, and how upset the other person felt when criticized.

This measure—"perceived criticism"—turned out to predict relapse in depression just as well as EE. Hooley and Teasdale found that every single patient in the hospital for depression who rated their spouse at 6 or higher relapsed within nine months of discharge. No patient who rated their spouse at 2 or lower relapsed during that period.

The simplicity of this measure, which could be assessed in less than a minute with the patient, led to a slew of studies connecting high perceived criticism with relapse in substance abuse, obsessive compulsive disorder, agoraphobia, and psychosis. Perceived criticism also predicted future hospitalizations for patients with bipolar disorder.

We would expect patients with verbally abusive family members to fare poorly. By comparison, the kind of criticism involved in these studies seems mild.

"Most people wouldn't see it as problematic. It's an expression of dislike: 'It really bothers me when he walks into the house and tracks mud on the carpet,'" Hooley told me. "This is highly predictive of bad outcomes. We were really curious about why that could be."

After all, criticism is an inevitable part of human life. It's how we learn. Our brains are inextricably linked to our social context. Certainly, you can't parent a child without some kind of critical feedback.

Something had to be going on at a deeper level for those individuals who were vulnerable to depression, anxiety, or another psychiatric condition.

Hooley started to investigate. Her lab recruited college students with a depression history. All had to have been stable for at least six months leading up to the study, with no current mood problems. They also recruited students with no depression history to serve as the control group.

Then Hooley did something that most people dread. With their permission, she recorded their mothers over the phone making critical remarks about them.

"The mother would begin by saying something like, 'Katherine, one thing that really bothers me is your tendency to speed. The way you drive. It worries me to think that you're in the car. I really wish you would slow down,'" she said.

Next, each participant went for an fMRI scan. The team played a recording of their mother's critical comments and analyzed the response in their brain.

"Their dorsolateral prefrontal cortex went offline," Hooley said. "The brain is taking a hit from criticism."

Only participants with a history of depression showed this response, according to the 2005 paper Hooley's team published. By contrast, the control participants showed no such decrease in activity for that part of the brain.

All this happened without participants being aware of it. Both the previously depressed participants and the control participants reported being mildly annoyed, despite the extreme differences in how their brains reacted.

"It's as if this is happening below the radar. They don't feel that was terrible. They were like, 'Yeah, yeah, that's my mother,'" Hooley said. "It's not too difficult to see how these soft punches could start to provoke a brain that is liable to depression to begin with. It creates these micro-stresses."

Hooley and her colleagues continued to investigate this phenomenon. In a 2009 paper, they reported that people who recover from depression may face higher risk for relapse if their relatives are critical, because such criticism helps to train brain pathways that are typical of depressive information processing. Basically, when people vulnerable to depression hear this type of criticism from their closest family member, their brain seems to snap back into a depressive mode of operating.

The test for perceived criticism captures both the actual criticism someone hears as well as their interpretation of the words used. People more vulnerable to mental illness often have trouble letting go of negative comments or managing their emotional response. It's as if negative comments are stickier for them.

Therapists can already harness the power of these findings. By measuring a patient's level of perceived criticism, they can gauge how vulnerable that person may be. They can adjust treatment in anticipation of these challenges.

The implications for parents are potentially profound. You may not yet know whether your young child or adolescent is vulnerable to mental illness, substance abuse, or an eating disorder. From Chapter 2, we know that at least half of children could develop one of these conditions. To be safe, consider limiting your critical comments to those that are absolutely necessary for redirection. Try to restrain your casual nagging and annoyed tone of voice.

When I first learned about this research, my chest tightened up in panic. I've been critical of my children and emotionally invested in their choices since birth! But I forced myself to relax. Tomorrow is a new day. I can always start fresh with a more tolerant outlook. Rather than regretting the past, I try to feel grateful for the chance to try reshaping the present and the future.

~~~

FROM THIS RESEARCH, WE KNOW that criticism hurts. But what helps?

Research scientists try to limit any variation in experiment conditions from one person to another so that the results will not be skewed by a factor that nobody thought was important. In a recent study of children with an anxiety diagnosis, one of the graduate students in a neuroscience lab directed by Greg Siegle at the University of Pittsburgh noticed that some of the kids asked for their mom to stand near them while they were being scanned. This is common practice in MRI scans of children, and the scientists allowed it. But they wondered: could that difference sway the results?

The researchers pulled the data for those children. Remarkably, the children with a diagnosed anxiety disorder had brain scans similar to those of typical children—but only when their mother was in the room with them. The anxious kids who were in the scanner alone had more activity around their hypothalamus, in the orbital frontal cortex and ventrolateral prefrontal cortex, all areas of the brain that integrate emotional and physiological reactions to fear and stress. When an anxious child's mother was physically nearby, these regions of their brain looked just as they did in kids with no anxiety.

"It was absolutely an accidental finding," Siegle recalled. "When we have another person with us, especially touching us, it seems to do a lot to regulate our emotional reactivity. It's returning us to a regulated state."

So does this mean Mom's presence can cure an anxiety disorder?

Not so fast. First of all, the treatment for anxiety involves small exposure to scary things, so that children's brains will experience that arousal-relief cycle that creates the ability to self-regulate. If the parent is always there, these kids miss the chance to begin that treatment.

Second, Siegle cautioned against taking a neuroscientific finding and immediately turning it into broad parenting advice before scientists have had a chance to study the impact of that parenting strategy. "Translating an association that we observe in neuroscience into a prescription is really hard," he said. "Just because something reacts does not mean that the causal chain went the way you thought it did."

However, it's a very promising area for research. And parents can do their own experiment with one subject—seeing how hand-holding or empathy may help their own child cope with distressing situations. If you can see a strategy helping your child, do you care if it's been proven to work for a representative sample of youngsters in a randomized controlled trial? As Siegle put it: "The neuroscience can tell us what rocks to look under for our kids."

This research is part of a growing body of scientific findings that when people experience empathy or social connection—or even the physical proximity of a supportive close relative—neurons fire in the areas of the brain that govern self-regulation. It builds on experiments showing the power of touch dating back to psychologist Harry Harlow's monkey studies in the 1960s. Many of the researchers I met while reporting this book have collaborated on the studies: Siegle and Hooley wrote the 2012 paper on perceived criticism together, and Nieves's boss, Wendy D'Andrea, and Siegle are collaborating on the study I observed at Columbia.

Another surprising result surfaced in an experiment conducted by Naomi Eisenberger at the University of California at Los Angeles: she found that when a study participant was excluded by other participants, the brain regions activated were the same as the regions that would have been activated if this person had been hurt physically.

This new science answers those who believe that kids are misbehaving because parents have become too soft. These critics want us to get tough on kids. This is the camp of Amy Chua, the "Tiger Mother," who recommends controlling children so that they excel in music, sports, and academics to win spots in selective high schools and colleges. Books like *1-2-3 Magic, The Strong-Willed Child,* and *Have a New Teenager by Friday* encourage parents to assert their power, promising that their kids' behavior will quickly improve. These methods may "work" if your only goal is to have well-behaved children, regardless of the effect on their mental health. The problem is that the methods of this tradition—yelling at, insulting, and restricting children—have been associated with increases in acting out and depression.

Tough love also reduces kids' intrinsic motivation. The University of Rochester psychologists Edward Deci and Richard Ryan, for example, found that teachers who aim to control students' behavior—rather than helping them control it themselves—undermine the very elements that are essential for motivating kids to self-regulate: autonomy, a sense of competence, and belonging. Subjected to such strong-arming, kids then have an even harder time learning self-control. When children and young adults don't have the psychological tools to regulate their emotions, they often find relief in external sources, whether acting out sexually or abusing drugs or alcohol.

Although corporal and verbal punishment may seem to improve children's behavior in the near term, both carry long-term risks similar to the risks of outright physical abuse of kids—drug and alcohol abuse, depression, heart and liver disease, suicide attempts, and sexual risk-taking.

<center>~~~</center>

BRAIN RESEARCH IS ALSO KEY to understanding why children misbehave in the first place. Neuroscientists know that the prefrontal cortex is central to managing executive function—our capacity to control impulses, prioritize tasks, and organize plans. Research suggests that the prefrontal cortexes of aggressive or oppositional children either haven't developed or develop more slowly than in typical kids; these children may simply not yet have brains capable of helping them regulate their behavior. Despite what some people assume, executive function doesn't correlate with intelligence; gifted children can also be impulsive or challenging, despite their intellectual strength and ability to articulate their thoughts. And even children who are right on schedule don't have a fully developed prefrontal cortex.

I first heard about emotional regulation and brain development at the Parent Encouragement Program (PEP), a parenting education center in Kensington, Maryland, near my home. My husband, Brian, and I went there for classes in 2010, when our youngest was in the throes of the terrible threes. Once I learned how her brain was firing in the middle of her tantrums, and that her prefrontal cortex had barely developed, I stopped taking the outbursts personally. PEP gave me a range of parenting tools to use in setting limits without harming the parent–child relationship. I took every class available. By 2011, I was assisting in classes so that I could stay immersed in the material. In 2013, I began to present parts of the curriculum and then to lead classes myself, eventually becoming a certified parent educator.

In one class I was leading, a student told the story of her three-year-old son coming home from preschool in disgrace for hitting a classmate. When asked why he did it, he said it was an accident. The mom was horrified, sure that this meant he was a liar or perhaps a sociopath.

"You can't hit someone by accident!" she said.

"Well," I responded, "to him it may feel that he doesn't have control of his actions. He may have responded to the impulse to hit without even thinking about it. Perhaps in his mind it was truly an accident. Or at least a surprise. That's probably developmentally appropriate."

She gave me a stunned look, but seemed reassured that hitting others in preschool wasn't going to lead her child into a life of violent crime.

As I taught parenting classes and read about brain development, the pieces slowly fell into place for me. Adult actions aimed at controlling children's behavior through rewards or punishment are counterproductive. For one, many children don't yet have the brain maturity needed to meet parents' expectations. And even those children who are ready lose access to the part of the brain where they can learn or exercise rational thought when they are in a conflict or having a temper tantrum. In that moment, neither threats nor rewards can reach them.

This doesn't mean we should accept bad behavior or excuse it. Children need signals and instruction on what's expected. They need practice exercising self-control over many years. But I believe that it helps adults to stop seeing a child having a tantrum or being disorganized as willfully disobedient, and instead to see that child as needing help self-regulating. In a sense, until children's prefrontal cortexes are fully mature, we adults must supplement their executive function. We must remove that support bit by bit, continually challenging their self-control to grow until they're completely independent.

The implications of this new wave of science are profound for anyone working with kids: adults can actually stimulate growth in the neural fibers that link the different parts of the child's brain that control emotional regulation by connecting with the child in the midst of an outburst. Children can literally reshape their brains when they learn and practice skills that support desired behavior.

Faced with a misbehaving child, adults have a choice with a far-reaching impact. We can take unilateral actions—declaring time-outs, offering bribes, yelling—that deepen the kid's dysregulation, disconnection, and despair. The research now tells us that repeated negative discipline experiences will take this child further down a path of misbehavior. Or we can choose to reinforce the relationship, help the child regain control of himself, and, often later, collaborate with them on a plan to reinforce those missing skills that will help them cope better with the situation or the trigger that led to the misbehavior. That's the option that will build the neural pathways in that child's brain for self-control, intrinsic motivation, and, ultimately, long-term success in life.

This combination—making connections, communicating, and systematically building capability—underpins all the successful discipline models I explore in this book and represents our best hope for raising and educating resilient, capable adults prepared to lead our society.

4

The Old Methods Don't Work

Kids, I don't know what's wrong with these kids today!
Kids, they are disobedient, disrespectful oafs!
　　—Lee Adams, *Bye Bye Birdie*, 1960

Men will dishonor their parents as they grow quickly old,
and will carp at them, chiding them with bitter words,
hard-hearted they, not knowing the fear of the gods. They
will not repay their aged parents the cost of their nurture,
for might shall be their right.
　　—Hesiod, 700 BCE

FOR AS LONG AS CHILDREN have grown into adolescents, parents have been complaining that *this* generation is the worst. This tradition stretches back at least as far as Homer. So I understand the skepticism when I become the latest in this string of doomsayers to attest that today's youth behave worse than ever.

Bear with me. As discussed in the previous chapters, the ability of children to regulate their own emotions and behavior is on the decline. And it's undeniable that our brains are being shaped by changes in media, technology, lifestyles, and other conditions of our modern society.

To understand why new parenting methods are needed for today's kids, let's start with a trip back in time.

Growing up in Connecticut in the 1950s, my father and his two older sisters followed strict rules. Every Sunday, the girls wore gloves

and hats to their Episcopal church, where my father sang as a boy so-
prano in the choir. Chewing gum and comic books were banned from
the house. Swearing was absolutely prohibited. They each took a turn
eating dinner with their parents in the dining room to learn proper
table manners, while their siblings ate in the kitchen.

They remember precious few instances of being disciplined, because they generally did as they were told and behaved as expected.
My Aunt Penny recalls using a bad word in a backyard sibling dis-
pute and being summoned to the kitchen door by her mother, my
grandmother Mary. With a fierce look, Mary seized Penny's arm and
marched her to the bathroom, where she proceeded to wash the inside
of the seven-year-old's mouth with a bar of Ivory soap. It tasted awful.
Penny didn't even protest.

"I couldn't imagine trying to resist the punishment," Penny told
me when I asked why she didn't clamp her mouth closed. "You didn't
do that. You might resent it afterward, but you're not going to keep
your mouth shut."

Then, when Penny and my father were raising my cousins and
me, they found that kids typically obeyed an adult command with
little protest or question. That's one reason grandparents today often
struggle to understand why we modern parents negotiate with our
children and tolerate emotional scenes. They remember the simplicity
of telling children what to do, giving a few choices, and being obeyed
with little question. The few instances of childish disobedience were
easily curbed by a stern look, a firm lecture, or a swat on the behind.
"It worked for me" is their common refrain.

They grew up in the era of *Father Knows Best,* when men ruled the
roost at work and women commanded the household with an iron fist.
Children were seen and not heard. Psychologists call that style of parenting *authoritarian,* and it worked in a time when people could devote
fifty years to a business in exchange for guaranteed employment and a
gold watch upon retirement. This was the era of "company men" and
lifetime pensions for faithful service.

So why doesn't that parenting style work now?

First of all, we are parenting in a different context. In schools,
workplaces, and government, we value collaboration and mutual respect far more than the command-and-control model of the past. On
college campuses, nineteen-year-old students are demanding apologies

for racial micro-aggressions and confronting faculty toe to toe. In this environment, it shouldn't be surprising that children challenge authority. They increasingly see themselves as equal to adults—or at least equally deserving of respect and a voice in decisions. Even preschoolers pick up on the attitudes of older children in their family and community, especially if they're exposed to smart-mouthed tweens on Disney and Nickelodeon.

Second, we simply want different things for our kids than parents did in earlier eras. In the parenting classes I teach at PEP, in the first session, I ask parents to share what they hope for their children when they turn eighteen. What qualities or values do they want them to have? What do they want their kids to be?

Nobody ever describes wanting rule-following children at age eighteen—as my grandparents had. The adjectives these parents use run much deeper: Independent. Compassionate. Self-confident. Responsible. Honest. Optimistic. Resilient. Dependable. Happy. Service-oriented. Courageous. Kind. Respectful. Hardworking. Creative. Wise. Emotionally healthy. Curious.

When parents are trying to build their children's emotional, psychological, and moral reserves, discipline is necessarily a more complex matter than simple compliance with adult commands. Parents today recognize that the pace of change is accelerating, and that their offspring need to adapt to whatever world exists when they emerge into adulthood. They want to raise thinkers who can understand the shifting rules of society and who don't just blindly obey authority.

～～～

It was 7:45 p.m. on a school night. The scent of instant coffee and hummus drifted across the carpeted room on the top floor of the Baptist church in Kensington, Maryland. Erika Roberts sat across from me in a circle of parents taking the PEP 1 class that I was teaching with my husband, Brian.

A tall woman with a resonant voice and easy laugh, she described to the group her struggle to figure out how to manage defiance from her five-year-old daughter, Emma, who didn't respond as cooperatively as Evan, now nine, had done at the same age. If Evan threw a tantrum in a public place, Erika would simply walk away. He'd then clam up and rush over to avoid being separated from his mother.

"With Emma, it doesn't work," she told the twenty parents around her. "She'll scream and walk in the other direction and just keep screaming."

Her husband, Tyrone, said that his biggest challenge was getting the kids to cooperate before he blew his cool. Other parents around the room nodded agreement. They took turns introducing themselves with a litany of concerns about their kids.

Sibling rivalry. Bedtime battles. Tantrums. Strong-willed children. Trepidation about the teen years to come. The need for strategies that weren't negative or punitive. The challenge of getting up and out of the house in the morning on time.

Eight of the parents were taking the class with a spouse. Three were single parents, and the remaining nine had a spouse at home managing dinner and bedtime. Their kids varied in age from three to fourteen, with the majority in the five- to nine-year-old range. Almost immediately, the parents bonded over their similar challenges and frustrations.

Later in the evening, Brian asked the group to brainstorm a list of qualities that the ideal parent would have.

Patient. Able to recognize which kid needs which strategy. Intuitive. Empathetic. Respectful. Loving. Creative and fun. Trusting. Supports effort. Never gets tired. Honest. Persistent. Present. Clear communicator. Willing to help. Willing to let go. Calm. Available.

"No pressure!" Brian joked as the whiteboard grew crowded with words. But the group wasn't done. They continued with the list.

Wise about the bigger world. Good teacher. Willing to learn more. Curious. Open-minded. Reflective. Loving unconditionally. Supportive. Willing to grow.

"When you look at this list here, how does that make you feel?" Brian asked.

"Tired," one mom responded.

"Like crap," Tyrone said bluntly.

"Exactly," Brian said.

"Imagine you're a five-year-old or an eight-year-old and you have tantrums," I said. "You forget things. You're always getting things wrong. Imagine if you had a parent who was always patient, who was intuitive, respectful, pleasant, a clear communicator, who was wise and calm and available, always willing to learn, empathetic. Every. Single. Minute. Of the day. What would that be like for you?"

The class laughed. "I want to vomit," one said.

"If you are a five-year-old or eight-year-old trying to figure yourself out and you have a parent who is just perfect, how can you see yourself growing into that person?"

"You'd probably be pretty dysfunctional because you're so on the other side of the curve," one mom said.

"I watched my much younger brother tell my dad, 'Well, you don't understand because it's all easy for you, so you don't understand what I'm going through,'" added Avery, an early thirties divorced mom of two girls.

"That's a great insight," I said. "One of the reasons we do this exercise is that even if you could be this perfect parent, boy, that would be discouraging to your imperfect children."

"Or your spouse," Brian chimed in, provoking more laughter.

"I think also it would give them a false sense of security about the world," said Ann, who had described her eleven-year-old daughter as a fierce contrarian.

"Right. No problems. Your way is paved. In this class we like to take that list, crumple it up, and throw it out, because none of us is perfect," I said.

"I think we should keep it," Brian joked.

"I'm not keeping anything that makes Tyrone feel like crap," I said.

"The core motto of the class is to have the courage to be imperfect," Brian said. "The idea is: there are lots of ways that might or might not work. You're going to try all of them. You're going to succeed and fail. The whole goal is you're going to learn by doing. Having the courage to be imperfect is plenty good. That's the goal. Just give a try."

"Being our own imperfect selves is how our kids are going to deal with their own imperfections and living in the real world and being able to accept their own limitations," I concluded.

The class was on its way. Over the next eight weeks, Brian and I introduced the basic principles of PEP's curriculum, based on the positive parenting model of the Austrian psychotherapist Alfred Adler

(1870–1937). We taught the parents techniques for connecting with their kids, communicating with them, and also building their ability to handle daily chores, strong emotions, and limits set by the family and enforced by the parents. Despite the demands of their lives, the parents kept showing up at the end of their long workdays to sit in uncomfortable metal chairs and make plans for improving their home lives.

~~~

ONE REASON PARENTS NOWADAYS FEEL strongly about tempering support with limits is that they've seen the damage done by parents who aspired to be their children's best friends and cheerleaders, not their bosses. In the 1990s, an overwhelming focus on self-esteem as the key to success in life prompted many parents to praise their kids no matter what. Little League teams awarded trophies and medals to everyone who showed up. Instead of punishing children, parents tried to placate them, in hopes of making them happy. Helicopter parents jumped in to negotiate on behalf of their children in school and activities—and sometimes continued to intervene through their kids' college years and first job.

This was the golden era of permissive parenting, defined by William Sears's *The Baby Book,* published in 1993. Research on the importance of early childhood development and secure attachment for lifetime success reinforced the importance of nurturing parents and set the stage for a cascade of writings on mommy guilt.

Whereas 1950s homemakers thought nothing of leaving Junior in a playpen for hours while they completed their daily chores, moms in the 1990s and early 2000s co-slept, wore their babies, and often had no privacy from their children, not even in the bathroom. (I plead guilty on the latter two.) As the name suggests, permissive parents struggle with setting boundaries, sometimes giving up on limits altogether.

In the mid-1990s, sociologists and psychologists launched a wave of new studies looking at the impact of permissive parenting. They contrasted parents who were permissive with those holdovers still practicing authoritarian, *Father Knows Best* parenting, as well as with a third style: authoritative. Authoritative parents combine warmth and connection with clear limits. Whereas the authoritarian parent tells a child to do something "because I said so," the authoritative parent

explains the reason behind the rule and may even be open to negotiation if a child presents a reasonable argument. Don't be confused
by the similar string of letters in *authoritarian* and *authoritative*—these
styles are dramatically different.

I read about these studies eagerly, hoping to solve a marital dis-
pute. I lean toward a permissive parenting style, and Brian leans toward authoritarian. Should we—*could* we—combine our strengths
and shed our faults to become two authoritative parents?

I combed through dozens of research papers about children's emotional health, level of misbehavior, and academic success under different parenting scenarios. Three caught my attention.

A team of psychology professors asked 272 Pennsylvania public
high school students a series of questions to assess their parents' style
and their own well-being. Questions associated with an authoritative
parenting style included: "How much does your mother/father really
know what you do with your free time?" They also assessed students'
answers to questions like: "When my mother/father wants me to do
something, she/he explains why."

From the answers, they labeled each parent in the study one of
four types: authoritative, authoritarian, indulgent, or uninvolved.
Both "indulgent" and "uninvolved" were types of permissive parenting, with indulgent parents being warm and connected but setting few
limits. Uninvolved parents were emotionally distant and rarely supervised their children, who in turn could do whatever they wanted.

After analyzing the results, the authors published a 2006 paper reporting that the teens with authoritative mothers experienced higher
self-esteem and life satisfaction and fewer signs of depression. The adolescents with uninvolved parents fared the worst, while the well-
being of kids of authoritarian and indulgent parents scored somewhere
in the middle.

The second paper looked specifically at alcohol and cigarette use,
antisocial behavior, and depression. Koen Luyckx, a psychologist at
Catholic University Leuven in Belgium, and Elizabeth Tildesley at
the Oregon Research Institute led a team working with the Oregon
Youth Substance Use Project. They created a prospective study, which
sets up questions and study parameters before gathering data. Such a
study is considered more reliable than a retrospective study because
there's less chance of bias or unrelated factors distorting the results.

They surveyed parents and their children in five different grades on an annual basis, beginning when the kids were in grades 1 through 5 and ending when they were in grades 8 through 12. A total of 1,075 parents and 1,049 kids participated, 40 percent of whom qualified for free and reduced meals and 86 percent of whom were white.

As they reported in a 2012 paper, they found that children of authoritative parents fared better than their peers on every behavior assessed. The gap was biggest for children of uninvolved parents, and it widened every year. By senior year of high school, these children drank and smoked twice as much as their peers with either authoritative or authoritarian parents.

The third paper I read, published in 1991, reported on a survey of 4,100 teenagers in Wisconsin and California and classified their parents as authoritative, authoritarian, indulgent, or uninvolved. The researchers looked at the kids' psychosocial development, school achievement, problem behavior, and "internalized distress," which means symptoms of depression, anxiety, and the like. "Psychosocial development" refers to the maturation of a child's individual personality within the social context of school and home.

They found that teens with authoritative parents scored highest on measures of psychosocial competence and lowest on measures of psychological and behavioral dysfunction; the reverse was true for those with uninvolved parents. Adolescents with authoritarian parents did pretty well on obeying rules, but experienced poorer beliefs about themselves than their peers. By contrast, teens from indulgent homes felt more self-confident, but more often abused substances, misbehaved at school, and underperformed academically.

I gathered that children of authoritarian parents behave better but may have worse mental health, whereas kids of indulgent parents experience fewer internal symptoms, but have more behavioral problems: they're more likely to act out with neglected academics, drugs, sex, and the like.

Those parents of the 1980s and 1990s, trying to improve on their parents' stern discipline and emotional distance, had swung the pendulum too far. In trying to be close to their children, they sacrificed important limits that kids need. It turns out that permissive parenting is even worse than authoritarian parenting in the long term. A slew of research studies from the 1990s to the present show that, with both parenting styles, children have an increased risk of depression and lower self-control, and that permissive parenting also is associated with lower academic achievement.

My research convinced me to walk that middle path: close emotional connection with clear boundaries. I would respect my children as individuals with their own goals and perspectives, while insisting that they contribute to our family and abide by our overall values and rules. I sorted through the many techniques that seemed to work, distilling their core principles into what I now call "the Apprenticeship Model" of parenting. All the successful systems in this book share these three threads: connection with children, communication about problems, and building kids' capability. Upon this foundation, adults and children together set healthy limits and boundaries.

Brian and I adopted this motto as a family value: work first, play later. As typical eldest children, we both willingly delay gratification when there's a big task in front of us. Our children are still in the process of deciding whether to embrace this mind-set. Rather than nag them into doing their household jobs, we simply state the rule: "When the dishes are in the dishwasher and your backpacks hung up, then we can go to the pool." Sometimes they jump into cleaning, but often they dawdle, read a book, do a puzzle, or play with the dog. Eventually they may decide to do their jobs. That's their choice.

We calmly go about our day, resisting the urge to lay into them. If they delay until the sun has set or it's too chilly to swim, we swallow our own disappointment. We're in this for the long haul: better to teach our kids responsibility for life than to get them to do their chores on our time frame this afternoon. When they're disappointed they missed the outing, we empathize. We don't say, "I told you so," or goad them with, "Next time you should . . . ." We let the experience do the teaching.

When I talk about authoritative parenting, some parents say they're exhausted just thinking about the time and effort it must take. But I'd argue that permissive parenting is actually even more work. With no children doing household chores, you're the one cleaning, cooking, shopping, and organizing the schedule, sometimes even into their young adulthood. Why not hand over responsibility as soon as possible, even if it takes more time to teach children to take on these tasks?

I have a similar view of authoritarian parenting. It may seem simpler to lay down the law, but that works only as long as children continue to obey. As they grow, they naturally will seek more independence, so you're likely to face tween or teen rebellion—either outright or sneakily, behind your back. I suggest setting up systems and habits for negotiating disagreements when the kids are young, so that by the time they start asserting themselves you've developed resilient ways to set limits (more on this in Chapter 9).

Regardless of the type of parenting we use, modern parents stand willing to put in the time.

Even as more women entered the workforce between 1965 and 2015, expanding the working mom population from 41 percent to 71 percent, mothers' time spent caring for children climbed from ten hours to fifteen hours a week. Fathers' time spent on child care nearly tripled over the same period, from two and a half to seven hours a week. Overall, parents have become more hands-on and collaborative in the last thirty years as attachment parenting and positive discipline increasingly replace command, control, and punish models. Although far from universal, these trends represent real shifts in the way large chunks of the middle-class population raise children.

Recent research shows, however, that kids need something other than additional time with their parents. The quality of the time matters.

In 2015, a team of sociologists tackled the myth of intensive mothering, the idea that moms should lavish their time and energy on their children to ensure their healthy emotional and academic development. They looked at data from the University of Michigan, which since 1968 has followed a sample of 18,000 people through their lives to evaluate their well-being. The surveys ask questions about the individuals' employment, income, health, relationships, education, and other topics every other year. Since 1997, these researchers have also been following the development of the children born to those individuals, with four additional surveys about their kids' well-being and behavior.

The Michigan data set yields especially valuable findings because, in addition to the large sample size, it relies on time use diaries. These are considered the gold standard for accuracy because they catch people in the moment they're doing something, rather than relying on their memories of what activities they engaged in at some time in the past.

Melissa Milkie, a University of Toronto sociologist, led a team that unpacked the data from 1997 and 2003, examining the impact of parental time on children's development. They looked at behavioral problems, emotional issues, and academic success. The behavior-related questions included whether the child cheated or told lies, argued too much, struggled to concentrate, bullied others, or appeared hyperactive. For teens, they also assessed risk-taking behaviors: drug, alcohol, and cigarette use and sexual activity. On delinquency, they asked whether teens broke curfew, stole items, damaged property, got in trouble at school, or had hurt another person badly or attracted police attention. They divided parental time into two measures: available time and engaged time.

Remarkably, they found zero association between the amount of time moms and dads spent with children under age twelve and any of these measures of behavioral, emotional, and academic performance. Zero. This held for both engaged time and available time.

When it came to adolescents, however, there was a split. Teens who spent more time engaged with their mothers reported less delinquency. And those who spent more time engaged with both parents experienced fewer behavioral problems, substance use, and delinquency. They also improved in math. Teens who enjoyed access to both parents were less likely to use drugs.

This research convinced me that quitting my job and lavishing every spare moment on my kids wouldn't help, even if it were financially possible. Rather, I would continue to learn how to be an authoritative parent. I would focus on the quality of time I spent with my kids.

Not only does authoritative parenting feel right to many parents, but it's supported by a growing body of research finding that autonomy, competence, and a sense of connection drive an individual's intrinsic motivation and happiness. We increasingly see how our first instincts—whether to punish our kids, offer them rewards, or rescue them—can backfire. A new wave of advice has been prompted by research by scholars such as Stanford's Carol Dweck, who shows how praise undermines kids' motivation and risk-taking, and the University of Pennsylvania's Angela Duckworth, who has detailed the importance of setbacks in developing resilience. Popular books like *How to Raise an Adult* and *The Gift of Failure* urge parents to worry less, let kids experience failure, and stop pushing achievement so hard.

Parents now are seeking the middle ground between the authoritarian style of an earlier era and the permissive parenting of the 1980s and '90s. But while they're increasingly skeptical of punishment and subscribe to the value of communication and mutual respect, the crucial piece that's often missing is discipline. When everyone in the family is respected, and with democracy being one of the highest values in our world, adults may feel awkward imposing limits. Authoritative parents-in-training often resist imposing their will on children until the moment when the whining or the messy house pushes them over the edge. Then they fall back on the authoritarian tones embedded in our collective memories.

When I started looking for answers about kids' behavior, the quest seemed useful and important. I was hoping to eliminate the daily meltdowns and the constant scramble for lost homework or belongings. But as I learned about the severe long-term impacts of parenting style, I grew more concerned about future generations. Visiting the nation's heartland convinced me that the country is already in crisis.

～～～

DARREN HENRY HAD THE SLOUCH of a man not entirely defeated by a hopeless task, but doubting that he would prevail. In his small office by the entrance to Leipsig Elementary School in Putnam County, Ohio, he reclined his chair as he considered my questions: Why do kids misbehave? What methods work nowadays?

"What seems to work? Do you have any answers for me?" he replied.

When we talked by phone before my visit, Henry had explained that he grew up in the rural Ohio community before becoming a teacher and then taking over as principal at Leipsig. The repeat offenders who turn up in his office are often the kids whose parents were chronic problems in his early years of teaching more than twenty years ago. The cycle of misbehavior makes it hard for him to believe that anything could change. Indeed, it seems to be getting worse. Compared to their parents, five-year-olds now arrive at school less able to sit still and more likely to grab or hit in response to a provocation. He sees a connection to the erosion of family life and community.

"Some of these kids go home and they're not worried about doing any homework, it's what kind of meal am I going to have, is anyone going to be home?" he said. I looked around his office at piles of school documents and crayon-etched thank-you notes from students.

Two decades ago, he said, he could walk through town and see kids shooting baskets, riding bikes, or playing together on the baseball field. Nowadays, that's a rarity, he explained.

"For a small town, we're lucky to have two different parks. You don't see kids in the parks as much," he said. "School is more than the standardized tests. We're trying to teach social skills and how to get along in a group. Kids need to learn how to play together."

The spring day I visited, a third-grade boy cooled his heels in a nearby office as Henry and I chatted. He'd received too many marks for bad behavior to participate in the class party to celebrate the end of the quarter. The boy fell in the middle of three brothers, all frequent fliers in detention.

"They are three of the smartest boys we have in their respective classes," Henry said. "They're tough. They're such tough cookies. When they don't want to do something, they're not going to do it."

This day the middle boy flatly refused when his teacher told him to go to the principal's office at the start of the party. She called Henry, who headed down to the classroom with some trepidation. He was tired of physically manhandling the boy out of the room—as he'd had to do earlier in the quarter when the boy was digging snot from his nose and rubbing it on classmates.

"I didn't feel good about doing it," he said. "I'm tired of dragging those boys out of the room. And I don't want to lose my job."

Instead, he tried a strategy he'd adopted in the last two weeks: smothering them with kindness. When he got into the classroom, he knelt down at the boy's level and asked him to come to the office.

"He bucked me at first a little bit. I said, 'Come on, I really need you to.' I patted him on the back. Trying to give him all the positives. He came down with me. That worked," Henry said. "I hope that keeps working."

To educators, when parents who can't control their behavior have kids of their own, it can seem hopeless that the kids will ever learn self-discipline. "Sometimes this position overwhelms me. You want to help them all and it consumes you," Henry admitted. "A lot of our kids, all they hear at home is yelling, so I find that just doesn't work. I try to get through to some of the teachers that yelling doesn't work. If you're going to browbeat them every day about homework and this and that, they're going to buck you even more. That's their mechanism."

I heard a similar story just a few states west from Henry's Leipsig Elementary, in Wisconsin. The elementary school teacher Mikki Retic had seen dramatic changes in both the families whose children she teaches and their behavior in the last two decades. In 1998, her first year, the vast majority of families had one stay-at-home parent. Now both parents work in most families, and many of the families are blended. "Mom and Dad may be married and in the home, but they're not around a lot. That is the single greatest factor because that causes the domino effect," Retic said. "The kids we see coming into school at four or five, Mom and Dad are carrying some guilt for not being around so much, so they want to be the little one's friends."

Not only are the children less obedient and respectful of authority, but teachers have a tougher time getting parental support when they need to call home about a discipline issue. "They say, 'My kid wouldn't do that!' or they look to blame other kids for their children's behavior," she said. "It's almost like the parents are afraid to discipline their kids at home and when they come into it at school it's a new thing."

More children will cry or throw temper tantrums than when she first started teaching. But the biggest change she sees is the way kids question directions and look to get revenge on other children when they think they've been wronged.

"They don't know how to play fair. They don't understand that to be given respect, *you* have to give it first," she said. "There's this entitlement that I should get my way all the time. That carries over to the classroom."

It can take forever to get through to children in the classroom with even a simple direction like "put your pencil on the desk." They continue chatting and seem to think the instruction doesn't apply to them, Retic said. Years ago, perhaps one or two children in the class-room would have needed to be redirected, but now it's the majority.

"They don't realize they're part of something bigger and greater. They don't realize their presence in the world can make it a better place. They're so egocentric," she said. "Everything is so instant grat-ification. There's no conversation anymore. I only care about you if you can do something for me."

In addition to the societal changes, she blames the increased use of technology in homes and the classroom. Children spend more time sitting or being still during the school day and also during their free recreation time. "The social interactions and personal responsibility that would naturally happen on the playground or at a park are now being replaced with one-on-one time with a device, where feedback is instant and you can hide behind a screen," Retic said.

~~~

As a PEDIATRICIAN, JEFFREY BROSCO often sees children who don't fit into the norm of expected behavior. When he started to think about the rising rates of ADHD—the percentage of childern receiving a diagnosis had doubled since the 1970s—he grew interested in whether changes in academic expectations might be skewing the picture. After all, ADHD is diagnosed by observing behavior in an educational environment and asking how well the child is able to learn, get along with peers, and follow the rules—that is, get along with adults. Since school has become more academic and sedentary over the years, it seemed reasonable to Brosco to ask whether more children are having trouble behaving themselves in that environment.

"When I went to kindergarten, it was half a day, we ran around, never had homework until I was probably in high school. There's been a large change in the last fifty years or so that says we need to be more academically rigorous with young children," said Brosco, a professor of clinical pediatrics at the University of Miami Miller School of Medicine. "We know if you look at the neurobiology of ADHD, it has to do with the maturation of your frontal and prefrontal lobes. Children with ADHD are less likely to resist their impulses, and they have more trouble focusing. They're not quite ready for what the environment demands of them."

Brosco and medical student Anna Bona pored through databases that got at the question of changing academic demands, like US Education Department statistics on the amount of assigned homework in each grade and surveys on how children spend their time. "They all pointed in the same direction," he said. "In pre-K, four-year-old kids are doing letters, numbers, and journaling. The demands on six- to eight-year-olds have gone up as well in terms of the amount of homework and lack of recess."

Brosco and Bona found a nineteen-percentage-point increase in the time spent teaching three- to five-year-olds letters and numbers over two decades, according to their study published in *JAMA Pediatrics* in 2016. In addition, more young children went to school for a full day: 58 percent in the mid-2000s versus 17 percent in 1970. In 1997, the paper said, six- to eight-year-olds spent more than two hours a week on homework, more than double the time spent on homework a decade earlier.

Looking at how quickly ADHD diagnoses have climbed, Brosco finds it much more likely that these significant environmental changes are playing a role than that the entire difference is due to changes in human brains. Moreover, with overall child health having improved dramatically, physicians and parents alike can now worry more about mental and behavioral health.

"Fifty years ago, children were dying from a whole set of infectious diseases," Brosco said. Today, "children are remarkably healthy, and this gives us the luxury of saying, 'He's not paying as much attention in school,' as opposed to an epidemic of polio."

So what's to be done now? Brosco's study and others like it support arguments for more physical movement and less structured academics for children in the early years of school. This research also provides a useful reality check in warning us to expect to see ADHD diagnoses rising when kids enjoy less activity and face more traditional academics earlier in their lives than in the past.

"If you are sitting still in a desk for hours doing tasks that are inherently boring, children with ADHD traits are going to show up a lot more than if their job is to run around and play," he said. "As we increase the academic demands on young children, we have to recognize that one of the consequences of that is that many more children will be labeled as having a disorder."

Homework has been debunked as useful for children younger than middle school. Notably, the Duke University psychology professor Harris Cooper analyzed 180 research studies on the impact of homework and found minimal association between assigned homework and students' achievement in elementary school. Even in middle and high school, Cooper discovered, there is only a small correlation between homework and academic achievement. So instead of battling their children over worksheets, parents should focus on physical activity, unstructured time, and connecting with their offspring in the nonschool hours. It's great if you can read together or include math facts as part of cooking dinner, but keep it light and fun.

"There's thirty years of research to show that homework doesn't improve academic performance. What I've found is parents take on the homework as their own, which eliminates any chance of independence," Brosco said.

Has anything changed for the better in the last thirty years? Certainly the eradication of childhood infectious diseases is wonderful for kids and the country. Another beneficial development has been the increasingly hands-on role taken by fathers with their kids, which improves kids' academic achievement and emotional health. Dads' unique approach to parenting can buffer children against anxiety—although fathers are also more prone to authoritarian parenting. Nevertheless, they provide an important counterpoint to the mom-dominated parenting that has been the hallmark of our modern era.

~~~

IT WAS THE FIFTH SESSION of my PEP 1 class, an eight-week class representing the first half of the center's core curriculum. The clock read 7:29 p.m.—almost time to start. The parents in the group entered the room casually. They collected name tags, grabbed a coffee, took a seat. They knew the routine.

I welcomed everyone and asked how the week went. In the previous session, they'd learned about the four types of misbehavior that children can exhibit, in the Adlerian framework that PEP follows. The first is seeking undue attention, as contrasted with useful and appropriate attention. The second is a power struggle. The third is revenge, and the fourth type of misbehavior is assumed inadequacy, when children simply give up.

Adler's theory maintains that all human behavior stems from a desire to belong. If people can't find a useful way to belong, such as leading or contributing to a group, they'll search for an unproductive avenue to belonging, like being the drama queen. The same holds for children.

I asked the class whether anyone was viewing their kids' misbehavior in a different way since last session.

"I stopped engaging in power struggles," announced Tyrone Roberts. I looked over in surprise. He was beaming, his six-foot-plus frame folded into the plastic and metal chair.

"You stopped engaging in power struggles," I said flatly. I'd never heard of a parent giving up power struggles in a week. It took me months to stop needing to win—and I still slipped up sometimes.

"It was hard because my natural instinct is: you just do what I say," he said.

"Yes. So can you give an example of what you would've done and what you're doing now?" I responded.

"Get dressed. Get dressed. Get up. Get dressed. Get dressed. Get up. Get dressed. Why aren't you up? Get up," he said, mimicking himself nagging his nine-year-old, Evan, in the mornings.

Instead, he explained, he and his wife, Erika, told Evan they would set an alarm for departure time. When it rang, they would simply leave the house to take five-year-old Emma to school. Evan could join them if he was ready. Despite being older, Evan seemed less capable of pulling himself together in the mornings. The whole family usually ended up waiting for him, which often made Tyrone late for his job in software support for an architecture firm and Erika for hers as a university professor.

Instead, Tyrone told him, "We're going to be downstairs. When the alarm goes off, we're going to leave. Just make sure you lock the door and take everything you need because if you don't, you won't have lunch at school. Okay, bye."

Tyrone told the class, "Every time we did that, he was downstairs before we were."

"Interesting. Wow. That sounds like magic," I said, a bit jealous.

"Yes," Tyrone said.

"We realized we seriously were just threatening. We were doing those fake threats. 'We're really going to leave,'" Erika said. "This time we were serious. We were nervous about it. We said, 'Go through the mudroom door. Lock it and then cross the street.' We gave him instructions like we were seriously going to leave him and you're going to have to get yourself to school. We would've done it."

"The only thing we didn't do was keep saying it over and over again. 'We're gonna leave. This time we're really going to leave.' We said it one time, and then we went on our way," Tyrone said.

"You acted instead of talking," Brian said.

That's a key piece of advice that PEP gives: act more, talk less. So if you're trying to train a child to stop dropping a backpack on the floor of the front hall, don't give a long lecture about the danger of tripping or how irresponsible the child is. Simply stand with an outstretched hand pointed toward the obstacle and say, "Backpack." With a smile.

Tyrone impressed me with his commitment to changing his parenting style wholesale. Overnight. I kept coming back to that, because I was curious about how he had accomplished the transformation. So a year after the class, I followed up with him and Erika to see how things were going.

Tyrone shared that, during the class, Erika had realized his approach to Evan was backfiring. He'd tease Evan to try to nudge him along in the daily routine or to motivate him to work harder. That behavior felt comfortable to Tyrone because he'd steered his own younger brother that way during their youth in Baltimore. As the two children of a single mom, they relied on each other for support—and his hard-headed younger brother needed his direction.

"I acted towards Evan more as a big brother than a father. I'd needle him, I'd antagonize him. I hadn't realized I was doing that," he said. "In me stopping that, I find myself falling back on some of the lessons from the class. I ask: 'How would Brian handle this?' and then I dial it back."

Tyrone's father lived with their family for a short while, but on the whole he grew up without a dad. Sometimes his younger brother would return home with a problem and they'd work it out together.

"Evan's not in the same environment we were, so he's not going to need it like we did. There was no one to look out for us, a protector of sorts. The world is scary," Tyrone said. "We had to learn the ropes ourselves through mistake after mistake. I thought I was helping him to teach him some of this, but I was taking the wrong approach."

Once Tyrone stopped being so aggressive and offered support instead, Evan blossomed. Their roughhousing became fun and joyous because Evan wasn't worried that his much-larger dad would take it too far. On the basketball court, Evan could take risks within his own comfort zone, without fearing that his dad would interrogate him for not being aggressive enough.

"Evan, in terms of who he is, those things push him away. Tyrone didn't want that," Erika said. "If Evan gets upset, I can see Tyrone catching himself. It won't even start. Evan will say, 'Daddy, why did you have to do that?' Tyrone will quickly notice it and apologize."

As a clinical psychologist, Erika easily discusses feelings with both kids, encouraging them to be emotionally open with their parents. Her parents immigrated from the Dominican Republic a few years before she and her younger brother and sister were born. Growing up in a small town in the Catskill Mountains, she experienced a safer, more tender upbringing than Tyrone's.

Tyrone now realizes that his children don't need the same toughening up that he and his brother required to survive in Baltimore, where they had to learn to carry themselves to ward off any attacks. "By the mask on your face, they could tell whether you were predator or prey," he said. "You guys have absolutely no idea how little boys were prepped for being men: being pushed to fight each other because you didn't want to be seen as weak or a punk."

Now he recognizes that Evan can be vulnerable or sensitive without being a target. But not in every setting. As a black young man, Evan will experience hard situations.

"There are things he's going to experience that I want to prepare him for. I still feel that's my responsibility, to make sure he understands that not everything is going to be rosy, you can't curl up in a ball in the corner. Face it and keep moving," Tyrone says. "He used to get really upset and couldn't control himself. I would say, 'You need to be able to control that because one of these days you're going to behave like that in a situation where you can't back up that explosion.'"

With coaching from both parents, Evan has learned to manage his emotions better. Neither parent can remember a recent temper tantrum. They've found a compromise between Tyrone's instinct to prepare Evan for a rough world and Erika's impulse to nurture.

~~

DURING MY CHILDHOOD, MY PARENTS saw me and my brother as the enemy in a struggle for control. If we misbehaved, the purpose was "to get attention," so they shouldn't reward the acting out with that desired parental attention. If we fought with each other, it was "sibling rivalry," behavior that—again—they dismissed as attention-seeking. When we chafed at a household rule or ignored their dictates, we were testing their limits.

When I first started raising my children, I easily fell into this frame of mind. Many parents I've interviewed also reflexively explain their children's behavior as limit-testing, manipulative, attention-seeking, or simply spoiled and bratty. Although there may be a grain of truth in this perspective—many sibling fights truly are a bid for parental attention—embracing this worldview merely sets parents up for a power struggle. If you view your children as trying to pull a fast one, or out to win a battle of wits, you've established an oppositional zero-sum game. For you to win means that they must lose, and vice versa.

When I discovered the teachings of PEP and the psychologists and educators you'll meet later in this book, my perspective began to shift. I realized that my single-minded focus on getting my kids to do what I wanted was keeping all of us from winning. Instead, I learned, I could view their inappropriate behavior as a sign that they were missing a skill or there was a problem in the environment, and together we could find a win-win solution.

I am not alone. As modern parents reach for a way of parenting that fits our era, we don't want to either punish or bribe our children into compliance. But today's parents can't quite figure out an effective model to replace the tactics of our parents and grandparents, what I think of as "the Obedience Model." Many devotees of positive parenting struggle with the notion of consequences, which can easily slide into punishment. This is where the lessons of neuroscience and positive psychology come in, pointing the way toward the Apprenticeship Model—an alternative model that gives our kids responsibility within ever-increasing limits that are agreed upon by parent and child.

Of course, putting this model into practice can get messy. Adults making all the decisions is simple. It's more complicated to teach our kids to use social media responsibly or to let them miss deadlines and lose items as they learn to organize themselves. We have to steel ourselves against their discomfort in those moments of failure, an inextricable part of learning.

Part 2

The Solution

5

The Way Forward

NIAMH GRANT PUSHED DOWN THE lever on the electric tea kettle. Her eleven-year-old daughter, Lara, sat nearby, hunched over a bowl of Cheerios at the dark marble kitchen counter in their home in Waterbury, Vermont. The faint early morning light filtered through the window.

"Can you help with lunch?" Lara asked her mom.

"You'll have to use a coupon," responded Niamh, a forty-three-year-old with curly brown hair just brushing her shoulders.

Silence. The Grant girls are responsible for cleaning out their lunch boxes and making lunch for school. For Christmas, they each received five coupons for a parent's help. Lara had hoarded those coupons. She wasn't ready to spend one yet.

Twelve-year-old Isabella slouched into the room, wearing mismatched striped pajamas, her dark blond hair pulled into a messy bun. She called their Golden Doodle dog Denali up to the couch for a cuddle.

Lara pointed to her lunch box, looking at her mom with raised eyebrows.

"Hey, Nali, wanna go for a walk?" Niamh said. She ignored the silent question from Lara. The dog leapt down from the couch and bounded over to the mudroom, where Niamh was pulling on a coat.

"What time is it?" called Isabella from the couch, abandoned by her fuzzy pillow.

"Time to get a watch," Lara said, taking her cereal bowl to the sink.

Isabella gave her an expressionless look.

"That's what you always say to me!" Lara responded with a smile.

Niamh disappeared out the kitchen door with Denali on a leash, cream hat pulled down over her forehead, avoiding a lunch box argument.

Lara brought her lunch box over to the sink. Isabella headed upstairs to change. Lara shoved some leftover food from the box into the countertop compost bin, a bit awkwardly. Some apple slices fell to the counter. She ran a sponge over her lunch box.

The girls' father, Rick, forty-five, came into the room, plopped down at the counter, and put his socks on. Lara grabbed a towel to dry her lunch box. Rick called upstairs: "Izzy, it's five of, hon."

Predictable routines, agreed on in advance, help the whole family avoid conflict. The Grant family, at a relaxed time, had talked through every single step and the time needed to get out of the house. When the kids were younger and balked at some point during the day, the parents had gently reminded them of the routine. They just pointed to the agreements posted on the walls or asked a neutral question like, "What comes next on our schedule?" By now, it was second nature.

Lara poured Smart Puffs into the lunch box. She took a red pepper from the kitchen island and started to slice it with a giant chopping knife.

"Careful," Rick said, hands in his jeans pockets as he watched Lara work.

She playfully stuck her tongue out at her dad. She wrapped the pepper carefully with plastic wrap, then brought the cutting board and knife back to the sink. While her back was turned, Rick put a single piece of candy into her lunch. Lara pulled turkey and cheese from the fridge and put them on the counter. Rick started to slice the cheese. Lara squirted yellow mustard all over two slices of bread.

Niamh came back from walking Denali. She pulled a block of yellow cheese from the fridge.

"Do you want this? You complain a lot about provolone," she said.

Isabella wandered into the room. "Do you know where my long-sleeved shirt is?"

"We need to leave in three minutes," Niamh said, the only reminder she gave all morning.

It felt like she injected caffeine into her children. Everybody sped up. Lara wrapped her cheese and finished packing her lunch. Isabella opened an English muffin with a fork and popped it into the toaster. Lara gave her dad a homework planner to sign. She sorted papers as he looked over the planner.

"I'll be in the car," Niamh said. She vanished out the door again. Later, she told me that she occupies herself when the kids are getting ready so that she's not tempted to nag.

Isabella tied her shoes. Lara zipped her backpack. She paused by the front door. "I feel like I'm missing something." After thinking for a moment, she left the house.

"Where'd the jelly go?" Isabella asked.

"I just put it away. I'm on food put-away," Rick responded. He walked away. A honk sounded from the driveway.

Isabella put her hair in a ponytail, buttered the muffin, then loaded jelly onto it.

Another honk.

"I'm coming," Isabella said to the empty room. She grabbed her bags and nearly collided with her mom coming back in the door.

"I left my phone," Niamh explained. "Did you hear Lara honking?"

And they were gone. It was 7:05 a.m.—just right to get to school on time. The morning had unfolded as you might expect in a household of kids finding their way to independence, with just enough support from parents resisting the urge to direct and correct.

~~

IMAGINE A FUTURE IN WHICH the Grant family is the norm, not the exception. Across the globe, children are productive, helpful, cooperative members of their families and communities. They take responsibility for household chores and their homework, and they play independently with each other in safe neighborhoods. They have harmonious relationships with their parents, working out disagreements through negotiations that address all family members' concerns. The climbing rates of mental, behavioral, and emotional disorders begin to fall. Adults abandon the persistent myths about why children misbehave—to manipulate or get attention—and instead look for the true needs underlying the misbehavior.

This is the Apprenticeship Model in action, and it is absolutely already starting to happen—but in scattered communities, alone or in groups of like-minded families. How can you join this movement?

Begin with a mind-set overhaul. Stop viewing your role as a parent as trying to control your children. From the time our children are born, we feed them and diaper them and rock them to sleep. We're 100 percent in charge. But as they emerge from infancy, our role shifts. We start relinquishing control and building their independence. We start to learn who they are as individuals and to realize that their temperament and preferences may lead them to different choices than we would make ourselves.

Recognize that your young children have a right to autonomy over basic functions like eating, sleeping, toileting, and physical activity. Look for ways to broaden their sphere of influence as they grow capable, to help them begin choosing their own activities, food, reading, friends, clothes, hairstyle, and the like. Teach them skills and social expectations, and then let them experiment. Before jumping in to correct or comment on their behavior, ask yourself whether what they're doing is causing any harm. They'll learn more from trying out different strategies than they will if you hand them the right answer.

In the fall of 2015, I started investigating parenting philosophies beyond the Parent Encouragement Program. From an easy chair in my bedroom, I watched a Skype transmission of the parent educator Vicki Hoefle leading the first session of her six-week parenting class in Burlington, Vermont. Downstairs I could hear Brian and the kids finishing up the dishes from dinner.

"Parenting is getting more difficult, not easier, as we find ourselves completely immersed in a digital age with information bombarding us all day long. It's so hard to figure out how to navigate this new terrain of child raising," Hoefle told the class of about twenty parents. She wore a black turtleneck sweater over a plaid skirt, with black tights and boots.

"It's even more important that we stop and give ourselves time to create a parenting approach that is based in foundational principles and it's something you've thought about and is intentional," she said, barely staying within the frame of my laptop screen as she strode back and forth in front of the class.

"So we land on an approach of parenting that is sustainable for us and sustainable for our kids. Then we can relax a bit and make more informed and thoughtful parenting decisions. The worst decisions are made out of fear. The worst decisions are made when we're not sure what to do but we think we have to do something."

Hoefle encouraged the class to take the next six weeks to hit the pause button and reset their parenting approach. They'd pull the things that are useful from the class. Their own kids would give them the information they need about what works and what's unnecessary. Over and over, they'd return to focus on relationship and independence—the two factors at the root of most family problems.

Parents need to talk less and listen more, Hoefle said. They must abandon the reward and punishment models that have merely served to encourage the pesky behaviors that brought them to the class.

"If talking worked, you'd have all perfect children and not one of you in here does," she said. "If spanking and punishing and consequencing and time-outing and counting worked, I would be out of business and none of you people would be here, because all of your children would be doing exactly what they're supposed to be doing, all the time. What you get is momentary compliance with that kind of parenting. [It's] not sustainable."

The goal, Hoefle said, isn't to lecture your children so that they never make a mistake, but to kick-start their critical thinking by asking them questions, drawing out information. The goal is to have a strong relationship and to encourage your children toward independence. That way, they'll see you as a resource rather than an obstacle.

"Mistakes are when learning happens," she said. "We want to create an environment where kids are making mistakes every single day and we are there to help them process."

Next, she introduced the technique that made her famous: "do-nothing-say-nothing week." That's seven days when parents resist the impulse to direct, nag, bribe, manipulate, yell at, bargain with, punish, reason with, or reward their children. They can't use guilt or turn on the TV as a distraction. The only parenting strategies they can use are to say thank-you, lead by example, notice, engage in dialogue, ask questions, and listen. Seeing skeptical faces, she asked:

"If there was a book out, a parenting book that said to you, 'If you want to raise emotionally healthy, well-connected, compassionate, thoughtful, self-reliant children, you should threaten them, punish them,' would you believe it? You'd never buy this book of parenting strategies, and yet this is what we do with at least 75 percent of our time."

She asked who was starting to panic. Hands popped up. One homeschooling mom motivated her son by rewarding him with computer time for expected behavior.

"So you manipulate," Hoefle said. "Done. No more manipulating."

"He will not learn for the next five days," the mom said.

"We don't know that. He's going to learn *something*," Hoefle replied. "How long have you been doing manipulation with goodies and treats?"

"It's one of the methods. I use that during home schooling," she said.

"It generally doesn't work," the man next to her interjected. I guessed that he was her husband, the boy's dad.

"If it worked, the problem would be solved," Hoefle said.

She encouraged the parents to list their fears. What could go wrong? Being late for work. Being late for school. Noise. Mess. Bad smells. Teeth falling out.

"All this fear is completely unfounded. We have no idea what will happen because we've never given it a chance to see what happens when we give this all up," she told them.

"Here's what's going to happen: You're going to sit them down and say, 'I am so sorry. I went to this parenting class, and evidently I am the problem. Not you. Who knew! I thought you were making my life miserable when in fact I am making all of us miserable.'"

This self-blame may be hard to swallow, but it's a disarming technique and true by definition. Since we're part of the parent-child relationship, we must own some part of any problem with it—as well as the solution.

Whatever dysfunctional parenting strategy you lean on, tell your children you'll no longer do it, Hoefle said. So if you're bossing them around, they're going to need to manage themselves. Walk them through the day so they can anticipate the decisions they will have to make on their own.

At the same time, take notes on what tasks your children can do without help and where they still need your support. Bite your tongue when they head for school and leave the lunch box sitting on the counter, or walk outside without a sweatshirt (and make a mental note to later help them create a plan for remembering).

"You're calm because you have a plan and you're gathering information about how you're disrupting the family by using all these strategies to force your children through the day," she said. "This is like the detox week, and detox sucks. It doesn't matter what you're detoxing from—it's a bad situation. It's going to be really hard."

That's why Hoefle put duct tape on her own kitchen counter, to remind herself to imagine taping her mouth shut when she was tempted to intervene in her kids' budding independence. That's why her most memorable book is called *Duct Tape Parenting*. "The thing that happened is, when my mouth went quiet, their brains flipped on," she said.

One mom asks: what if it's time to go to work and school and the kid won't put on his pants? "Do you take them without their pants on?" she asked.

"I guess so," Hoefle responded. "If somebody makes a choice not to put their pants on. You offered and they said no. I guess they're serious about no pants."

Same with a concern about kids refusing to brush their teeth. One week won't make a difference. Better to solve the problem now than to argue for their entire childhood. A dad asked what to do when it's time to brush teeth.

"I'd say, 'I'm going to brush my teeth, anyone want to come?' Everything turns into an invitation instead of a directive. If you keep directing, you're never going to get out of that job," she said. "Say: 'If you want a book, I'll meet you in the bedroom.' You have to start to change your language. You guys are going to have to dig deep and think about how you talk to other people in your lives to make things happen. So it's going to be awkward for all of you."

A mom raised the challenge of getting her three kids, ages two, four, and six, to bed by herself. Usually they bounced all over each other. She'd hand one a phone to watch a TV show while she rubbed another one's arm. Eventually one would fall asleep and she could turn to the other two.

"I would decide on one thing you're going to do differently to break this up. It's not going to be pretty. They're not going to be like,

'Wow, we have just been obnoxious at bedtime, Mom.' It's going to be detox for them too. You can do it now or you can do it later. It won't magically solve itself," Hoefle said.

For example, the mom could say she's willing to read to all three for a half-hour after teeth brushing and pajamas. "If not, I will tuck you in and I'm done," she said. "There's no scratching, there's no TV, none of that. You get this whole thing much more streamlined. Bedtime should be a ten-minute proposition."

The parents seemed panicked for sure. What about school? Hoefle reassured them that most of the teachers in Burlington knew all about "do-nothing-say-nothing week" and supported the long-term investment in responsible, self-sufficient children. At home, trash and dirty dishes might be left sitting out. But soon enough, the family would figure it out. After fielding some more "what if" scenarios, she sent them into the night with instructions to have fun.

If Hoefle's no-excuses philosophy seems too extreme, don't worry. It's just one of four models of discipline that you can choose from. The others are PEP, which you've already heard about; Ross Greene's model of collaborative and proactive solutions, described in Chapter 7; and the PAX game discussed in Chapter 8. You'll also learn about additional techniques being used in Columbus and Boston to help children self-regulate. But these four methods are the core focus of this book because they represent a comprehensive approach to discipline that contains all three steps that I've identified as critical: connection, communication, and building capability. That's the Apprenticeship Model.

The following three chapters—Chapters 6, 7, and 8—will go over each of these three steps in detail. They're sequential. You must first connect with your kids to get them in a state where they can cooperate. The next step is communicating with them about the problem or issue at hand. This could mean learning what's going on from their perspective or sharing with them the impact of their actions. The final step is building their capability by coaching them on both practical and social and emotional skills. Only after taking these three steps can you successfully set limits, the subject of Chapter 9.

Replacing the Obedience Model with the Apprenticeship Model doesn't give kids a license to disobey rules. The Apprenticeship Model is simply a different perspective on reaching an orderly, collaborative household, one that works for our modern times.

Repeat this three-step pattern—connection, communication, and capability building—as more problems crop up and as your children grow. You'll set limits or implement routines to keep each solution in place. You will see progress and some back-sliding and then more progress as you identify new challenges. The goal of parenting is to work yourself out of the job of parent—to steadily relinquish responsibility and control to your ever-more-capable children.

You may find that different elements of Hoefle's system or PEP's teachings appeal to you. That's fine. Begin wherever you see an opening to apply these examples in your life. Each family is likely to have a different starting point. PEP promotes a gradual ramp-up to the Apprenticeship Model, whereas Hoefle's method can feel like a Band-Aid being ripped off. Ross Greene's model works well for children ages five and up, especially those who are most oppositional. Adults must be patiently persistent as kids learn to open up and understand their own needs. And though the PAX game is designed for classrooms, you can apply its principles of fun and systematic skill-building in your home. Most likely, different pieces of these different techniques will resonate with you and you'll end up with a patchwork of strategies—as I have.

Each of these philosophies returns the word "discipline" to its true meaning: to teach. According to Webster's dictionary, using the word in the sense of "instruction" is obsolete. Call me old-fashioned then. I'm taking us back to the Latin word for "pupil," *discipulus,* with all its lovely associations. When I think of discipline, I think of the time and practice we all need to commit to as our children study the ways of the world and the results of their actions and slowly learn to control themselves.

~~~

EMILY DAVIES CRINGES WHEN SHE remembers how she and her husband berated their son Christopher for being lazy at schoolwork and for not reaching his potential. Although they knew he had ADHD, they didn't realize he also had a learning disability that made it hard for him to process written material.

"We were in this mode of taking away privileges and taking away technology, saying, 'You're going to sit at this table for an hour and work,'" she recalled. "We came to understand that this child is not going to learn the same as we did, as his sister does, as his friends do.

I spent too much time trusting what the school was saying." Now Emily and her husband give Christopher extra support in organization and more time to complete his homework.

Before changing your parenting wholesale, consider the health factors that may be impacting your children's behavior. Are they getting enough sleep, exercise, nutritious foods, vitamin D, and omega-3 fatty acids? Could an overload of electronics use be contributing to unwanted behavior? Could your child have a behavioral or learning disorder that would benefit from a diagnosis and treatment, like Christopher Davies?

Sleep, in particular, may be a culprit. Adults and children alike are remarkably sleep-deprived these days, and busy family schedules and electronics overload often contribute to this problem.

The National Sleep Foundation recommends that elementary school–aged children sleep 10 to 11 hours a night, but according to its poll, on average they sleep 8.9 hours on a typical school night. Older children should sleep 8.5 to 9.5 hours a night, but young teens sleep only about 8 hours a night and older teens average 7.1 hours a night.

Scientists have connected lack of sleep with mood disorders, especially anxiety and depression. Sleep problems in early childhood often predict the development of depression, anxiety, inattention, and hyperactivity. Experiments that restricted sleep caused problems in emotional regulation, mood, and attention.

Omega-3 fatty acids play an important role in the development of the central nervous system, which itself is crucial to healthy brain and emotional functioning. These are the good fats found in fish and many plants, such as kale and flaxseed. You can supplement your child's diet or simply look for foods heavy in omega-3 when you shop.

Researchers are looking at the impact of omega-3 fatty acids on depression, anxiety, ADHD, and other neurological conditions. Although nobody yet recommends replacing traditional therapy with a dose of salmon, a slew of recent papers suggest enriching your family's diet with omega-3 fatty acids. After all, these healthy oils also protect against cardiovascular disease. Talk to your children's doctor for more information, and while you're there, share any behavioral concerns you have.

After reviewing your family's health, wipe the slate clean so that everyone gets a fresh start. Apologize to your kids for having the mistaken impression that you were the boss and that they were to do exactly what you said—for hewing to the Obedience Model. This will disarm them and make them more open to some of the seemingly less pleasant aspects of the Apprenticeship Model, such as taking responsibility and doing chores.

Assess your lifestyle choices. Can you downshift your work or the family schedule—or team up with neighbors—to leave more time for free play and relaxed family interactions? Try to re-create some of the conditions that set up kids for mental and emotional health in previous generations. You may find that it's easier to make changes than you think—even tiny shifts and simple tweaks have a way of snowballing.

That's the path taken by Colin and Camila Cullen, whom you may remember from Chapter 1. Camila came to my PEP class struggling with the hot rage she felt whenever her children refused to cooperate. Having been raised in Nicaragua by a single mother who worked all the time, Camila had grown up with few rules. She did her homework if she felt like it, or she goofed around. Though infrequent, discipline was harsh and sometimes physical. She wanted more consistency and warmth for her own kids, but didn't know how to get there.

In PEP 1, she and Colin learned skills and strategies for being kind and firm leaders of the family and encouraging Mariana and Alejandro to contribute to the household. As discussed in Chapter 4, PEP's parenting education curriculum is rooted in the Adlerian theory that people are motivated by the need to belong and be significant. Adler pioneered the concept of "social interest"—an individual's contribution to the welfare of others—and believed that individuals could solve any problem through cooperation.

Instead of sticker charts, promises of ice cream or toys, praise, time-outs, and punishments, Camila and Colin began to rely on reflective listening, respectful language, routines set by the entire family, and consequences agreed upon in advance. To build stronger relationships, each parent started regularly expressing appreciation for the children's actions and spending one-on-one "special time" with each child. (I'll have more to say on all of these tools in the chapters ahead.)

The Cullen family created a laminated "Listo Para Hoy" ("Ready for Today") with pictures of each step in the morning routine and hand-drawn clock faces showing the time for breakfast, brushing teeth, hand lotion, and sunscreen. They turned one wall of the kitchen into a chalkboard where they wrote the afternoon routine and the kids' favorite activities for special time.

Both parents adjusted their work schedules and the family cut way back on the kids' after-school activities to make room for more relaxed family time together. They also began to create their own community of support, recruiting several parent friends from the kids' public charter school to take PEP classes and swapping books with people whose ideas about parenting resonated with them. As a volunteer room parent at school, Colin shared PEP ideas via email and in person. Gradually, positive ways of interacting with children were taking root at the school and in the community.

You can benefit from these ideas without changing your life wholesale. Certainly, there's no need to discard something that's working for you. Look for incremental change as you adopt new habits. And please read this whole book before dismissing certain notions— you'll soon see how they play out.

Under an authoritative parenting model, some of the strategies may look similar to your previous parenting style. For instance, my children may enjoy thirty minutes of screen time after school once their household jobs, homework, and music practice are done. This routine doesn't seem that different from the computer reward that the home-schooling mom in Vicki Hoefle's class felt reluctant to give up.

The key is that under the Apprenticeship Model, parents negotiate agreements about responsibilities and privileges ahead of time, in discussion with their children. They don't dictate limits unilaterally. Whenever possible, the rules apply to everyone, not just the kids. So if a parent's chores are incomplete, they also must finish up before relaxing in front of a screen. And the agreement is consistently enforced— it applies all week and all month. Screen time after responsibilities are taken care of, for instance, is not a reward the parent pulls out simply to motivate a child to perform one task on a given day.

The psychologists Edward Deci and Richard Ryan of the University of Rochester first showed how connection, competence, and autonomy motivate people more strongly than a reward-punishment scheme. Indeed, rewards actually undermine an individual's intrinsic interest or motivation.

For example, in one study, researchers rewarded one group of people for finding the word "Nina" in drawings by the artist Al

Hirschfeld, while offering no reward to a control group also tasked with looking for the word. Then they pretended the experiment was over but left the drawings, along with other materials, in the room while study participants were waiting. They found that the group that had received a monetary reward for finding Ninas spent less time looking for Ninas for their own enjoyment than those who had not been rewarded. Performing the task in exchange for the rewards seemed to drain the joy out of an otherwise fun activity, reducing intrinsic motivation.

Rewards have the same impact on children. Whether given for grades, household jobs, or behavior, they erode the child's interest in the activity and risk turning a potentially fun challenge into a task to be dreaded.

~~~

LINDA JESSUP GREETED ME IN stocking feet. Opening the sliding glass doors to her modest rambler in Silver Spring, Maryland, the otherwise elegantly clad seventy-four-year-old explained that she lent all her dress shoes to be shined at the recent "Can Do Kids Fair," an annual PEP event that teaches children a variety of useful household skills in a fun environment. She would retrieve the shoes later that evening at the final session of the eight-week parenting class she was teaching.

With the help of a polished, dark wooden cane, Jessup crossed the large open central room of the house, her head almost perpendicular to her chest, a legacy of childhood polio. A white and gray collie trailed her. "Now, Promise," she told the dog firmly as we seated ourselves on the sofa. "We're going to be sitting here talking for a bit, so you must lie down at my feet."

Promise obediently flopped onto the hardwood floor as we began to chat, but couldn't resist lifting her nose and inching closer to the human legs beside her. Soon she rose on all fours and her back knocked over a lightweight table. "Dogs can be like children," Jessup said with a rueful smile, as we righted the table and restored the colorful centerpiece to its spot. "She's in undue attention."

"Undue attention" is the mildest of the four types of misbehavior that children exhibit, which psychologist Rudolf Dreikurs described in his writings on Adlerian psychology. It happens when the child doesn't really need the parent's attention, Jessup told me, as opposed to when the parent is teaching skills, reading, connecting, or engaging in another useful activity. Jessup calls it "undue attention getting" because the child is seeking attention in a socially useless way. We all deserve attention from our loved ones, after all, and it should be built into our daily and weekly activities.

The classic example of undue attention is when your child is playing quietly while you putter in the kitchen, but as soon as the phone rings and you start talking, they come over and start whining for your help. If a child grows more discouraged, undue attention can morph into a power struggle, such as refusal to put on their shoes to leave the house.

If your toddler throws that shoe at you—or your tween slams the door—they could be seeking revenge, the third type of misbehavior. The most discouraged children simply give up, feeling they are inadequate—the final category. This is the child who simply stares at a sheet of math homework with slumped shoulders, or says they'll never learn to tie their shoes.

All these actions are attempts to belong, but in each case the child has come up with a useless or harmful way of belonging. That's why Dreikurs labeled these four kinds of misbehavior "mistaken goals." The child mistakenly thinks, *I belong when I'm the center of attention* (undue attention), or, *I belong when I'm the boss* (power struggle). If a child's unwanted behavior occurs repeatedly and provokes a strong emotional response in you, it's probably a mistaken goal.

Over a dinner of tortilla soup and spinach salad served on vibrantly colored dishes evoking the American Southwest, Jessup and her husband, David, reminisced about the early days of PEP. The house in which they parented three biological and four foster children served as PEP's office for the first eight years. Once, when David threw out his back, the volunteers continued their usual practice of putting together class packets on the couple's bed. "We told him to lie very still as we collated around him," Linda recalled, her vivid blue eyes crinkling as she smiled at the memory.

The conversation drifted further back, to Linda's childhood in a Quaker-Methodist family of four girls living in Mormon-dominated Utah. "I was a troublemaker in school, fighting, and just not able to sit in a seat for any length of time," she said, speculating that she probably had undiagnosed ADHD. "My two older sisters navigated socially by being smart and well behaved, and I navigated socially by fighting. Kids gave me a hard time and I fought."

This early tendency toward mischief inclined Jessup to try to understand her own children when they started acting up. She first discovered Adler through a book discussion group at the Individual Psychology Center, focused on Dreikurs's book *Children: The Challenge*. Soon she was teaching classes out of her home. She taught parents that in order to understand their child's misbehavior, first they had to notice their own emotional response. If they felt annoyed or irritated, the child was probably seeking undue attention. If they felt angry or challenged, it was a power struggle. If they felt hurt or desire to punish, it was most likely revenge. And if they felt despair or hopelessness, the child's assumed inadequacy was the problem.

It's a bit counterintuitive. You may think that your reaction will differ based on your mood or personality, but this Adlerian framework is actually a remarkably accurate way of diagnosing misbehavior regardless of individual characteristics. That's because we are so deeply connected to our children, and so much a part of our family system, that we play out the same patterns repeatedly. You should help your child find positive ways of belonging that address their specific mistaken goals. You might redirect a child who is seeking undue attention or set up routines to avoid the annoying situation. Because a child seeking revenge is feeling hurt, you might assuage that hurt by apologizing or showing that you care. The goal is to shift the child from trying to *get* something—whether undue attention, power, or revenge—into being able to *contribute* something to the situation or family needs.

At age nine, Jessup contracted polio in Brisbane, Australia, where the family spent a year during her father's Fulbright fellowship. "Polio was a really good experience for me, in a lot of ways," said Jessup, who was paralyzed for weeks by the virus. "For a really hyperactive kid, it brought me to an abrupt halt. I was isolated at home since I didn't need to be in an iron lung, when they weren't sure how it spread. We always say I discovered my brains."

Those brains serve her well at PEP, where Jessup is legendary for her wisdom about how to handle thorny parenting problems. She can hold a class spellbound with a story of her creative solution to a recalcitrant child. She acts so realistically in classroom role-plays—perhaps channeling her own rebellious youth—that she can reach parents who are resistant to PEP's methods and not persuaded by lecturing.

She's also famous for committing herself so completely to the present moment that she loses track of time. That's where we found ourselves now, as David Jessup asked what time she had to leave for class.

Linda Jessup glanced quickly up at the wall clock. "We have to be gone now," she said calmly. "Don't forget your shoes," her husband reminded her. We were soon hurtling along the road in Jessup's maroon Nissan Rogue, seeming to hit every pothole possible. A dozen parents were gathering at the Kensington Baptist Church to pour their troubles into Jessup's sympathetic ear.

~~~

When talking to parents about discipline, I regularly field a range of objections to replacing rewards or punishments with democratically agreed upon limits. One dad told me that time-outs worked with his four-year-old and six-year-old. The kids stopped misbehaving because they were scared of the time-out. I responded that I wouldn't call that "working." "Are you really teaching children what they need to survive in life? Or are you teaching them to be sneaky so they don't get caught?" I asked him. Surely, he was in a parenting class because something needed to be tweaked—could the disrespect and noodling he complained about on the first day of class be evidence of clever children taking revenge for punishment?

He conceded that he'd signed up for parenting education because he was tired of always being the enforcer and wanted quieter, more loving family moments together. "Are time-outs nurturing their relationship with you, or creating distance?" I asked. "And even if they do work in the moment, do you want to succeed by instilling fear in your children?"

So how do you get the kids to do what you want? The painful secret of this book is that you, the adult, truly have to give up control of the outcome. Let your child struggle with life and its real consequences, rather than battle you.

That's possibly the hardest thing for a parent or teacher to do—to have faith that an inexperienced child will grow in the right direction without us guiding every step. But the lessons of experience stay with a child longer.

Take the situation of a child refusing to carry a coat on a chilly day. If you nag him into bringing a coat—or say, "I told you so," when he gets cold—he focuses on the annoying parent. If he experiences being cold without a comment from you, he may be more likely to decide to bring a coat next time. Some parents ask: what if he doesn't care? Then you have to stop caring about the coat too. (And you have to stop caring about what other people—whoever that means in your life—will think of your parenting when they see your coatless child.)

No matter where you are in the parenting journey, you can start using the Apprenticeship Model today. Customize your actions to your child's age. If your children are under three, your focus will be on connecting with them, encouraging independence, redirecting strong emotions, and beginning the routines that will eventually turn into household jobs. By ages four and five, children become more logical. Defuse tantrums by offering them limited choices; do household work alongside them, and give them as much independence as possible in dressing, bathing, and other daily tasks. Although this is an exhausting phase of parenting, you're lucky to be able to start with positive messages while your young children are still extremely impressionable.

I came to PEP when our middle child was five, and my heart sank when I learned that by this age children have already formed their beliefs about who they are and where they fit into the family and the world. Maddie was often in a power struggle with us because her frequent mistaken goal was to belong by being the boss. It was our fault—both Brian and I are control freaks at heart, so we imparted the message to her that power is valuable.

But starting later, when your children are older, doesn't mean the cause is lost. Ages six to eleven present many opportunities to engage children in problem-solving, coach them through emotional struggles, and enlist them in cooking and cleaning while they still think it's fun to work alongside you. With their greater capacity, you will find that their help is actually useful—unlike the contributions of younger children, whose assistance takes more supervision and time than if you had done the work yourself. This is also the prime time to make sure your kids master all the elements of self-care, from bathing and dressing to organizing and caring for their belongings. If they're overwhelmed by the quantity of clothes or toys they need to tidy, give some away. They may simply own too many things.

Ages twelve through eighteen are often seen as a more challenging time for parenting, as children focus more on their peers and less on their parents and seek independence in a way we may misinterpret as rebellion. But in a sense, this is your last chance to build a strong relationship with your children before they venture beyond your orbit. Seize it. With teenagers, the key is to respect their privacy and independent identity, being very clear about your expectations and the consequences for breaking family rules. Think of your growing teens as being surrounded by a set of limits and family agreements, with the boundary expanding as soon as they show they are able by accepting greater responsibility. Instead of looking for ways to constrain them because you fear they're not ready, look for ways they can demonstrate responsibility and increase their freedom. Remember to focus on your relationships with your teens as well. Don't be dissuaded if they sneer or seem dismissive of your opinion; keep reaching out. They still want to be asked for hugs and special time together, even if they accept these ways of connecting only rarely.

At every age, remember always to take a long-term view. It may seem crucial to solve today's bedtime drama or ensure that the math test goes well. But the lessons of responsibility, accountability, and organization that your child could learn today are ultimately more important than one night's sleep or a single grade. We have a bias toward action in our culture, but in many scenarios, wise parents simply do nothing. Let things unfold and don't be afraid of a messy outcome. Like Niamh Grant, you may find that you need to leave the room, or house, to escape your impulse to intervene. Take note of what works and persevere. Just as your kids are, you are learning self-control and new patterns of behavior. Your patience in the moment will pay off in the end.

6

Connection

MADDIE DASHED AWAY FROM ME on a crowded New York City side-walk. I grabbed Ava's hand and speed-walked to catch up with Mad-die. We dodged a hipster college student in line for the food truck. Maddie's dark mop of hair came into view.

I grabbed her shoulder.

"Maddie, let's get some food," I said. "We'll all feel better after lunch."

"I'm not hungry," she snapped at me. She pulled her body out of reach.

"Look, there's a Chinese dumpling food truck," I said, relieved that she'd stopped running.

Anger had sometimes sent Maddie stalking away from the family, out of sight even on unfamiliar city streets. Now she stood a safe dis-tance away from me, face knotted in a scowl.

Ava and I ordered three different kinds of dumplings and noodles. We perched on a nearby bench. Ava devoured the food. I picked at the cheap, doughy noodles. Maddie sat with us, but spurned the food. I urged her to eat. It was the spring of 2016, when she was twelve years old and Ava was nine. We'd just left the Developmental Affective Neuroscience Lab at Columbia University, where Nim Tottenham, an associate psychol-ogy professor, attaches electrodes to mothers and their children, measures their saliva, and scans their brains to assess their emotional connection.

I didn't need a scientist to evaluate my connection to Maddie right now. Any of the random passersby looking at her rigid back and clamped-shut mouth could have seen that it was strained.

Sweat dotted my hairline, from the humid air and the fast walk. And perhaps also because my plans for the weekend—for reporting this section of the book—had just fallen apart.

~~~

THE DAY HAD STARTED SO well.

I'd brought the kids to New York City on their spring break to see my brother and also to visit Tottenham's lab. Her research builds on decades of studies that have found that maternal neglect harms growing children by asking the opposite question: how does a healthy, nurturing relationship affect the brain? They were studying how children learn from their mothers' responses and how mothers' physiology affects their children's heartbeat and stress levels. To help them in that effort, Ava and I had signed up to have our parent-child bond judged by an fMRI machine and a battery of psychological tests.

Why did I agree to let a team of scientists assess my connection to my child? To some moms, it would be anathema to have your parent-child relationship clinically judged.

One reason was that signing up for the assessment was the easiest way to get a glimpse inside Tottenham's lab without jumping through hurdles to protect patient confidentiality. It's what she suggested when I asked to observe the study; she herself, she told me, had participated in the study with her two similarly aged girls. And I was eager to understand her work because I had a growing conviction that the adult-child connection is the single most important pillar of effective discipline.

Connection can transform a fierce conflict—like the stand-off between Maddie and me on that New York City sidewalk—or a child's meltdown. As discussed in Chapter 3, these are the moments when your child's amygdala is flooding their body with stress hormones, when holding hands can help them self-regulate. If you connect with your child, you stand a chance of helping them calm to the point where they can access the problem-solving parts of their brain. Indeed, the moment when your child seems most unlovable is exactly when they need connection the most.

Even when you can't interrupt your child's dysregulation, you can model how to stay calm and regulated in the midst of conflict. For sure, you want to avoid yelling or getting amped up, which your child is likely to mimic, whether consciously or because of the biological forces that Tottenham and other researchers are decoding.

One caveat: putting the relationship first doesn't give you an excuse to back down from enforcing an agreed-upon family rule. It gives children a sense of security to know that the boundaries are solid, even if they respond by raging against them. Your job is not to make your kids happy all the time. You can connect with a touch and an empathetic word even when you're saying no or upholding a rule. This is key in the Apprenticeship Model.

The day began with us filling out paperwork in the lab, whose rooms looked like a nondescript doctor's office. Ava leaned forward in a low armchair, listening to the explanation of the day ahead. She wore a baggy T-shirt and sweats, her long brown hair pulled into her typical messy ponytail.

"In this lab, we're very interested in emotion and brain development," explained Bridget Callaghan, a postdoctoral scholar with a perky Australian accent. "We're really interested in how kids learn about particular things, how they respond emotionally, and also how their parents help them to change how they think and feel."

This first day, Ava and I would be playing computer games and taking psychological, language, and math assessments, often while our heartbeats, sweat production, and hormone levels were being measured. The next day we'd go to Columbia's medical center for mother-daughter fMRI scans, Callaghan explained.

"Have you ever been in an MRI machine before?" she asked Ava.

"I've seen pictures of one," she responded.

"An MRI machine is pretty cool," Callaghan said. "It uses magnets which turn on and off really quickly to take photographs of your brain. It's very special because it's able to see beneath your skin to show you what your brain looks like."

Lab manager Kaitlin O'Sullivan gave Ava a piece of gum and asked her to chew it until it was "juicy" and her mouth filled with enough spit to be soaked up by a wad of cotton. That would give a baseline measurement of Ava's cortisol level, an approximate measure of stress, to compare to another spit test in ninety minutes.

Next, we answered a battery of questions to screen for metal that might be in our bodies, which could be dislodged by the powerful magnets in the MRI machine. Ava had never worked as a machinist.

She had no cochlear implants, shrapnel, or bullets in her body. Callaghan reassured Ava that nothing painful would happen to her. "You're volunteering your time, and we're really happy you are," she said. "It's really important that if you feel uncomfortable or there's anything you feel you can't do, just let us know."

Callaghan took a photo of me that they would show to Ava later in the study. She and O'Sullivan hooked us up to EKG electrodes to measure our heart rates, one stuck to each shoulder blade and one on the belly. Thin wires clipped to the electrodes snaked out of our clothes and around our bodies. Then they left us alone in a tiny exam room with nothing but a couple of kids' magazines: *National Geographic Kids* for me and *Highlights* for Ava. As we read silently, a line tracking our heartbeats rolled across the nearby computer screen for the scientists to review later and determine whether and how our body rhythms were synchronizing.

I felt very aware of the wires enmeshing me and didn't want to move my body or disturb the web of cords. Ava seemed perfectly comfortable and relaxed. She came across some knock-knock jokes—her favorite. She read them to me, just as if we were sitting on the couch at home. It was an odd but sweet experience to share with her this glimpse into the minute detail involved in data-gathering for neurobiological research. After a few minutes, Callaghan returned to unhook us.

Then we separated. Callaghan hooked me up to new wires to measure my sweat response, while O'Sullivan took Ava to perform computerized tests in another room. I sat in front of a computer with earphones on so that I could hear an annoying sound that periodically played while I watched different-colored shapes appear on the computer screen. A camera videotaped my reaction—a scrunched-up face and slight startle when I heard the noise—to play back for Ava while she was inside the fMRI machine. The goal: to see if she could learn about threats more effectively from watching her mother's experience rather than a stranger's.

As Callaghan connected the wires and set up the experiment, I asked what had brought her to Columbia. She had originally worked with rodents, and she found that when baby rats were separated from their mothers, they experienced accelerated neural development. That's the kind of brain change that leads to overly anxious, reactive adults. At the time, Tottenham's lab was beginning to publish similar findings in humans. It seemed a natural fit.

Scientists can look at the brains of children—whether rats or humans—when they're separated from their mother and see reactivity in the amygdala, which controls the fight-or-flight response. When the mom comes back, the scientists have observed, the children's brains return to normal.

It's not just brain activity. The mother's presence helps regulate infants' body temperatures, heart rates, sleep, and elimination habits.

A Columbia psychiatrist named Myron Hofer discovered this by accident when he arrived at his lab to find that a mother rat had chewed through her cage and escaped. Her rat pups were shivering in the nest, their body temperatures having dropped to less than half of normal. They were unable to snuggle next to her warm body. Thinking that the pups simply needed to be warmed, Hofer tried doing so with a man-made heat source—but the pups still showed sluggish heart rates. He tried stimulating the babies with a cloth that smelled like their mother, and he tried grooming them; each of these efforts helped, but the pups' overall metabolic activity remained subdued. Hofer's research led to a whole body of work on early infant separation in humans and mice and helped support developments in attachment theory that traced emotional and behavioral problems in adulthood back to infancy.

In further experiments in the 1970s, Hofer showed that pups' fear response could be switched on by the mom's behavior. Remarkably, rat pups responded even when scientists piped the scent from their fearful rat mother into the cage. Similarly, human babies look to their mothers for cues as to whether a new situation or object is safe. This is one reason, researchers believe, that conditions such as anxiety, depression, and mood disorders are so often passed down from parent to child, not just genetically but owing to environmental factors as well. When a parent can't effectively regulate their own emotions or their sense of fear, the children don't learn to do so.

Although behavioral scientists have observed the intergenerational transmission of mental illness, researchers like Tottenham are just beginning to understand the biological mechanisms that underpin mental health and dysregulation. The key is to figure out the impact of the parent-child interactions you can observe with your eyes on the cellular changes that require microscopes and MRI machines to document.

Remember from Chapter 3 that as a child's brain is developing, it's healthy to experience an arousal response—whether fear, anger, or another strong emotion—followed by regulation. That toning is like a workout for your brain because it creates neural pathways that help you manage stress and anxiety. Scientists believe that it's advantageous for a developing brain to stay plastic and flexible as long as possible— to allow this regulation pattern to take hold, among other reasons.

Researchers are trying to incorporate into this framework the findings that when children are neglected or raised without a reliable parent, their brains mature prematurely into a less-flexible state. On the one hand, this helps the children to manage situations—without the help of an adult—that other children their age couldn't cope with. On the other hand, it seems also to bake into the brain a tendency to overreact to threats and be less able to differentiate true danger.

Something about the way the child's regulatory system learns about threats in the environment during development has enduring effects into maturity. Just as rats or monkeys isolated from their mothers early in their development become fearful and aggressive, young children who grow up without a secure attachment to a stable adult are more likely to be anxious or risk-taking adults. As part of understanding how this works at the level of the brain, neuropsychologists like those in Tottenham's lab are looking closely at all the mechanisms in securely attached, typically developing kids and their parents.

Once I completed the annoying noise video, Callaghan turned off the videocamera recording me and gave me a final task on the computer. As pictures of animals flashed across the screens, either scary or cute, I realized that I was taking the implicit bias test. I'd taken the test before, when I was writing about unconscious racial bias. The test was designed by Project Implicit at Harvard University, based on social science research about unconscious racial bias. Because US society treats white people more favorably than black people, many people— including me—internalize that bias. As a result, even if I do my best not to act in racist ways, my first, split-second response to a black face is likely to be negative—either fearful or rejecting. Sure enough, the animal images gave way to black and white faces, to which I had to react quickly.

When I finished the implicit bias test, she set me to work filling out a long questionnaire about my child-rearing practices, demographics, general health, and Ava's health and development, as well as psychological assessments to evaluate Ava for anxiety, grit, depression, and behavioral disorders.

Finally, I regrouped with Tottenham to talk about how her interest in biology, emotional development, and parent-child relationships had come together over time. She was chic in black pants, tank top, and shirt, a trim woman with a neat, dark chignon and the energy of someone whose to-do list exceeds the time in the day. As we talked, she periodically glanced at the time on her Fitbit to be sure she wasn't late for her next appointment. Like me, Tottenham has an Asian mother (Korean) and white father (Irish-English).

"Studying children who have an extreme disruption in caregiving makes it clear that parents are important," she explained. Her inflection was low and controlled, the habit of a petite woman determined to be heard and taken seriously.

"We certainly knew that from decades of work, but we don't know why parents are important. What are parents actually doing on a moment-to-moment basis to sculpt our emotional biology? We have these micro-interactions with our kids all day long—that's really what parenting is—so what effect does that have in childhood?"

Every test that my daughter and I took would help the lab get at a different question: Could Ava learn to avoid a shape that triggers an annoying noise from watching my emotional reaction? Would she learn faster watching me as compared to a stranger? When we sat together, how quickly did our heartbeats and breathing synchronize? If I was in the room, did she perform better on a computerized task?

"From a neuroscientific vantage point, you want to get to the level of mechanism: if you pull this lever, what happens?" Tottenham said. "The parent's presence is a powerful buffering effect against a lot of arousal in the emotional brain region."

The results of all the experiments that Ava and I participated in would help the lab piece together a picture of how a parent's influence and simple physical presence can help children learn and self-regulate. Eventually scientists will understand how parents can protect children from threats at the neural level—as well as how parents unwittingly pass along anxiety, depression, and other pathologies to their offspring.

Unfortunately, Ava and I wouldn't get our individual results—all the study participants would remain anonymous and be lumped together.

As Tottenham and I finished up our chat, she asked about a casual comment Maddie had made while I was filling out paperwork. It turned out that one of the many questions I answered—which Maddie knew about—disqualified me and Ava from participating in the fMRI study the following day. That's what had led to Maddie's bad mood. She thought she'd ruined my book.

～～

IN THE SQUAD ROOM OF Boston Police District B-3 in Mattapan, nearly two dozen police officers lined the walls of the room, wearing pressed blue uniforms. Their insignia sparkled. They folded their arms across their chests or clasped their hands together over their belt buckles. They were listening. It was moments before roll call, when they usually received an update on overnight crime and instructions for the day to come.

Today the professor was in.

Ronald Ferguson, a Harvard University economist, was lecturing about the importance of holding babies and talking to them. He urged the officers to share his words with the young men they encountered on the streets of Mattapan and North Dorchester, one of the most violent districts of the city. That year to date, Mattapan had tallied nineteen shooting victims—more than any other district. Roxbury was coming in second, at fourteen victims.

"Most of you know that the majority of people behind bars are high school dropouts. A lot of the seeds to becoming high school dropouts were planted when they were little bitty kids. We're trying to nip it in the bud," said Ferguson, a tall black man with a small, graying goatee.

He explained that Harvard's Achievement Gap Initiative had boiled down decades of social science research into "the Boston Basics": five things that parents should do with babies to build secure attachments and lay the foundation for school and life success. I'd traveled to Boston to see whether public policy wonks and nonprofits could change how new parents across the city nurtured their babies. This initiative seemed poised to build the parent-child connection from infancy.

The first of five steps in the Boston Basics framework is maximize love and manage stress. The security that babies feel from being held and having their needs met builds their ability later in life to "be able to form an intention and follow through on it, which is called executive function skills," Ferguson said.

The squad room could have been a classroom, with its dull checked linoleum floor, simple tables, and institutional color scheme. The students here were patrol officers who usually only connected with members of the community over negative incidents, like a domestic incident or a noise complaint. The police were trying to change that through community outreach and initiatives like turning the station into a haunted house for Halloween or giving out gifts at Christmas.

Ferguson stood a few steps from Wendell Knox, a Black Philanthropy Fund trustee; an even taller black man, with a sharper suit, Knox had introduced Ferguson. Next to Knox were the Boston police commissioner, William Evans, and Mayor Martin Walsh, both cleanshaven white men. Walsh wore a blue AUTISM SPEAKS puzzle pin on the lapel of his charcoal gray suit.

The second Boston Basics bullet point: talk, sing, and point. From three months before they're born, babies can hear the sounds around their mothers from within the womb. They're born preferring their mother's language to any other. So from the beginning, parents should narrate life to help babies develop verbal skills.

The importance of early language exposure came to light in the mid-1990s when the University of Kansas researchers Betty Hart and Todd Risley tucked voice recorders into babies' blankets and carriages so they could count how many words the infants heard. They found that babies from low-income families heard roughly 30 million fewer words by age three than children from upper-income families.

Early in his career, Ferguson studied programs aimed at keeping African American and Latino students from falling behind in high school and college, a persistently stubborn problem. While 88 percent of white public school students graduated from high school in 2015, only 75 percent of their black counterparts received their diploma, according to the National Center for Education Statistics. Poverty compounds the inequity.

The more time Ferguson spent on this seemingly intractable problem, the more complex the web of historical and institutional factors that kept students of color from pulling even looked to him. It seemed ever more daunting to raise achievement levels while narrowing the disparities.

Ferguson kept coming back to two statistics. In humans, 80 percent of brain growth occurs in the first three years of life. And by age two, the achievement gap already exists. At nine months, there are few discernible differences in a baby's behavior or learning based on race, family wealth, or parents' education. But as early as eighteen months, Hispanic and black children—and the kids of less-educated parents—already show lower average scores in vocabulary, listening comprehension, and sorting skills. The best classroom-based efforts to combat the achievement gap—even as early as age three in Head Start—come too late to do the most good. This fact hits home in Boston, one of the most racially segregated cities in the country.

Ferguson continued the lecture in the squad room.

The third Boston Basic: count, group, and compare. "That's laying the foundation for mathematics," he said. "It's an intellectual breakthrough for a toddler when they understand that numbers correspond to groups of things. Four is not just a word you say after three and before five."

Fourth: explore through movement and play. "We want to tell parents: pay attention to what your kids are interested in. When they're playing, they're not just wasting time."

The fifth Basic is to read and discuss stories. "People talk a lot about reading to little kids, but they don't talk about discussing things with little kids, getting those thinking wheels turning in their heads," he said. "Ask them, 'Why do you think the character did that? What do you think's going to happen next? How would you finish writing the story?'"

Each of the Boston Basics grew out of decades of research on optimal child development. Each one builds a strong connection between parent and child. Each one lays the foundation for verbal and math skills, secure attachment, physical fitness, and mental health.

The Achievement Gap Initiative aims to blanket the city with these five simple messages and to reinforce them in multiple venues, including doctor's offices during well-baby visits, churches, barber shops, housing developments, and community health centers. In maternity wards, nurses teach parents the Boston Basics before they're discharged with a new baby. And now beat cops would share them as they patrolled the neighborhood.

"We're not trying to fix anyone. We're not saying people are broken in any way. We're just saying we know some stuff, and if you do this, your babies can have better lives," Ferguson told them. "This is an opportunity for all of us. We're trying to saturate the entire community. We want it to be impossible that if you live in Boston you don't know about the Basics."

The effort builds on a model of social pediatrics in which health care providers and civic leaders join together to help parents change their behavior in ways that benefit children. One famous example is the "Reach Out and Read" campaign, which enlisted pediatricians to combat illiteracy. Dr. Barry Zuckerman founded Reach Out and Read in 1989; he's also involved in the Boston Basics.

Ferguson and his colleagues have developed a website and videos in English, Spanish, and Haitian Creole. They're creating an app that will push out suggestions for activities and interactions at each stage of a child's development—sort of gamifying the infant-raising process. Already, interest in other cities, including Ossining, New York, and Chattanooga, Tennessee, has led to parallel efforts, as well as an umbrella group called The Basics National Network. Ferguson hopes that eventually the Boston Basics will become part of the standard routines of each institution that becomes a partner in propagating the Basics.

"What the society needs is something that can go to scale, something that can reach everybody," Ferguson told me on the phone, when I was planning the trip. "People's lives are already crowded with folks trying to get them to do stuff."

Ferguson's grandmother—a special education teacher—made sure to enrich his childhood in Cleveland in the 1950s and 1960s. When he was twelve and learning the clarinet, she took him to a Duke Ellington concert. She brought him and his three brothers to events with her college sorority. Her encouragement led him to art and dance lessons at Cleveland Karamu House, a black arts center. She herself had benefited in her childhood from exposure to the broader world and culture at the Phyllis Wheatley settlement house, which became her after-school refuge. Then she met and married Ferguson's grandfather, a dapper man who was refined but liked to drink and smoke cigars.

"She didn't go as far in school or do as much in life as she probably would have if she hadn't met my grandfather," he told me later in the same day he spoke to the Mattapan police. We were sitting together in his Harvard office. "In some ways, I was the realization of aspirations that she had had but never completely lived out."

He recalled visiting in her living room with her stepfather, a former Pullman porter who was about ninety-four years old at the time. Ferguson was perhaps twenty-five, had a bachelor's degree from Cornell University, and was enrolled in graduate school at the Massachusetts Institute of Technology. He was the wonder child, carrying the family's hopes.

"He had watched me grow up. I was in the PhD program at MIT, and I was doing well. I think he identified vicariously and thought about where I was compared to what he had experienced in life. There were things that he wasn't allowed to do, but I was being allowed to do them," he said.

Ferguson wrote a poem about that conversation, "Sacred Words from a Great-Grandfather." He swiveled to the computer screen and pulled up the poem.

When I was in my twenties
Like you,
There was a lot'a things
They wouldn't let a black man do.
Now that things have changed,
My life is nearly over.
But I'm not sad about it.

Your soul and mine are one,
And we're still gonna make it.
I want the best for you;
And I want you
To want the best for yourself.

Don't stop tryin'.
Don't stop believin' in yourself.
Don't stop scratchin' and clawin'
And pullin' and sweat'n

And above all
Don't stop
Don't stop rememberin' –
That I love you.

Ferguson writes a lot. He and project coordinator Jocelyn Friedlander wrote the script for every Boston Basics video. He narrated the English-language ones too. As he shared more of his poetry with me, I realized I was receiving a tour of his career of the last twenty years. As I evaluated him, I gathered that he was sussing me out too.

Ferguson is a preacher as much as a poet; he often writes a few verses to deliver in a speech to preschool teachers or math educators. Every piece carries a message, sometimes explicitly linked to a concept in educational theory. One poem responds to educators who are reluctant even to discuss underperforming students' problems, for fear of seeming racist, and who focus instead on the positives.

Later in the day, we drove to a "fatherhood summit" sponsored by the Massachusetts Department of Children and Families at a nondescript Doubletree hotel in Westborough, a western suburb of Boston. Driving down the Mass Pike, Ferguson pointed out a digital billboard, with huge images of the Boston Basics, on the site of another partner, WGBH, the New England PBS affiliate. At the conference, he schmoozed with nonprofit and local government officials, all of whom were seeking to engage fathers more deeply in the lives of their children and convince them "to give up trying to get over, and shift to trying to get ahead," as Ferguson said to one small group of attendees. ("To get over" is slang for exploiting a situation or the system.)

Ferguson left the event with the business card of a facilitator whom he thought could be a good Boston Basics trainer as well as a contact from the Cape Verdean community who might be able to recruit a volunteer to narrate the videos in Cape Verdean Creole. (I later learned that facilitator became the program director managing dissemination of the Basics in Boston.) With limited resources and a long timeline—it would take perhaps three years for the program to permeate Boston—Ferguson was always looking to win allies and volunteers to the cause of nurturing parents.

In the nine hours I spent shadowing Ronald Ferguson, he consumed only food purchased from Dunkin' Donuts while hurrying from one meeting to another—an egg-and-cheese sandwich with orange juice for breakfast and chicken salad on flat bread with apple juice for lunch. By the end of the day he was tired—it was a Monday but felt like a Friday, he said.

～～

A'ZAYAH RUSSELL RUSHED UP TO the couch where I was sitting with his mom, Jasmine. His tiny fist clutched her phone. Bare brown legs thrust forward in that unbalanced, stiff-legged walk typical of toddlers. He wore a diaper and a lime green Boston Public Health Commission T-shirt.

He slipped, then started wailing.

"Whoopsies," Jasmine said. A'Zayah pushed up to standing again. "You okay? Did you have a boo-boo?"

In response, he grabbed Jasmine's second phone. "As long as he don't call 911, I'm fine. Or call anybody from the Boston Housing Authority," she joked.

Dashing away, he slipped again. *Thump.* This time the cries were about pain, not protest.

Jasmine reached down and pulled A'Zayah onto her lap.

"You okay? Are you okay?"

A'Zayah said something I couldn't understand.

"You hurt your knee? Okay." Jasmine gave him a big cuddle, gauging the weight of his diaper at the same time. "Did you already wet your diaper?"

He mumbled again.

"I know, ba-ba," said Jasmine, a thirty-four-year-old woman with dark-rimmed librarian glasses, long braids, and a snug T-shirt over bedazzled jeans.

Apparently comforted, he pushed away from his mom. He grabbed for the Thomas the Train set on the floor of the dark living room. A wet breeze floated through the open window.

Young children touch base with their parents constantly throughout the day, to get information or reassurance. This healthy give-and-take, the blend of connection and encouragement, will build A'Zayah's ability to self-regulate.

Jasmine was telling me about her first exposure to the Boston Basics. Her advocate at the Boston Public Health Commission, Lori

Caiby, showed her one of the videos and told her to pick up A'Zayah as much as she wanted.

That surprised Jasmine. Her relatives always warned her that you'd spoil babies by picking them up every time they cried.

She seized on Lori's encouragement to disregard those voices. It felt natural to respond to her baby's needs. From the time he was born, she loved stripping them both down for skin-to-skin contact, which studies have shown reduces infant crying, improves mother-baby attachment, and boosts successful breast-feeding. She ignored her grandmother's concern that he'd catch a cold. She just bundled them both in a blanket.

But she was still figuring out the "manage stress" part of the first Basics point. She's a single mom taking care of a sick boy, living in a housing project in Charlestown with only her grandmother for help. When she discovered she was pregnant, she'd had to leave the rooming house where she was staying because of a no-family policy. "When you're pregnant, it's supposed to be one of the happiest times in your life," she said. "That was the hardest time."

She bounced around on friends' couches for about a year before getting the subsidized apartment in Charlestown, when A'Zayah was five months old. A'Zayah has a metabolic disorder, and at the moment was sick with bronchitis. That was on top of ear surgery in February, just a month after he turned two. It was April now.

"He was going deaf. He had tubes put in," she said. "He had about ten ear infections in one year."

"Mommy, Mommy," A'Zayah interrupted, holding up a train.

"Those are some of the stressors," Jasmine said.

"Mommy, Mommy."

"Yes, my baby. Did you want Mama?" Jasmine looked over to admire A'Zayah's construction.

"High-five," she said.

They slapped hands.

"Awesome work. I love you. High-five."

Another hand slap. "Choo choo," A'Zayah said. He turned back to the trains.

"The thing that struck me. A lady by the name of Betty, she found a thirty-million-word gap or something to that nature. That struck me."

"Choo choo."

Jasmine's phone rang, but she silenced it after a glance.

"When we have disadvantaged children, they hear less words than children that are more advantaged," she said. "I kind of knew from my background with children that you read with your child, when you're pregnant. They start to hear you at five to six months, in utero. I read to him when I was pregnant. I used to always grab a book, any book I could get my hands on. He's very, very smart, even though he's a tad delayed on communication, due to his hearing."

Jasmine knows about child development from working for years at different schools, from preschool to third grade, in addition to assorted customer service jobs. She served as a substitute teacher in a Catholic school in Brockton and then ran the after-care program. The school called her back as a paraprofessional in kindergarten for two years. Between 2003 and 2009, she earned forty credits in early childhood education at Massasoit Community College and Quincy College, a community college in Dorchester. She hopes to go back to school and get an associate's degree.

Nowadays, she helps out at Jump Start while A'Zayah is in day care, in return for a stipend and credit for performing community service. So far, that's satisfied the Department of Transitional Assistance requirements to continue her food and housing benefits. She contributes to the Jump Start team planning meeting, preparing lessons on reading for enjoyment and reading for reconstruction. They supervise preschoolers in dramatic play, puzzles, writing, arts, and other areas.

Jasmine is fortunate. Some low-income moms can't manage to get vouchers for day care, Caiby told me the previous day when I visited her office at the Public Health Commission. Without day care, children start kindergarten seriously behind their peers—unless the parents take their babies out, socialize them, and expose them to enriching activities.

Jasmine also fields nonstop emails and phone calls in her role as president of the community board, which is negotiating a redevelopment of the community with the housing authority and developers. And she runs a popular playgroup in Mattapan, about an hour away by bus. That's how I first saw her name: on the playgroup flyer distributed at the Mattapan police station.

Other Boston Basics points come naturally to Jasmine. "I try to talk to him as much as I can, especially when we're outside."

She's teaching A'Zayah sign language. Since ten months of age, he pointed to everything, the first developmental step in associating words with objects.

While we were talking, A'Zayah was fussing under the couch. Then he disappeared into another room. He returned now with a plastic light saber. I tried to play Jedi with him, but he was not having it.

"No!"

I looked at Jasmine, puzzled. A'Zayah swept the light saber through the skirt of the couch. Not exactly attacking it. Not playing pretend. Frustrated.

Comprehension dawned on me. I took the light saber and used it to fish under the couch for a lost train.

A smile broke across A'Zayah's face. He grasped the train.

"Say thank you," Jasmine said.

"Ta ta."

"That's how he says thank you," she said.

"That's his little broom," explained Dorothy Russell, Jasmine's grandmother, who had been sitting in a nearby rocking chair.

A'Zayah's upbringing differs from Jasmine's own. Her mom got pregnant with her at age sixteen, then proceeded to have nine more children, the youngest of whom is now ten. Taking care of her siblings probably kept Jasmine from getting into trouble herself, but it wasn't much fun for her as a teenager.

"How I grew up? Very rough. I don't mean for my life, I just mean in the sense of being a household of ten people," Jasmine said. "I was the live-in babysitter for my mom, taking care of all my brothers and sisters. There wasn't really a life for me. I was always in the house."

She wants A'Zayah to have a different experience. Already, they go out whenever she can—to museums, the aquarium, playgroups, or even just for a walk. She has signed up for every free study and intervention she can find, from "Healthy Baby" through the Public Health Commission to "Smart from the Start" and Union Capital Boston, a loyalty program that gives social and financial service rewards when participants are engaged in the community.

Jasmine doesn't understand friends of hers who sit around indoors with their babies or feel reluctant to express physical affection.

"I'm all over my son. I'm hugging him, I'm kissing him," she said. "The bonding starts there."

~~~

CAMILA CULLEN SAT IN A rocking chair in her children's darkened bedroom on the third floor of her townhouse in the quickly gentrifying Petworth neighborhood of Washington, DC, listening to the faint strains of Pandora's "Hipster Holidays" channel playing on an iPad in the hallway.

"My love, what was your favorite part of the day today?" she asked Mariana, seven, and Alejandro, four. This is the kids' bedtime routine, what Mariana calls "the debrief," when they share their favorite and least favorite parts of the day, one thing they did well and one thing they could improve. They all talked in quiet voices, Camila in Spanish and the children answering in a mix of Spanish and English.

Mariana didn't like getting sick with a fever after school. Alejandro didn't like when a car nearly hit him, backing up. Mariana liked the afternoon with Mama. Alejandro was proud of cooking dinner. Mariana congratulated herself for taking a break in a different classroom instead of just wandering off in the hallway when she was feeling overloaded at school. Camila punctuated their comments with questions and murmured remarks. Then she said a gentle "buenas noches" and, with a sigh of relief, slipped into the hallway, where I was waiting.

What a change in just a few months. Earlier in the fall, about six months after finishing the PEP class, the family had truly gone off the rails. The kids dug in their heels at every normal part of the routine: mornings, after-school, homework, bedtime. Everything was a battle. After their parents put them to bed, the kids would turn on the lights, play music, dance around their rooms, and make a mess. If Camila and her husband failed to notice, the kids would inform them the next morning: "We were angry, we threw a party." (That had brought Camila to the low point described in Chapter 1.)

Mariana seemed mad all the time. "I was in a really bad place. I had gotten to where I didn't like her. She didn't like us," Camila recalled.

When the "screws came off," as Colin put it, they quickly realized they had fallen away from their new PEP parenting skills and routines. Under the time pressure of a two-career household with no relatives nearby for support, they'd stopped holding family meetings.

Those weekly opportunities for each family member to appreciate the actions of the others—and to discuss any problem issues—had been an important way to keep everyone on track.

At bedtime, their tactics verged on coercive. They delivered ultimatums and threats to get the kids into bed. Then they overcompensated and became too permissive, agreeing to lie down with the children, only to fall asleep themselves. Camila became so exhausted that she'd easily sleep all night on the floor of the kids' bedroom.

Mariana and Alejandro were so angry and uncooperative all the time that Camila felt her relationship with them was broken. Even though she knew rationally that things had to improve, at the time it seemed impossible.

Slowly, Colin and Camila had righted the ship. First, they removed all the rules and requirements. They stopped worrying about the schedule and instead focused on special time, connecting with their children, and encouraging them in the household.

PEP teaches each parent to schedule appointments for regular special time with each child, during which there are no screens or distractions. The child picks the activity, whether Candyland or playing house or art. For perhaps twenty minutes for young children to as much as two hours for a teenager, the parent is completely focused on connecting with the child. The Cullens also instituted weekly family fun, an activity decided by consensus, such as board games, ice skating, charades, playing soccer in the yard, or painting pottery. (If you spend family time playing video games or watching movies with your children, enjoy yourselves, but don't let these activities crowd out the screen-free moments that decades of research show build self-regulation and learning.)

Without a controlling parent to push against, Mariana and Alejandro stopped being so resistant and defiant. Once the family had reconnected emotionally, Colin and Camila gradually brought back the routines, including the collaboration that's crucial to the Apprenticeship Model, rather than dictating rules. They became more adept at diagnosing the children's misbehavior and calmly choosing the most effective parental response.

For forty-five minutes earlier on this December day, I had watched Alejandro help Camila wash blueberries and raspberries; chop patty pan squash, zucchini, and peppers; cook pasta; and warm Peruvian chicken in the oven. They worked closely together, with Camila giving her son a constant stream of information ("the top of the squash is edible") and offering choices: "Melon or raspberries?" Camila, a slim brunette with chin-length curly hair, spoke in a low voice that often dropped to a whisper or rose in playful singsong. Instead of directing Alejandro, she invited him to participate—a key difference. When he tired at the half-hour point and announced he was done, she accepted it calmly. He came back a moment later, eager to help find a top to cover the chicken.

Camila reminded me that when Brian told the PEP 1 class that our kids were cooking eggs for themselves at age eight, she couldn't imagine letting young children manage a flame and pan. But here was four-year-old Alejandro wielding a knife—a sharp one, as PEP recommends, to give him real-life practice being safe—and helping her move the pasta water onto the stove. "We're doing more and more at the stove, and they like to be there," she said, noting that they've taught the children how to be safe with knives and the stove. "He's very careful."

We have eighteen short years to build a mutually respectful relationship with our children that will last for a lifetime. We must strike the balance between being involved and taking over what is truly the kids' domain. Don't let a battle over homework or clothing choices corrode the parent-child connection. Remember how that bond helps children learn to self-regulate.

I'd learned from PEP, the neuroscience research, and my child development interviews the importance of systematically building connection with my kids. It's the first, necessary step in the Apprenticeship Model.

The phrase "connect before you correct" reminds me that learning cannot happen at the moment a child is upset. It took me years to train myself to stop reacting with high-volume criticism when I walked into a room and saw my children doing something unproductive. Now I look for a way to connect with them—even something as small as a hug or a compliment—before asking about the screen agreement or guiding them back on track.

"Wait a minute," you might say. "I already spend a lot of time connecting with my children!" You probably do. You care enough to read a parenting book; you spend time with them. Indeed, parents in our generation spend far more time with our kids than parents in previous decades, as we know from Chapter 4. I had this same response when I first learned about positive parenting techniques like special time. I already spend so much time with my kids—why should I make this extra appointment?

But ask yourself how that time is spent. Are you bossing your kids around? Hovering over every precious step? Distracted by the ding of your work email every five minutes?

Once you start asking yourself these questions, you can nudge your parenting toward a balance between connecting closely with your kids while giving them enough independence to make their own mistakes. You'll begin to recognize the moments when your inattention is interrupting an opportunity to build your relationship. Your kids' behavior will let you know if they need more quality time.

Parents should notice children's interests and creations with specific attention to what the kids bring to it, rather than indiscriminately praising their work. This ties back to research by Stanford's Carol Dweck, who found that blanket praise undermines intrinsic motivation, whereas noticing effort and kids' interests builds their enthusiasm.

Show appreciation for their contributions, even when they're small. A child has to start somewhere when it comes to household chores, so merely fetching items from the fridge or helping crack eggs is a boon to the family. Schedule special time with each child. Hold weekly family meetings that focus on appreciating each other and planning fun family activities. Even small children can sit for a few minutes with parents to be thanked for their actions that week and to vote on an outing.

The hours we put in now—empathizing with our kid in a tantrum, teaching how to match freshly laundered socks, digging in the backyard mud, patiently reinforcing rules—will pay off as our children increasingly take charge of their lives and learn respect for everyone in the family. And eventually our adult children will actually want to call and visit us, after they've launched successfully into the world. Sure, there will be moments of conflict and disagreement along the way. But as long as we focus on empowering our children to become more independent and to figure out their own path—instead of imposing our will on them—we will create authentic relationships with them that endure for life.

~~~

BACK ON THE NEW YORK City sidewalk, I was feeling helpless. I wouldn't be able to experience an MRI scan. I had left Tottenham's research team on the hook for the cost of a scan—about $600—but with no usable data to show for it. Although I know that participants occasionally have to be excluded from any given study, I still felt guilty.

But more pressing: my twelve-year-old and I were at odds. After we walked out of the lab and said good-bye to the photographer who accompanied us, I'd turned on Maddie. I'd yelled at her for chattering about our personal business, which led us to be excluded from the study.

Now, looking at her stiff back, I knew we had to reconnect.

"Maddie, it's okay," I said. I put an arm around her shoulder. She let it rest.

"It's not okay," she shouted. "I ruined your book! I'm always messing up."

"You didn't ruin the book. I'll find a way to write around it. Or I'll find another lab that will let me observe. The important part is describing the research," I said. "I was wrong to blame you. Once they read through all my answers on the questionnaires, they would've called to tell us not to come tomorrow. We wouldn't have been able to participate. This actually helped us plan to have a fun day tomorrow."

She turned to face me. Lip thrust out. Eyes wet.

"Why don't you have something to eat?" I said.

"This food is disgusting," she said. But she picked up a fork. She chose a noodle from the corner of the white Styrofoam container, without any meat sauce on it. Slurped it into her mouth.

"I really appreciated your help," I said. "You took pictures for me in case the photographer's don't come out. You were so patient during the boring sections when Ava and I were both occupied."

She wasn't smiling. But at least she swallowed another noodle. And then another.

"What should we do now? Do you want to go back to Uncle Chris's apartment and build some Legos?"

Both kids agreed. I wrapped up the remains of the Chinese food and grasped Maddie's hand.

We walked to the subway entrance. Together.

7

Communication

It was a Friday in November like any other Friday. Bryony Daly was hurrying through the dishes and household chores, making the most of having three kid-free hours before picking up her five-year-old from school at 11:00 a.m.

Then she got a call from Maine's child and family services.

"A report has been filed about concerns regarding abuse in your home," the caller said. "I need to come out to talk to you."

Daly's breath caught in her throat. Her kids were both safe at school. Had a stranger reported that she'd briefly left them in a car during an errand run earlier in the week? Or maybe one of her neighbors in the apartment building had complained about the boys' cater-wauling during a sibling tussle.

"Can you tell me what this is about?" she asked.

No, he said. He offered to visit her home that day, but she declined. The apartment was a mess. Laundry draped around the kitchen, her bucket of fiber piled up next to the sofa, waiting to be spun into yarn.

"I cannot wait a whole weekend without knowing what's going on," she said. "Do I have to sit here worrying about what's going on for the whole weekend and not knowing anything?"

"I legally can't tell you anything," he responded.

"I don't understand why you can't legally tell me anything when it's about me," she said, voice breaking. They made an appointment for him to visit her home on Monday, and she hung up.

She burst into tears.

Could it be something to do with school?

Her older son, Quinn, seven, had struggled since starting Central School in South Berwick, Maine. After just a few weeks in kindergarten, his teachers recommended moving him to pre-K. Understanding academics wasn't the issue; the routine of the full school day challenged his self-control. He'd yell, or run out of the room. The shorter pre-K day and abundant playtime fit his needs better. The next year, in first grade, the school adapted his schedule and routines as best they could. Regular time with the school's learning specialist seemed to help. Now, in second grade, it seemed two steps forward, one step back.

Quinn's behavior had previously led to a child services report, when he pulled his penis out of his pants in front of a teacher. It was a joke, but it hadn't gone over well. But in that case, Quinn's counselor called Daly first to warn her about the report.

Daly emailed Nina D'Aran, Central School's principal, asking if she knew what was going on.

Quinn was "that kid." Every school has a few of them: That kid who's always getting into trouble, if not causing it. That kid who can't stay in his seat and who disrupts class and has angry outbursts. That kid whom other kids are quick to blame for a recess tussle, and who can make a teacher's life hell.

Quinn knew he was that kid too. He was smart enough to realize he was causing problems, even though he couldn't seem to stop himself from getting into trouble. He'd run out of the classroom when upset, occasionally pushing over a staff member in his haste to find a comfortable place. Impulsive, he'd sometimes lash out physically at a child who'd bothered him in the past. Daly was already meeting weekly with his teacher to review and troubleshoot his most recent actions. The school gave him a lot of latitude to calm down in the learning center or a buddy classroom, where any students in the class could work temporarily. He could use fidgets—little stress balls and gadgets—when he was feeling overwhelmed.

A few years earlier, educators at Central might have responded very differently to an outburst or tussle, perhaps sending him home for the day or taking away future recess time. Quinn towers over his classmates, taking after his tall mom and dad. In a typical school, a kid who seems to be threatening others would probably be physically restrained, segregated into a special ed room, or even sent home.

Quinn has a special education plan, which puts him in a category of students more likely to face punishment. Children with disabilities are suspended at twice the rate of their peers and incarcerated at three times the rate of the overall youth population, government data show. Like 95 percent of Central's student body, Quinn is white, so he is at less risk of punishment than his peers of color. For black kids with disabilities, the national suspension rate is 25 percent.

America's schools treat chronically misbehaving children as though they don't want to behave, when it's increasingly obvious that they simply cannot. Central has gone a different way, however, by adopting a pioneering new approach created by Ross Greene, a Harvard-pedigreed psychologist with a near-cult following among parents and educators who deal with challenging children. Just as Dr. Spock taught a generation of mothers to trust their instincts, Greene's disciplinary method has become a go-to resource. Parents of kids with ADHD or oppositional defiant disorder often pass around his books, *The Explosive Child* and *Lost at School,* as though they were holy writ.

Kids will behave well if they can, Greene teaches.

His model was honed in children's psychiatric wards and battle-tested in state juvenile facilities; in the mid-2000s, he brought it into dozens of public and private schools, including Central School. The results thus far have been dramatic, with schools reporting drops as great as 80 percent in disciplinary referrals, suspensions, and peer aggression. For Greene, disruptive children lack the skills, not the motivation, to meet behavior expectations. Under his philosophy, you'd no more punish a child for lashing out in class or jumping out of his seat repeatedly than you would if he bombed a spelling test. You'd teach self-control skills in the former cases, just as you might review word patterns in the latter. The goal is to get to the root of the problem, not to discipline a kid for the way his brain is wired.

Quinn was still a work in progress.

After a few anxious hours of waiting on that November morning, Daly heard back from her social worker that, indeed, the child services report had come from school. Quinn had been using his active imagination to describe a scenario at home where Daddy and Mommy beat each other, and his little brother too. Nothing about it was true, the social worker told her, but she was required to report it. After four months of home visits, child services cleared the Daly family—and Quinn learned a lesson about the power of his words.

When I discovered Greene's track record in 2012, I experienced the first epiphany that led to this book. I realized that the educators who continue to argue over the appropriate balance of what we now call "incentives" and "consequences" are debating the wrong thing entirely. After all, if a child simply hasn't acquired the brain functions required to control his behavior, what good is a suspension—or for that matter, a gold star? And as we know from Chapter 5, even those who have developed the ability become less motivated in a reward-punishment environment.

I visited Central School on a crisp fall day in 2013. The school day began with 450 children from pre-K through third grade pouring through the front doors. They greeted principal Nina D'Aran, a slender brunette and mother of four, with hugs and high-fives. As they streamed into their classrooms, D'Aran rejoined her staff in the open-floor-plan main office, which hummed with the restrained tension of a fire station between calls.

D'Aran had no sooner taken a seat than the intercom buzzed with a teacher in crisis. D'Aran hurried down the hall to find a boy sobbing under a desk in the third-grade classroom. His teacher hustled the rest of the class out of the room.

A quiet conversation revealed that another boy had slapped him on the bus and said "the big bad words." The bad feelings made him think of his dog that died. When D'Aran asked what might help, he suggested wearing his ghoulish Halloween hoodie zipped up over his face for the ride home. D'Aran counter-offered that he wear the hoodie over his head, but leave his face uncovered to keep from scaring the little kids. Solution in hand, the boy rejoined his classmates.

"Teachers have so much to do, it's amazing," the principal acknowledged when I asked how she and her staff balance the needs of the entire student body with the demands of the more challenging kids. D'Aran combines the perkiness of a Disney princess with the calm wisdom of her previous job as a guidance counselor.

In spite of the challenges, the decision to adopt Greene's model was paying off. D'Aran now could spend more of her time planning, and classroom teachers could spend more time on instruction and a lot less time dealing with these sorts of mini-crises. Problems that once took days to resolve could often be handled much more quickly, sometimes in minutes, and often proactively.

Some of Central's teachers and staff were skeptical of Greene's model at first. Our desire, as adults, to see children suffer over their bad behavior is deeply held and hard to dislodge. Greene's method hinges on retraining staff to nurture strong relationships—especially with the most disruptive kids—and to give all kids a central role in solving their problems. That part is critical. Not only does it provide the kid with a stake in the solution, but it often reveals the underlying difficulty.

For instance, a teacher might see a challenging kid dawdling on a worksheet and assume that he's being defiant, when in fact the child is just hungry, having missed breakfast that morning. A snack ends the impasse. Before Greene's model, "we spent a lot of time trying to diagnose children. Just talking to each other isn't going to figure it out," said D'Aran. "Now we're talking to the child and really believing the child when they say what the problems are."

The next step is to prioritize each student's challenges—whether it be transitioning from recess to the classroom, keeping hands to themselves in the hallway, or sitting with the group in morning meeting—and then tackle them one by one, revisiting the plan as each skill is mastered. It sounds like a no-brainer, but it requires some shuffling of resources and a completely different mind-set.

At Central School, the administrators used building improvement funds for renovations that would facilitate problem-solving conversations, turning one classroom into an open work space for D'Aran and the main office staff, with couches and tables where kids could relax, play, have a snack, cool down, or have a heartfelt chat. They divided another classroom into a resource room and a special ed room. The school committed to twenty weeks of teacher training, with frequent coaching from Greene's trainer via Skype. After all, coaxing a recalcitrant second-grader to express their needs can be a lot like enticing a shy kitten into your lap—teachers needed support as they learned to broach these difficult conversations. By recording their interactions with students and reviewing them with each other and the trainer, the teachers improved their skills through reflection and feedback.

Ross Greene and Central School's educators discovered the power of the second pillar of the Apprenticeship Model: communication.

We can mimic their success in changing adult behavior and breaking through communication barriers. Their conversations with children are a model of nonjudgmental listening. Although these strategies are most effective with children ages four and older, you can convey even to a toddler your sincere interest in his input and your support of his growing independence.

Just as the Central teachers learned to listen and draw out children, I began to prioritize communication over compliance. When I first started on this path, it shocked me to realize how often I was directing, reminding, and bossing my kids. That's not communication. I had to learn to listen more than I talked. I had to stop jumping in with my solutions or lessons. It was amazing how many tantrums in the grade-school years ended when I simply reflected what the kids were saying and showed that I understood where they were coming from.

～～～

"MY CHILD DOESN'T LISTEN."

"How can I get my kid to listen to me?"

"You weren't listening when I told you to put on your shoes!"

When we parents make these comments, we aren't really talking about listening. When we say "listen," we really mean "obey." We're talking about compliance. It's the Obedience Model at play.

But as we saw in Chapter 4, the days of blind obedience to parental commands are long gone. Instead, we must aim for mutual cooperation, which is more challenging to build but also more powerful. We need a communications overhaul.

It begins with a mind-set change: you must genuinely accept that your child may know something you don't about the problem or situation. When a child misbehaves, instead of getting angry, get curious. The outburst or misbehavior is a puzzle, and your child holds the solution. The behavior is communicating something to you; it's up to you to decode the message.

Our role as parents isn't to preside over an always peaceful household; it's to see disruptions as a chance to better understand our children and help them grow. The home is a learning lab where our children can experiment, fail, and eventually succeed, not a shrine to perfection.

Use focused and reflective listening to be sure you really understand what your kid is saying and feeling. Ask questions. Show faith in their ability to handle their own problems. Speak to children with the same respect you'd give a friend or coworker. For persistent problems, engage children in active communication and problem-solving. As you might expect, it can take time for your kids to contribute their ideas if they've experienced years of being told what to do.

To learn to truly listen, you may need the equivalent of a parenting detox, like Vicki Hoefle's "do-nothing-say-nothing week."

I visited Hoefle's class, held in a classroom at Champlain College in Burlington, Vermont, the week parents returned to report on the detox. This was the second session in the six-week class that I'd listened to over Skype a week earlier. Energized by her no-nonsense delivery of her parenting principles, I came to see the magic in person. A mother of six grown children, Hoefle uses plain, sometimes salty language to make her points, her humor softening the hard messages. The parents are the problem, she believes, because we talk too much, use strategies that don't work, and try to control our kids.

This night I saw her in person, standing at the front of the classroom, before a whiteboard mounted on a brick-red wall. With her shining silver bob tucked behind her left ear, Hoefle had dressed for comfort in a black waterfall cardigan over a maroon blouse and dark blue jeans. She welcomed the two dozen parents as they settled into seats, and then gave a brief overview of the evening's material: a focus on relationships and fostering independence. Then she asked what the parents had learned about themselves and their kids in the past week and what they would do differently going forward.

"What I learned about myself was that I was quick to boss or deliver a threat to get him to do something," said one mom. "I learned my child was more capable than I thought he was. What we're going to do differently is try to stay on this path and keep it consistent, because we had a very successful week."

"Boom!" Hoefle said. "How many of you figured out you're too bossy?"

The majority of the hands in the room went up.

"How many of you relied on threats to get things done in your house?" Half the hands. "How many of you noticed your kids are more capable than you gave them credit for?" The majority of the hands shot up. Another mom confessed to being a cheerleader. A third discovered she was raising a praise junkie. With each revelation, at least half of the other parents said they'd had the same experience.

"We're all in the same boat," Hoefle said. "Everybody's getting the same kinds of results. It does make us a community of people who are experiencing many of the same things. We just don't know how to talk about it. We talk about what's going wrong instead of trying new things and talking about the results we get so we create this momentum, this forward-looking momentum of possibility and developing the courage to try new things and seeing that they work, which inspires us to do more."

That community is growing in Vermont. Hoefle has been teaching classes for twenty-five years and estimates that she's taught more than 5,000 parents. When she starts a new session of her class, the teachers in the local elementary school know because the kids arrive late, without lunches, or with only partially completed homework. The teachers don't complain. "They're all for this because what we're doing is raising a generation of kids who are responsible, who are capable," she told her class. "Isn't that what we want? Nobody wants another generation of kids who can't take care of themselves. Enough with that, already. If you tell people, you'll get a lot of support from your community."

From the second row of the class, Lisa Rowley, age forty-eight, raised her hand to confess the "guilt-driven parenting" she recognized using with her eight-year-old daughter, Ella, whom Rowley and her husband, Brian, had adopted from China at one year old. Rowley had followed Hoefle's suggestion at the first class session that she apologize to her child for ordering her around. She reported to the class that she told Ella: "If Mommy's getting too bossy, tell Mommy to go read a book." To her horror, Ella responded: "But, Mommy, I know that's how you love me. You don't love me if you're not bossing me around."

"Yeah. Amazing. So what are you going to do different?" Hoefle asked.

"To show her other ways that Mommy loves her," Rowley said, a rueful smile on her face.

"Your job is to redefine what a healthy, loving relationship is. It's going to take a lot of work, because you were really committed to making sure this little kid, who had a terrible first year that she doesn't remember—you were going to somehow make up for it, which is impossible. It's going to take a lot of diligence on your part and a lot of open conversation about what does it really mean," Hoefle said, moving across the room with sweeping arm movements to punctuate her words. "So, lovely! You've got this great thing to be working on for the next twenty-five years. I'd rather be working on that than table manners."

She reached the board and circled the words "relationship blueprint." Other parents chimed in that they were struggling to find alternatives to delivering commands or using their other favorite parenting crutches. Hoefle suggested taking five seconds before responding to their kid's misbehavior. Or confessing, "My brain is really tired. I'm having a hard time not barking orders at you." That models for a child how to take responsibility for your feelings and also how to regroup under stress.

One mom complained about her struggle to find creative ways to remind her child about the dog needing to be fed without giving an order. "I'm saying, 'The dog looks so hungry, oh poor dog,'" she said.

"It takes a lot of work," Hoefle agreed. "Here's what I want you to remember. Do you know how hard kids work every damn day to get out of bed, make you happy, figure out what kind of mood you are in today, are they going to get away with the sweet cereal or are they going to have to eat the leftover Brussels sprouts because you threatened them the night before? . . . We've got to be in the trenches with them."

~~~

WHEN WE'RE UNDER STRESS, WE tend to fall back on patterns of behavior and communication that we learned as children. If you grew up in a dictatorship, this is when you start yelling and bossing. If your parents desperately wanted to be your friends, this is when you open negotiations with your children. It's time to learn a new communication style. You're probably doing some of this already, by instinct. But some elements of the Apprenticeship Model may feel uncomfortable. Give it a chance.

In the second week of the PEP 1 class, Brian and I teach an exercise that brings home the difference in parenting styles. We play-act being the adult and tell the students to expect three different experiences. In each scenario, we hand a lump of clay to the parents in the class.

First, we tell them to be creative. We heap on the praise. We gush over everything they mold. Second, we sternly hand them each an equal chunk and demand that they create clay plates. We bark instructions, step by step. We order them and deal harshly with anyone who's misbehaving, sometimes sending them to time-out. In the final scenario, we explain clearly that the class will be making doll house furniture for children at a local homeless shelter. We tell them how long they will have to work and give specific feedback on their creations—not over-the-top praise.

One of the great mistakes of the self-esteem movement was the idea that adults could instill self-esteem in children simply by saying they were unbelievable, amazing, the best, and showering them with trophies. Children see right through this nonsense. The only authentic way to build self-esteem is to face real challenges and overcome them. The good news is that these challenges can be the ordinary challenges of daily life.

Remembering Dweck's growth mind-set research showing that specific praise and a focus on effort motivate children, I teach parents to use specific language to observe their children's interests and accomplishments. For instance, when they show you a picture, you may be tempted to say, "That picture is so beautiful!" Instead, describe what you see. Ask questions about the child's choices or intentions. This stimulates their own sense of judgment and evaluation of their work—rather than training them merely to seek your empty praise. You could say, "I see orange, yellow, and purple in the sky. What interesting choices! Tell me more about how you picked those colors."

Focus on your child's progress rather than the end results. When debriefing a soccer game, instead of praising them for scoring a goal, notice that they've improved their passing accuracy or have become more vocal in telling teammates that they're open for the ball. Being specific is harder work, but it shows true interest and evaluation, not blind praise. Eliminate phrases from your vocabulary that center on your own parental judgment rather than your kid's, such as: "I'm so proud of you," or, "I like how neatly you're stacking the dishes. Good job!" Instead, you could say, "I notice you're stacking the dishes neatly so nothing will break. Thank you." You could always ask a question rather than saying, "Good job," such as, "What did you think about your performance?"

The dramatic experience of using clay to illustrate three different parenting styles often gives parents taking PEP 1 an epiphany about how it feels to be a child on the other side of permissive, authoritarian, or authoritative parenting. In one class, the authoritarian scenario showed a mom of two named Leanne that she probably came across as a tyrant to her children.

"I felt totally uncomfortable. I could hear my own voice in what you were saying. It was very uncomfortable. It was stressful," she said.

"This was an epiphany exercise for me when I took PEP 1," I told her. "When you're saying: 'Hurry up, hurry up, put your shoes on, it's time to go,' to the kid it's like: 'What happened?' Because you know your schedule in your head as the adult, you know what the next thing is. They're coming from a different perspective. They may not realize we have fifteen minutes, we have to leave now to get to where we're going."

"When you said, 'Have you done it yet?' that's when I really got it. We are rushing all the time," Leanne said.

For me, Leanne, and many parents, better advance communication with our children solves a lot of the family tussles. Instead of barking at them that we have fifteen minutes to get ready, we review the day's schedule—often the night before—and ask them how long they think they need to prepare and what they need to bring to school. Then we calmly let the day unfold. Expect that the first few times kids will underestimate the time they need or get something wrong. Use that as a learning opportunity.

By planning ahead, we manage the daily bumps more easily.

When my children were younger, whenever they wanted my attention, they wanted it instantly. Somehow this always seemed to happen as soon as I picked up the telephone—even if they'd been playing quietly by themselves a moment earlier. So we agreed on a nonverbal signal for them to use when they wanted me to pay attention. They'd put a gentle hand on my forearm (meaning "I want to tell you something"), and I would cover it with my other hand (meaning "I'll be with you in a moment"). That physical contact was reassuring.

Even better, I was able to turn around this interruption signal and use it when I needed their attention. So instead of yelling from the kitchen, "Dinner time!" while they were playing, I would walk over to where they were, put a hand on each forearm, and wait until they looked up. This may seem like more work, but it was actually faster than yelling from the kitchen, being ignored, blowing up, everyone crying, and finally eating dinner twenty minutes later.

Another cue we used was the sign language for "wait," which is both hands held palms up and curved, and fingers wiggling. I could use this sign at the store, when I was in conversation with another adult, or even when I was finishing a bite and couldn't speak. Not only did they love the intrigue of a secret sign, but being able to communicate with me when I was busy with something else strengthened their ability to wait.

As you begin implementing these new parenting tools, you probably will notice when you're about to do the "wrong" thing, like yelling or ordering your child. But you may not know what to say instead, or perhaps you're too angry to respond calmly. This is a perfect time for the "mumble and walk away" technique. Rather than engaging with a misbehaving child, act as though you've just remembered a pot on the stove, or heard a knock at the door, and dash out of the room. This buys you time to think over the response you want to use, or even just to take ten deep breaths and become centered before responding. After all, your children's annoying behavior is bound to repeat itself over and over until you figure out how to extinguish it; if you take the time to think up the right response, you will surely have another opportunity to use it.

Parents are primed to act. When a child misbehaves, we want to know what to do in that instant. But often the best response is to wait and observe. To say nothing. To see how it unfolds, and when the crisis is past, to think through how to handle it next time. As discussed in Chapter 3, adults and children alike lose access to the learning and problem-solving parts of the brain when they're emotionally ramped up. Get brain science on your side by saving your thinking and planning for a calmer moment.

There is one time when it's okay to jump into action: when it helps you talk less. It's often more powerful to act than to speak. If your child is watching TV when hot food is sitting on the dinner table, don't stand there yelling at them to turn off the set. After you've stated the family limit once ("TV off during dinner time"), walk over and turn it off yourself. Place a firm and friendly arm around your child's shoulder and gently move toward the dinner table.

This is just one alternative to saying no—the ultimate communication blocker. Saying no shuts down conversation with your children and often becomes an invitation to them to dig in their heels for a power struggle.

Another substitute for no is "when-then." If a child is begging to play outside when the living room is a mess of baby doll parts, you could say: "When the floor is clean, then we can go to the park!" This strategy works best when it reinforces a family routine or rule, such as chores before playtime, or brushing teeth before the bedtime cuddle. Resist being drawn into a negotiation—simply repeat the phrase with a smile.

Hoefle tells parents to suggest to their kids: "Convince me."

If children are begging for a later bedtime or a new toy, you're in a prime position as a parent. You can harness their desire and use that energy to get done whatever the family needs. Let the kids do the heavy lifting in making a case for the new privilege—it'll build their problem-solving skills.

Lay out all your concerns: a later bedtime, for instance, could make it hard for them to wake up for school, and you'll end up with limited quiet adult time at the end of the day. Give your child a day to think about your concerns and come up with a solution that truly answers the issues you've raised. (The answer can't be: "Mom, stop caring about it.") Get your child working with you to solve a problem you both care about, rather than just fighting against your no.

For something big, like expanded technology access, ask them to show you ways they can self-regulate so you know they'll be able to manage greater freedom. When we were considering getting a dog, the children had to keep their belongings off the floor for ninety days in a row. After all, puppies chew up loose shoes and notebooks. We kept track on our calendar. Their tidier habits stuck—not perfectly, but they were vastly improved—even after the trial period ended and we adopted a puppy.

Use these strategies with confidence and a pleasant demeanor. Take a few deep breaths and make sure you're in a calm state of mind first. Be warned: it's easy to turn a "when-then" statement into a threat if you use a tense tone of voice or seem angry.

~~

THE PARENTS SAT, PERFECTLY SILENT. Vicki Hoefle was blowing their minds again.

"The words we use to describe our kids, it's like you feed them," Hoefle said, pacing up and down the aisle in the center of the rows of chairs. "They're either positive words that describe cooperative, compassionate, thoughtful, flexible, creative kids, or you're grouchy and you noodle and you take too long and you're stubborn and you're defiant and you're being sassy, and you always hit and you never listen and you're unreliable."

"Every time you use a word, a kid swallows it and it becomes part of their self idea."

Listen to the words you use, even in those moments of complaint to your friends, and ask whether you want your children describing themselves that way. If the answer is no, drop that language. "If you don't want to hear your kid say, 'I'm the defiant one in the family,' stop feeding them the Kool-Aid," Hoefle said.

A mom raised her hand to ask whether she could say, "It's disappointing when you do that," or, "That behavior gave me a headache, please stop."

Hoefle's not a fan. We all need to take responsibility for our feelings. Tying kids' behavior to your approval or your emotions can backfire in one of two ways. You might end up with children who blame their own headaches or frustration on other people—or who spend their lives catering to other people's feelings. Instead, simply respond the way a nonrelative would respond to the behavior.

"Pick a few things you want to work on. How do you want your child to describe himself at twenty-five? Those are the words I want to start introducing," she said.

Lisa Rowley asked how to convey ideas like intelligence if you're hoping your child will value smarts and hard work in school.

"Intelligence, you can't do very much about it," Hoefle said. "Intelligent is like, you're left-handed. That has nothing to do with the kid. You want them to be thinkers.

"So you say: 'You're such a good thinker? That's using your brain?' What do you say without it being praise?" Rowley asked.

"Here's the strategy you guys are going to use," Hoefle said. "You're going to identify the trait and anchor it with the activity. When you see a child being thoughtful, you say, 'You were so thoughtful when Michael came over and XYZ.'"

Then your children not only recognize the trait in themselves but start to truly understand what being thoughtful means. Once you do that three or four or a half-dozen times, your children start to think of themselves that way.

Kids are hungry to hear more substantive feedback than just: "'You're good, I like that, it's pretty,'" Hoefle said. "Suddenly you have a kid who has a new picture of himself. This is powerful stuff. It's so easy."

Instead of trying to correct the things you don't like about your kids, just focus on the tiny signs of progress, the traits you want to encourage. Even if it's a fleeting moment when you see them being flexible, or using self-control, seize it. "They have to be fed this constant diet of: 'These are some of the character traits that I see in you. I notice this about you. I can tell you exactly when you did it.' It's not fluff," Hoefle said. "Just start practicing."

Her advice aligns with the research I saw at Columbia and the psychology I learned through PEP. Even positive labels can become a trap for children. Children always labeled "happy" or "responsible" may feel that they can't express any negative emotions or be less than perfect. Instead, see your children as they are and let your language describe how they've grown and changed. Track their progress, whether in tying shoes, helping with family chores, or cooling down from a tantrum. For example: "A month ago, you were only making the loop on your shoe. You stuck with it, and now you're making two loops and tying them together. That's what I call persistence!" Or even a simple comment like, "I noticed you're doing your household jobs before you start playing, as we agreed. Thank you."

Another mom asked Hoefle what trait will encourage a child who's hitting whenever frustrated or thwarted.

"I'm going to look at the moment that the kid has a fleeting second of self-control and say, 'You really used a lot of self-control this afternoon when I told you that you couldn't have the popcorn, and I know you wanted it.' I'm not saying 'I'm proud of you, I like that you did that,' I'm just making an observation," Hoefle said. "It's slow, teeny tiny steps. Over the course of a couple of weeks, you see kids begin to explore other kinds of solutions."

That's when you can help your children think through other ways to handle the wash of anger that comes over them. Stop taking it so personally, Hoefle said, and don't say things like, "You can't hit. We are a family that's nice to each other." Then, she warned, "the kid's like, 'I'm not a part of this family? Because I hit.'"

A new mom asked how to handle a nineteen-month-old who started hitting when he was overtired. At dinner the previous night, he had slapped her across the face.

"Of course, Daddy swoops in and says, 'That wasn't very nice.' Grandma was there and says, 'He's just overtired,' and tries to justify it. I'm stunned," she said. "For a nineteen-month-old, how do you say to him, 'That's not appropriate.'"

"You don't. There's no words," Hoefle responded. "So what would the action be?"

"Picking him up and just getting him ready for bed," the mom suggested.

"No," Hoefle said.

Other parents murmured, "Walk away." Hoefle nodded.

"Nobody hits me. I don't care how little they are," she said. "I put mine down and walked away. I already had a solution for this. All kids hit, bite, push, pinch, spit, and say 'fuck you.' I'm not one of those people who thought mine wouldn't, so I was ready for it."

Don't lecture or yell at the child, Hoefle said. All that energy and attention just feeds the behavior. Show the child what happens to the relationship when they're violent.

"A lot of this is about thinking before it happens. Kids are predictable. There are patterns of behavior that go on in your home so by the time your kid is two you can predict what's going to happen," she said. "Have a nice calm plan. Put them down. When you're ready to engage, come back."

The mom had an objection. "In our case, when you put him down or you walk away, he has a meltdown," she said.

"I don't know what's wrong with a meltdown. I don't see a problem with kids being frustrated and crying. That's a natural part of childhood," Hoefle said. "That gives kids' brains a chance to relax and move forward. I hit, somebody stops playing with me. If I throw myself on the ground, they come back to take care of me. It's all cause and effect with the kid. Give them good information. You don't have to be mad at them. They recover so quickly."

Perhaps the most positive thing you can communicate is confidence in your kids' ability to navigate their own lives. You can build independence through phrases like, "That's a tough one, but

I'm confident you'll figure it out!" or even, "Sounds like you have quite a friendship problem. Would you let me know how it goes tomorrow at recess?" Rather than solving your child's dilemma, give them first crack. (Be sure to use your most sincere voice and facial expressions, so they don't mistake your hands-off attitude for a lack of concern.) Only by having the space to tackle their own problems can our children make mistakes, experiment, and eventually succeed on their own.

Children live up or down to our expectations. Not always at the moment, but in the long run. Stop predicting doom through negative comments like, "If you don't finish your chores, you won't be able to play basketball with the neighbors!" Instead, convince yourself that your child will go along with the plan and express this confidence in phrases like, "As soon as you've finished your chores, you can go play basketball with the neighbors!" Act as if all will go smoothly, and it often will.

~~~

A COUPLE OF MONTHS AFTER I observed Hoefle's class, Lisa Rowley told me that it had dramatically changed her family dynamics. Instead of focusing on the to-do list and the mechanics of each day—is Ella on time to school? is her homework done?—she was making the connection with her child the priority. Ella now made her own breakfast and lunch and relished the opportunity to try new independent skills, such as going solo into the grocery store to buy bananas. Rowley recalled the heart-sinking moment when she realized that she'd raised Ella to define love as controlling behavior. Now, "she knows she's loved because of the boundaries that she has, but also because of the freedom she has. Mom and Dad care enough to try to do this differently," Rowley said.

Rowley originally came to Hoefle's class after a standoff with Ella over a simple request to clear the table after Sunday lunch, which the girl refused to do. "Okay. Then you need to go up to your room and spend a few minutes just thinking about what's happening and why you're not cooperating with Mommy and Daddy," she told her.

"No!"

"Ella, you need to go to your room," Rowley said, putting a guiding hand on her shoulder. Ella swatted it away. She glanced over at her husband, Brian, fifty-seven, the cue for him to step in.

"Mom has asked you to go to your room, and I don't like the way you're talking to Mom. That's not respectful," he said, grasping Ella's arm and escorting her to her bedroom.

The parents looked at each other, hoping the confrontation was over. But Ella popped back out over the threshold. "I'm not staying here!"

Furious now, Brian walked into the room with an overly calm voice.

"Ella, we're going to take some things out of your room. I'm going to take Dumbo," he said, snatching her favorite stuffed animal and brushing past her, still standing in the hallway. She walked back into her room and burst into tears. But a moment later, she came back over the threshold, standing defiantly in the hallway, still crying.

"Okay. I'm going to go back in and take your pillow."

That was it. Ella leapt into action. She started picking up all her favorite things: pillows, a snuggly blanket, toys by the armful, and carrying them out of her room to dump them at her father's feet.

"Here you go, Daddy. I don't care!"

Brian walked back into the den, where Lisa had retreated, and the two looked at each other in panic as they heard the faint sounds of Ella emptying her room of belongings. They'd played their last card. How could they be out of parenting tricks and their kid was only eight? They started researching resources and decided that Lisa would go to Hoefle's class and both parents would implement what she learned.

Occasionally, Lisa and Brian Rowley do find themselves slipping back into their old, bossy habits. Then they know it's time to revisit "do-nothing-say-nothing." Just twenty-four hours of biting their tongues is enough to get back on track.

You can try do-nothing-say-nothing week yourself. Use it as an opportunity to understand how much you rely on commanding, directing, and controlling your kids. You'll learn that your children don't need your voice in their ear as much as you think they do. They'll be challenged to figure things out for themselves and will enjoy the independence.

～～～

WHEN YOUR CHILDREN ARE BABIES, you can tell from the shape of their yawns whether they are hungry, sleepy, or gassy. But as they grow, they develop lives of their own. You may think that you always know what they need or are going to say, but increasingly they surprise you. Leave room for this possibility by listening with an open mind to what they tell you.

I mentioned reflective listening earlier. This involves more than just parroting back what the other person said to you. It requires restating what you believe you heard and asking for confirmation or clarification. For instance, "I'm hearing that you felt sad after Charlie refused to play four-square with you at the playground. Could it be that you were embarrassed?" You may learn that your child actually felt hurt or angry—not embarrassed. Because you're making a tentative guess, the child feels free to fine-tune your understanding of their feelings. It's a powerful way to connect and develop empathy with your child.

Not only does reflective listening strengthen your connection to your child, but it helps them develop a feeling vocabulary. Instead of just feeling "angry," your child can refine the experience and understand the difference between "feeling humiliated" and "feeling hurt" and "being left out." Don't be afraid of bad feelings or deny them—this merely teaches your children to stuff their feelings down rather than acknowledging them. Reflective listening can be especially difficult when your child says something like, "I hate that stupid head Kathy! If she comes over here, I'm going to spit in her face," using words you don't allow in your family and maligning a friend you know to be a sweet kid. But some reflective listening may extract that Kathy has been excluding your child.

Communication is more than a feel-good skill. Chapter 3 described the power of empathy to reshape the brain and strengthen self-regulation. Decades of social science research show that people who are socially connected have lower rates of obesity, mental illness, high blood pressure, and other health challenges. In particular, researchers find that people with high empathy for others actually experience less stress, anxiety, and depression themselves.

Sara Konrath, an assistant professor at Indiana University, designed a study to assess whether mothers with higher levels of empathy experience more or less stress. Researchers told mothers to prepare a speech and told them their remarks would be recorded and evaluated by a panel of experts. They measured stress levels in saliva during and after the speech preparation. It turned out that moms who scored higher on a psychological test for empathy were better able to weather the stress of preparing for public speaking, which consistently ranks at the top of most-dreaded tasks. "People with greater empathy actually are feeling a smaller biological stress response," Konrath told me. "It's almost like that empathy is buffering them."

How do you develop empathy in your child? Reflective listening and thoughtful conversation provide a good start. The more your children are able to feel empathy, the more protected they'll be from depression, anxiety, and other health problems. The more you can help your children develop a rich emotional vocabulary, the better prepared they'll be for the storms of adolescence and early adulthood. These benefits are especially important if you have a family history of mental illness.

Try this at home. Consider the instructions you're accustomed to giving your children and how they might hear and interpret the words. When you say, "Be careful," to a child climbing on a high slide, he may hear, "I don't believe you can climb that safely." If you say, "It's okay, it's just a scratch," to your child who's scraped his knee, he may hear, "I don't believe you're in pain," or even a broader invalidation of his feelings. The best encouragement may be to stay silent, simply to express empathy, or to ask questions. Resist offering a solution or downplaying your child's negative feelings.

Misunderstandings happen in the other direction too, as we often assume we comprehend the meaning of our kids' words. If you have a toddler, it's natural to struggle to understand what he's saying. As children grow and lose their charming lisp, their words may be easier to comprehend, but the meaning can become opaque. What exactly do our kids mean when they say "friend" or "popular" or "I don't like it" or "Do it myself"? We may think we get it, but some focused listening can reveal a different meaning altogether.

For instance, when your kid says, "It's a waste of my time" in reference to math or visiting Grandma, you may hear a rude, entitled child and start worrying that they'll drop out of high school or grow up to neglect elderly relatives. Your hackles rise, and you come down hard with a lecture or an order to comply.

Instead, you could get curious about what your child means. Maybe your kid is struggling with the current math unit and doesn't like to admit it. Or perhaps you have a high-energy child who needs an hour of hard play before being able to tolerate sitting still for a conversation with a seventy-two-year-old. If you listen with an open mind and ask probing questions, you may be surprised by what you learn.

Don't blow off comments like "It's boring" or "I don't care." Our kids know exactly how to push our buttons. They've studied us for years. They may be trying to provoke a lecture in order to hide the vulnerability or pain or insecurity lurking behind their reluctance to cooperate.

How do you draw out a reluctant talker? First, pick the right time for the conversation. Make sure you feel unhurried and ready to be patient. Then, be persistent but not aggressive. Ask open-ended questions like "What's up?" or "Tell me what that's like for you." Use silence to your advantage—your child may well fill the empty space with an explanation. If they persist with non-answers like, "I don't know," ask them to take a guess at what might be going on. You can even make some educated guesses yourself, and learn much from their response. If the first conversation is a bust, try again later.

With many children, sitting close together and looking into their eyes will convey trust and effectively break down communication barriers. But other kids feel intimidated by that much eye contact and will open up more on a car ride or while doing dishes together—when you're not staring into their face. Experiment to find what works best with your child.

～～

THE TEACHERS AT CENTRAL SCHOOL discovered the power of listening as they became more comfortable with Greene's problem-solving conversations. They learned that Quinn often made up stories or ran out of the room when he was embarrassed. Indeed, anxiety seemed to lie at the root of many of his difficulties. His special education plan gave a vague diagnosis, "other health impairment," because his symptoms fell all over the map: some seemed to indicate autism, some ADHD, and some a sensory processing issue.

Mornings could be a disaster. Quinn grew riled up just being in the gym with crowds of other pre-K and kindergarten students waiting to file to their classrooms. He couldn't sit through morning meeting.

His teacher and D'Aran began a series of conversations, intent on figuring out the solution. Talking to a seven-year-old requires a special kind of patience. They may fall off the chair during your discussion. You're guaranteed several monosyllabic answers. You have to be prepared for a long session, without any guarantee of progress, and probably a follow-up or two.

Quinn's teacher often would begin a conversation with an apology, for whatever her part was in the outburst or misunderstanding. This helped put Quinn at ease. Then she'd broach the issue at hand, using a phrase like, "I notice that sitting at morning meeting is hard for you. What's up? What's up with sitting at meeting?"

When she first asked what's wrong, he'd usually say, "I don't know." She and D'Aran used observations like, "From your body, it looks like this is uncomfortable to discuss," to draw him out and help him name the emotions he was experiencing. They'd reassure him that he wasn't in trouble. Then they'd ask again, building on any tiny comment he had made, any way in which he had participated. They'd bring up past successes to remind him of his capability. They'd hypothesize about what might be going on, listening for his agreement or dismissal of their ideas. They'd suggest different solutions, to see what might help.

By listening to him patiently, and relying on Greene's communication training, his teachers figured out that the chaos of the morning simply overloaded his system. They agreed to try a plan where he would skip the noisy gym and go into the classroom first, with his teacher, to begin to acclimate to the school day in quiet. He thought that might work.

It did. Mornings became more tranquil and less agitated. But meeting time still challenged Quinn. Sitting near the other kids just seemed too much for him. After another conversation, they tried having him sit one-on-one with a teacher to share individually. That helped.

Slowly but surely, Quinn learned to trust that he wouldn't be judged and that his teacher and the school staff would help him work through issues to find solutions. For months they focused only on keeping him safe in the building and not a danger to others.

Trouble often rose out of his misperception of a situation. He might think that his aide was making fun of him, or that a teacher was mistreating another child. By debriefing him, his teacher and counselor learned that many of his outbursts stemmed from a mistaken idea that someone was being victimized.

As Greene's teaching took hold, the staff stopped delivering personalized praise like "I love that you walked safely" or "It made me happy," and instead used phrases that emphasized Quinn's decisions and attributes: "I noticed that you made a choice not to run. Way to go." Or, knowing that Quinn felt fearful of strangers, "I noticed you were very brave about talking to the visitor today."

They created affirmation cards to give to Quinn and his peers, a physical representation of this kind of positive feedback. The kids called them "awesome cards."

One day last fall, Quinn got off the bus in front of their apartment complex. He greeted Daly with a big smile.

"I had a terrible day, Mom. My day was so bad," he said. This was their running joke, that if he had a great day for behavior, he'd pretend it was awful.

"Oh, really," she replied with a smile.

"Just kidding."

He pulled an awesome card out of his pocket. With shock, Daly read that Quinn had been able to listen to an entire concert at school. This boy couldn't even sit in music class for more than ten minutes. The noise and acoustics overwhelmed his system. He couldn't stand the different voices clashing, with some people singing off-key. At the previous year's "Hike Through History"—a huge schoolwide event celebrating the town's past—he couldn't even remain at an *outdoor* sing-along.

And here he was now, sitting at an indoor concert for forty minutes straight.

"Quinn, that's amazing! Did you enjoy it? What was it about?"

"Yeah, it was okay," he said.

Another big smile. He ran off to play with the other kids milling about the apartment building.

Daly felt relief. Slowly but surely, her son was learning to manage his issues. More and more, he could say, "I need to express my feelings," instead of screaming. He could tell his teachers he needed a break instead of bolting from the room or building.

From Greene's perspective, that's the big win—not just to fix kids' behavior problems, but to set them up for success on their own. Too many educators, he believes, fixate on a child's problems outside of school walls—a turbulent home, a violent neighborhood—rather than focus on the difference the school can make. "Whatever he's going home to, you can do the kid a heck of a lot of good six hours a day, five days a week, nine months a year," Greene said. "We tie our hands behind our backs when we focus primarily on things about which we can do nothing."

This holds true in our homes as well. Instead of bemoaning our children's faults and shortcomings, if we focus on the distance they've come and find hope for their future progress, they will follow our lead. This can only happen if we understand our children's perspective and communicate with them effectively, the second step in the Apprenticeship Model.

8

Capability

BAY AND JOSIAH JACKSON LIVE in a simple, two-story house in rural Lincoln, Vermont, with their seven-year-old son, Zealand, and four-year-old twin daughters, Scarlet and Magnolia. They milled the posts and beams themselves when building the house, and they left the exterior unpainted except for a bright orange door. The town rests at the foot of Mount Abraham and offers stunning views of the New Haven River through the trees.

On a brisk fall afternoon, Zealand finished an after-school snack of eggs and toast while Bay helped Scarlet mix yogurt and granola at the kitchen island a few feet away. Magnolia darted up to the kitchen table to show me how she could write her name, then padded back to investigate the food situation. All three children sported fine, red hair, a lighter shade than Bay's auburn. Magnolia wore a brightly colored striped cloth hat over a chin-length bob. A pink barrette held Scarlet's longer locks away from her round face.

Seated at the table with me and Zealand, Josiah explained that he and Bay used to see groups of parents coming to the local pub after Vicki Hoefle's parenting classes. When Zealand, at age three and a half, started throwing tantrums and resisting transitions between activities, it made sense for them to sign up too.

Hoefle compares misbehavior to weeds, which either grow, if watered with attention, or shrivel up when parents instead focus on building the relationship and supporting kids' small steps toward independence. Instead of telling kids what to do, she advocates taking a coaching and training approach—giving them the information and practice they need to become increasingly more competent.

"The first couple of times we went to her class, it was so clear it was a lifestyle choice, and it was much more about us as individuals than fixing our kids. There's nothing wrong with them. They're just mirroring and reflecting what we feed them," Bay told me. "It resonated with us both in a big way. It felt very natural and right."

While I chatted with his parents, Zealand seamlessly transitioned from snack to homework at the kitchen island, tucking his plate into the dishwasher without being asked. Scarlet chopped her own nuts for a bowl of yogurt and granola—with a mammoth knife—before beginning to fold laundry with her mom on a futon in the corner of the room. All three children dress themselves, pack their own lunches, and clean up after themselves, as well as helping the family by cleaning the bathroom, cooking, emptying the dishwasher, feeding the animals, bringing in wood, and starting the fire. Hoefle taught the Jacksons to give these chores the positive name of "contributions."

"There's a level of pride they all take because the contributions are not catered to them as kids, they're real-life contributions, like cleaning the toilet and cleaning the shower, things that oftentimes kids are not encouraged to do," Bay said.

"We need to heat our house and we need wood," said Josiah. "Zealand was lighting fires when he was two."

When Zealand began to prepare for his soccer game, the first hint of a cloud hovered over the serene afternoon. Magnolia begged to come along, but her parents wanted her to rest at home since she was getting over a cold. It was November in New England, and the weather was chilly.

She proceeded into a heartfelt and full-on meltdown as her initial wails and whines escalated and she burst into tears. Bay pulled Magnolia onto her lap. She stroked her back and comforted her without judgment, just giving quiet empathy. Seconds after the door closed behind Josiah and Zealand, Bay proposed bike riding in the driveway. Tears still on her face, Magnolia agreed.

And like that, the storm passed. Magnolia brushed tears from her cheeks and ran for her sneakers. She came back to show me how she could tie the beginning of the bow, the bunny ear. Bay finished tying them, and they both pulled on jackets to walk outside. I rose to leave as well.

It wasn't until I said good-bye and was reflecting on the cozy after-school routine that I realized that not once in the ninety minutes I'd been visiting had any member of the family picked up an electronic device. Josiah had leafed through a Patagonia catalog as the kids puttered around him, but the emphasis had clearly rested on connecting as a family while completing the daily tasks—all within the kitchen that comprised most of the 560-square-foot ground floor. The afternoon had unfolded like a well-choreographed dance, with every family member knowing their part. The parents didn't nag or yell, but merely offered to help or asked questions to move the action along.

~~~

I FIRST HEARD VICKI HOEFLE speak in October 2013, at a gathering of PEP teachers where she delivered a fiery denunciation of parents as the problem underlying misbehavior. By then, I'd taken all the PEP classes and was beginning to teach portions of the curriculum. Brian had joined the PEP board with an eye to making the organization more dad-friendly. We were fully sold on Adlerian parenting and agreed in theory with most everything in Hoefle's book, *Duct Tape Parenting*. And yet Hoefle's conviction that parents are the problem shook me. I was too scared to try even a week of "do-nothing-say-nothing," much less commit to parenting that way forever.

By late 2015, two days in Burlington immersed in Vicki Hoefle had won me over. I realized that I couldn't teach my kids to face life with courage if I was parenting from a place of fear. And frankly, I was a bit humiliated that the three Jackson kids—all under age eight—were doing more household chores than my nine- and eleven-year-old children.

I arrived home primed and ready to build my relationship with my kids and to stop being so tyrannical. I started taking notes about the kind or helpful things they did for each other and the family, so I could thank them in order to emphasize their contributions and capability. At our next family meeting, I brought up the issue of family jobs. Brian and I and the children had been rotating through the usual set of kitchen and front hall tidying jobs earlier in the school year, but we had let them slide as homework and activities heated up.

We all agreed to resume the jobs, and Brian and I offered to teach the kids to do laundry, cook a new meal, or help tidy their rooms. To my delight, Maddie took Brian up on the offer to learn how to cook crepes, and Ava jumped at the chance to have Mommy help put her clothes away and organize books. Within a few days, they were back in the routine of sharing the household work: dishes, cooking, cleaning, tidying, and caring for the dog. We started having ham and cheese crepes for dinner once a week, an event spearheaded by the kids.

Over the following months, whenever the family seemed to be in a jobs rut, I would change the method of dividing up responsibilities. Once, I turned a shoebox into the "Secret Box of Jobs," from which the kids could randomly choose a chore. Another time I wrote the jobs on slips of paper and put them in an elegantly scalloped glass. By not taking it personally when the jobs started to slide—or seeing it as a sign of my children's future irresponsibility—I avoided a power struggle.

Whenever my good humor threatened to slip away, I reminded myself of the simple rule: before taking any action as a parent, ask yourself whether it will be relationship-building or fracturing. If you're about to harm the relationship, stop. It's better to do nothing than to damage your bond. You'll surely have another opportunity to address whatever issue is at hand—give yourself breathing room to think it out.

I kept telling myself that the kids beginning to act up or the chores slipping by the wayside weren't signs of our failure as parents. Instead of seeing a tantrum as a disruption to be eliminated, I now viewed it as a signal that something was wrong—and a message for me to switch into detective mode. Perhaps the uproar was prompted by my child not having a skill needed to handle the situation, or maybe she needed support in building frustration tolerance or getting organized. Maybe my child was bored and needed more challenge and responsibility. (It's counterintuitive but it works: give a misbehaving child a truly difficult job and their behavior may suddenly improve.) I would simply keep coaching and leading them into the next area they were ready to master—saving and spending, planning their time, organizing their belongings, or whatever the next mountain to climb might be.

Researchers such as Heidi Riggio, a psychology professor at California State University–Los Angeles, have found that when children help with the work of the household, they develop a belief in themselves as capable and effective. Riggio interviewed a few hundred young adults about when they started doing chores and how they felt about themselves. She found a significant correlation between regular housework and their sense of competence. If they began chores at an older age, the connection was weaker. On average, people in the study started doing family jobs at age nine.

Similarly, Marty Rossman, professor emeritus at the University of Minnesota, analyzed data from a study that followed children from preschool to age ten, to age fifteen, and into their midtwenties. Those adults who started doing chores in preschool were more likely to complete their education, start on a career path, enjoy healthy relationships, avoid drugs, and be self-sufficient, as compared with people in the study who'd had no chores or who started them as teenagers. One caveat: some researchers have found that children who shoulder too many chores because their parents are absent or busy with work may lose out on academics. It's a balance.

Other researchers have found that household jobs have the most positive impact on kids' well-being when they have a say in which household jobs they do and autonomy in deciding how and when to perform them. It's good for parents to stretch their children's abilities, and time management skills, by teaching them household tasks and expecting them to complete them. Children gain confidence and a sense of meaning when they're responsible for walking a dog, setting the table, cooking dinner, and other daily jobs. When Brian and I started presenting these jobs in a matter-of-fact way as part of every family member's responsibility, the kids went along, with only a modicum of complaining. You may need to switch from a chore chart to a wheel to a mystery box from time to time, but stick with it.

~~~

So where do you start? It depends on your children and what seems reasonable to you. If Vicki Hoefle's do-nothing-say-nothing approach resonates, try that. Be guided by your child's interests and age, rather than what you'd like them to handle themselves. Some children just love to sort and stack—they're well suited to organizing plastic containers in the kitchen or storage areas of the garage. Cleaning out the pencil sharpener or changing the printer ink cartridges will appeal to kids who adore doing anything mechanical. Be sure to start with a manageable task, so you can build on success.

Sit down together in a quiet moment and ask your child whether there's anything they'd like to learn to do for themselves. Be enthusiastic and positive, to capture their interest. Look for ways to make household tasks fun or even a game. When we were trying to get our kids to sit still at dinner and use good manners, we brought home a PEP suggestion that we pretend to be in a fancy restaurant. The kids ran with it, creating the "Lewis Family Restaurant" game, complete with kid-created menus and a host stand where guests could check in. Dinner took longer, but was both more orderly and more fun.

Make a plan for teaching your child the agreed-upon skill. Always begin a training session by asking what the child already knows—from logic or from watching you—and build on that. Talk through the steps before handing over the knife for slicing vegetables or the sheets for placing on the bed.

If you have toddlers, this is a prime age for getting them involved. I bet you've already heard "I do it myself!" more times than you can count. The willingness is there, just not the skill. That's okay: your goal is to encourage your child to contribute and to get in the habit of helping, not to have chores performed perfectly. Make sure to leave extra time so you can go at your child's pace. Guarantee that the first attempt will be a success by picking a realistic goal—tidying up a few stuffed animals, for instance, rather than the entire collection of Playmobil toys. You can make it even more fun with silly songs, sing-along music, or funny voices. Even with young school-age children, the appeal of doing things with Mom or Dad usually overcomes any reluctance to get off the couch and help. Let them pick the job they want to master.

Roping tweens and teens into household tasks may be more challenging. The key is to stay one step ahead of them in level of difficulty. Teach them something at the edge of their comfort zone: cooking with an open flame and a pan that sizzles, or measuring pressure on all the bike tires and pumping them up. Use real-life needs rather than invented tasks so they see the impact of their work.

Maddie always loved cooking. As early as eight, she regularly made herself and her sister fried eggs and pancakes on the stove. So naturally, Ava hung back from meal preparation. Why compete? I kept at it, gently urging her to help whenever I could without nagging. One week she even helped me make simple ham quesadillas, though grudgingly.

A few days later, I was driving home late from work, stomach grumbling, with only a few minutes to change my clothes before I needed to leave for an evening meeting. I called the house, and ten-year-old Ava picked up.

"Honey, I have an emergency. I'm running very short of time and I'm hungry. Would you be willing to pull together some dinner that I can grab when I stop in the house in about twenty minutes? You can make some extra for yourself and Maddie."

"Okay," Ava responded instantly, to my surprise. "What do you want me to make?"

"Could you make me some turkey quesadillas like the ham ones we made earlier? Just grab some tortillas from the fridge, put turkey on them, put cheese on top, and then—"

"Wait a minute," Ava said. "Let me get a piece of paper and a pen. Can you tell me the steps, one by one?"

Delighted, I waited. Then I listed each step in making quesadillas. I arrived home to find two warm quesadillas on a paper plate for me to consume in the car en route to my next commitment. Next to the plate was a neatly printed recipe in her round handwriting:

1. Get ham/turkey
2. Get gouda
3. Get tortilla
4. Slice gouda
5. 1 tortilla 3–5 peices gouda
6. 5 slices ham
7. Microwave 40 sec
   (Make 4–6)

If you're not sure where to start when it comes to household jobs, take a look at the age-appropriate chores for children at the end of this book. Pick a few, or even show your kids the list and ask them if they see a task they'd like to master. (Are you surprised by what's on these lists? Perhaps your children are older and you're not sure they can handle such challenging jobs. You will never know until you try.)

If they're willing, you're in luck. Teach them the task, step by step. Be sure to appreciate all that they do, and resist correcting them at first. As they practice, they'll get better. After a few tries on their own, ask if they'd like feedback on how they're performing the task. If they say no, keep your mouth shut. Be patient as you look for progress, not perfection. New chores represent an opportunity for them to learn a skill and spend time with a parent, rather than something to be dreaded.

What if your child is resistant to the idea of chores? Bring it up another day. Introduce humor. Ask them to give it a try for a week. Tell them you honestly need help. If all else fails, start very small and look for the tiny contributions they do make—like just picking up a coat—while inviting them to learn more. Even shifting 5 percent in the direction you want to head is an improvement. Focusing on the positive contributions they do make will work better than lamenting all that they don't do.

Remember to have appropriate expectations, based on your child's age, abilities, and temperament. A three-year-old isn't going to be as responsible with belongings, or as considerate of others, as a ten-year-old.

As children grow, they should increasingly take over responsibility for self-care: brushing their teeth, bathing, feeding, and dressing themselves—and caring for their belongings. We went through a terrible power struggle with Ava over brushing her teeth and taking her asthma medicine, until I thought of inviting her to join me in brushing teeth. She's much more cooperative when we're doing something together, as opposed to me tapping my toes waiting for her to finish washing up. My rule of thumb is that by age eleven children should be able to completely care for and feed themselves. You may do more of the cooking while they do easier chores, but they should be capable in a pinch. And anytime you do something for children that they can do for themselves, you're stealing the opportunity for them to feel more capable.

Children also need dominion over some portion of the house. In my family, that means that the kids can decide how messy their room gets. When the floor beside Ava's bed gets too crowded with stacks of books, I may just stand at the door of her room and blow her a kiss good-night—since I don't want to risk tripping. The next day she may be more receptive to my offer to help her organize her library so that we can resume our bedtime cuddles.

In your home, their area of control may be a basement playroom. If your kids have trouble keeping their clothes and toys tidy, they probably have too many. We regularly sort through both for donations to charity or for a garage sale—which my kids enjoy because they keep half the proceeds. When new toys, books, or clothes enter the house, we aim to shed the same amount through donations or garage sales.

It's a little puzzling to me that my kids need so much training and support when I don't recall my parents ever spending so much time on chores. But then I realize that we're so much busier and more isolated than in previous generations. For a time, my grandmother lived with us and helped us learn to cook and clean. My friends and I spent a fair amount of time underfoot in the kitchen, watching our moms run the household; today kids are often out of the house at activities and only reunite with their parents just before dinnertime and bed. Whatever the reason for these changes from one generation to the next, you can start your children on household tasks today.

The arena of life skills and contributions to the household is just one of two ways in which adults build children's capability. Even more important is working on their social and emotional skills. I saw this vividly at a public school in Ohio.

~~~

BRANDY DAVIES'S HEELS TAPPED QUICKLY down the halls of Ohio Avenue Elementary School in Columbus. I followed, a bit breathless. For a short woman, she was fast. The school was well maintained and full of windows. Nestled in a rough neighborhood—I passed a pawn shop and discount grocery stores as well as boarded-up buildings—the Ohio Ave ES building itself feels safe, orderly, and joyous.

Davies reached the door of the gym before I did and huddled to talk with the physical education teacher, a tall man standing in the doorway. A handful of children squeezed around his body. A girl with a neat bun of hair on top of her head and a piteous look on her face held out her arm for Davies to inspect.

Something had gone down in PE class.

Davies had warned me that might be the case. A majority of the twenty-four third-graders in her class had experienced trauma in their short lives—a parent incarcerated, a parent's death, or exposure to violence, alcoholism, or drug abuse. And those were just the incidents she knew about. They had also endured the stress that comes with poverty: a majority of children in the Columbus school district qualify for free and reduced meals. The need is so overwhelming that the school system simply provides breakfast and lunch to the entire student body. In schools like Ohio Ave, children struggle with the most basic social emotional skills: impulse control, emotion management, empathy, and decision-making.

As a result of these children's experience with trauma, a fight could break out at a moment's notice. A sideways glance or an accidental nudge could easily provoke something bigger. The girls in particular this year seemed like a tinderbox. At Ohio Ave, adults building kids' capabilities focus on these missing social emotional skills—a parallel to how the parents in Hoefle's classes work on their children's life skills.

The girl who held out her hand, Jayliana, had moved to Ohio Ave from another school, one where the norm was defiance and fights. She arrived full of rage. It didn't help that her mom and dad were splitting up and her dad had recently moved out, Davies told me earlier.

"You have to watch your girls. All of them want to fight together," the PE teacher told Davies. A boy grabbed Davies around the waist and leaned in for a hug. Accusations flew through the air.

"They was throwing beanbags," one boy said.

"It was your beanbag," one girl accused. The girl she looked at denied being involved.

"You was too, dude," the boy said.

"Why are you all out in the hall? I'm not talking to you, so this is not your concern," Davies said.

"People trying to smack me. And I'm not having it," Jayliana declared, her round face fierce.

"You always talking about people's families!" the boy said, voice rising in outrage.

That prompted a burst of angry comments.

"Stop right now," Davies said. "I didn't ask you. I didn't ask you, and I haven't asked you yet." A stern glance at each complaining child punctuated each "you."

"Okay. Now explain something to me." She leaned close to Brianna, a tall girl with short dreads and a light blue polo shirt. They were almost the same height, even with Davies in high heels.

"They're trying to hit me a lot, and I'm trying to move, but I can't if they keep hitting me and hitting me," Brianna said.

"That's a lie," commented Brayden, a boy in a dark blue polo shirt.

"Why are they trying to hit you?" Davies asked.

"That's a lie. That's a lie," Brayden repeated.

"Do you want to be honest about that?" Davies asked Brianna.

"I know why they trying to hit her," Brayden offered.

"So then I'm going to ask them as well," Davies told him. "We'll give them their turn. Go to the entrance please."

She stepped back. Jayliana, Brianna, a girl in a pink Aero T-shirt, and a few boys lingered. The children who had been in the gym piled out, forming a rough line against the far wall. More accusations flew.

"They hit me first."

"You hit me."

"She touched me, dude."

Girls hugged Davies as they passed by on the way to the line. Every time I visited Ohio Ave, I noticed how the students connected to their teachers, gravitating toward them and often wanting a hug or other physical reassurance.

Jayliana was still proffering her scratched arm, comforted by Keelin, the girl in the pink T-shirt. The PE teacher shut down the kids' begging to go to the nurse's office. Keelin started walking toward the line of children, which was beginning to move down the hall. Jayliana, tears on her face, stood immobile.

"Just go. Go, Jayliana," Keelin urged her.

Davies started the children taking turns at the water fountain. She walked up to Jayliana and cupped her face in both hands. Jayliana was full-on crying by now.

"Look at me. If you talk like that, it gets you into trouble and I have to write you up," she said. I hadn't heard what Jayliana said to the PE teacher, but it must've been bad.

"You can't say things like that. Get in my line for me," Davies said kindly.

Jayliana hung her head. Dragged one leg after the other as she slumped down the hallway.

As intense as the scene seemed to me, Davies explained later that a few years earlier it probably would've escalated into throwing things and physical fighting. At least one child would've been sent to an in-school suspension or possibly sent home. As in many urban schools, even five-year-olds would curse or talk back to adults without blinking an eye. Slapping or punching a classmate came easily to them. Their trauma history made them prone to misinterpreting someone else's actions as aggressive, known in the psychology literature as hostile attribution bias.

All that changed after Davies started playing the "PAX Good Behavior Game," which research has shown to cut disruptive classroom behavior by 70 percent or more.

Here's how the game works. Before any given activity or transition, the teacher and children discuss and agree on the behavior that leads to PAX—which stands for peace, productivity, health, and happiness—as well as behavior that is unwanted, which PAX gives the made-up name "spleem." For instance, during independent work, PAX behavior might include keeping your hands on the task, resting your eyes on your papers, and not speaking in a voice that can be heard more than three inches from your mouth. Spleems might include fiddling with water bottles, taking lip gloss out of the desk, or getting into off-task conversation. The classroom is divided into teams of five or six kids each.

Each game begins with a gentle blow on Davies's harmonica. At the end of the game, any team with fewer than four spleems gets to participate in a celebration drawn from "Granny's Wacky Prize Box" or from a choice that Davies gives them. These prizes are silly activities that last only a minute or two, but the kids love them. The prizes that Davies's students like include dancing to a GoNoodle video, playing Mrs. Davies Says, and doing calisthenics, like high knees or stretches.

Because PAX relies on key principles of child development and motivation, the game avoids the pitfalls of reward schemes. Teachers aren't demanding that kids meet unilateral standards—the children agree as a classroom on desired and undesired behaviors. The rewards aren't tangible bribes, but rather physical experiences that celebrate the group's successful cooperation. The movement alone contributes to self-regulation by releasing stress. Even the name "spleem" avoids the baggage that might come with labels like "misbehavior" or "bad choice." Saying "spleem" curves your face into a slight smile, which helps avert negative feelings. PAX is the Apprenticeship Model in a nutshell.

The kids loved the game. They got excited when they thought it was coming. Jayliana and Keelin in particular became really invested in it. During the game, they'd encourage their team to behave so they could win the prize.

As the children built their ability to control themselves in the game, this skill extended to other parts of the day. Before the game, Davies had to move students out of the classroom for dangerous behavior as often as ten times a day. Now days could pass without one of her students losing control—whether throwing objects or fighting—to the point where she needed a second adult to help her restore order.

This is how adults teach behavior control and emotion regulation. This is how they build children's interpersonal capability.

Kids usually act up because they're feeling useless—not able to contribute to the family or the classroom—or because they lack emotional awareness and skills. Chores and social and emotional training help solve the problem. In your home, look for opportunities to work on these skills, whether managing anger or navigating social situations.

You could start with something as simple as playing pretend with a preschooler before meeting relatives or attending a grown-up event. Talk through the scenario and ask what behavior your child thinks is appropriate. It's especially fun if you play-act the inappropriate behavior, giving your child a chance to correct you. One trick you can teach children who feel shy about looking into adults' eyes when greeting them is to look in the middle of their forehead. The adult can't tell the difference, and the experience becomes less intense for the child.

It may also help to come up with code words when you're training kids in social skills. PEP's Jessup taught us one technique that we use to this day. Since good manners are the keys to success in life, when our children forget to say "please" or "thank you," we might whisper "keys" to remind them. That way we don't have to nag them publicly: "What do you say to that nice compliment from Grandma?"

～～

Dennis Embry founded the Tucson-based PAXIS Institute to create and distribute the PAX game and other science-based programming that fights mental illness, often in partnership with the Johns Hopkins Center for Prevention and Early Intervention, where Embry is co-investigator on several studies.

"We have an epidemic of mental, emotional, and behavioral disorders. It makes the polio epidemic look like nothing," he told me. In today's numbers, the polio epidemic—which mobilized every state in the union—would have caused 6,000 deaths and 120,000 cases. That's dwarfed by the 44,000 annual suicide deaths and half a million self-inflicted injuries seen in emergency rooms today.

Embry considers the PAX game to be a behavior vaccine for classrooms that helps to build children's self-regulation, thereby boosting their school success and reducing mental health problems, addictions, bullying, violence, and crime over the long term. Indeed, for some children the game effectively eliminates their ADHD, which is diagnosed by observing behaviors like distraction and impulsivity. By the end of one year with the game, many children no longer display those behaviors, thanks to their increased self-control.

I met Embry in October 2015 at a teacher workshop in Columbia, Maryland, where Johns Hopkins maintains a training center. Embry had the look of an aging elf, or perhaps Willy Wonka. He sported Elton John glasses, a small soul patch, and thinning hair with a tuft on top. This day the theme was blue: turquoise disk earrings and a royal blue skinny-cut suit with a light blue floral shirt and a darker blue floral tie. Pins attached to the breast pocket of his suit jacket resembled a set of military medals, but close up I saw that the pins were candy-colored playful shapes that would look at home on a carousel seat or a preschool playground.

Embry's fingers clicked on his MacBook as he set up his slideshow presentation. He scoffed at my suggestion that doctors might be too aggressive these days in diagnosing disorders and that kids today have similar struggles as in the past. He pointed to the 30 percent increase in the teen suicide rate over the last decade—and the 50 percent increase in the suicide rate of children ten to fourteen years old. "Dead bodies are hard to overdiagnose," he said.

"Something has gone dreadfully wrong in behavioral genetics in our world. Anxiety disorders are driving the suicidality and the opiate and much of the marijuana addiction. As younger and younger generations come on board, they're having earlier depression, and a larger percentage of people are having depression."

Teachers began to filter into the room, clutching coffee cups. He greeted each one with a cheerful handshake and word of welcome.

The room filled with nearly three dozen teachers, most of them female; only three were male. Then the presentation got under way. Embry described the research supporting the PAX game, including a finding by a Johns Hopkins postdoctoral fellow that just one year of playing the game changed gene expression at ages nineteen, twenty, and twenty-one. Children carrying a gene linked to aggression, depression, and ADHD—who played the game in first grade—showed less impulsivity and aggressive behavior at college age. Your genes may incline you to be impulsive or aggressive, but you won't display such behavior if those genes aren't expressed. So the fact that the game dampens gene expression is potentially life-changing.

Embry talked about the importance of teachers building a strong relationship with the students in their classrooms. "If you do [things] *to* children, you get a foul response. If you work through and *with* the children, you tend to get much faster implementation and behavioral effects," he said.

As he taught, Embry seemed to be in as constant motion as the children I would later see in Davies's classroom. To illustrate different points, he did push-ups on a desk, twisted his nose at the thought of something gross, and lay down on a chair and waved his arms madly. During breaks in the training, when the teachers were writing a reflection, he would pace the room, walking up and down the aisles and often coming back to whisper an insight or research reference to me. He led the teachers through an exercise they would do with their students to start the year: he asked them to imagine the most wonderful classroom and to list what they would see, hear, feel, and do in that classroom. "For children to have a vision of a future, they must develop a sense of trust and reliability in peers and other adults, such as their teachers," he said.

～～～

THE TWENTY-FOUR THIRD-GRADERS CROWDED ONTO the carpet at the front of Brandy Davies's classroom. They gyrated. They jumped. They giggled. They aligned their bodies with the flickering shadows of dancers on the smart board. Then the board went blank. Instantly, they streamed back to their desks, panting and smiling.

This is self-regulation learning in action. Since Davies began using the PAX game, she'd seen a steady increase in her students' ability to control themselves. When they win one of the nontangible prizes—like a minute of dancing to a GoNoodle video—they enjoy it to the fullest and then switch back into learning mode as soon as the minute ends. The harmonica at the beginning of each game commands their attention without triggering their alarm systems, as a series of claps or a teacher's raised voice might do. Training on the impact of trauma has given the Ohio Ave teachers an understanding of their students' vulnerabilities. With a grant, the school bought exercise bikes and fidgets—stress balls, finger toys, and other gadgets that the kids can manipulate with their hands as a way to calm themselves down. The students often ask to bike for five minutes or to use a fidget when they feel agitated.

"It has been such a benefit to these kids in bringing their anxiety levels down and getting them focused on their work," Davies said. We stood together looking at the line of kid-sized exercise bikes in the hallway. A row of raised knobs and plastic animal shapes dotted the walls at waist level, their surfaces worn smooth by children's fingers.

Teachers can't just hand over these toys—different tools work best for each child, she said. First, teachers need to have a strong relationship with the children so that they can learn whether dysregulation is the culprit or whether misbehavior stems perhaps from something as simple as hunger. And of course, they've taught the kids to use the toys and the bikes only for stress relief, not when they're merely bored. During a quiet moment in the classroom Jayliana and Keelin crowded around me to explain the fidgets. "When you're mad or sad, you can have a fidget. Or you can go pedal," Jayliana said. "Or you can stay in the classroom, and then you can squeeze and squeeze until you get your stress out."

I asked how the fidget toy helps her. "It's soft and everything, and it makes me not feel mad or sad, because if you mad or sad and try to act like you mad or sad, you get in trouble and they gonna call your mom," she said. Later in the day, she and another girl exchanged heated words as one of them crossed the room. I saw Jayliana return to her desk and pick up a squishy pink ball. She squeezed it, tugged the center, and finally pressed it against her forehead, closing her eyes. Then she went back to her work.

This year Davies's students had experienced their share of trauma. Kids had been bounced around from Mom's house to Grandma's house, eagerly awaited news of their dad's release from prison, or struggled through their parents' separation. One girl had lost her step-dad to a fatal shooting while she was in the same house, supposedly sleeping; the teachers suspected, however, that she heard the argument and commotion that led to his death. Another girl's mother had disappeared and turned up dead. "It's a handful," Davies said. "Something will strike her or it's a time of day, maybe if I've said something, tears will just start pouring down her face. If that happens and I see her with tears on her face and she starts coloring and writing, if that's what she needs to get settled, I don't mind. She's not listening anyway."

At recess, I found the Ohio Ave principal, Olympia Williams, overseeing a playground of children dancing, playing ball, or chasing each other around the jungle gym. She places her priority on teaching behavioral skills through the PAX game, before academics. If the children can't sit still or are persistently fighting, they're never going to learn. She also supplements with trauma-informed lessons that teach kids language for their emotions and social skills. "Yes, on the front end you are giving up time. We're not getting to curriculum on day one. We're not. But just like you teach the kids what you want to do in reading centers, you really have to teach them about their feelings and give them vocabulary words to describe their feelings."

Embry likes to describe his debate with officials at a state department of education, who have bought four different reading curriculums over seven years. "How's that working for you?" he asked them. "Regardless of the curriculum, PAX made reading better. As the child changes at school, that changes the parent-child relationship with the school. You have fewer calls home, not as much spanking, etc., for getting in trouble in school."

The PAX chart that collects what the children want to see, hear, feel, and do in their classroom becomes a visible reference throughout the year. "Just like they have an anchor chart for reading and math, they have this anchor chart they can look up to as a reminder, these are the things you guys said you wanted to see more of in the classroom. The teacher didn't make that up. The principal didn't make that up. This is your community, and this is what you guys agreed to," Williams said. "It pushes the ownership and accountability onto the students. A lot of time teachers try to take too much of that, and kids feel like they have no power. They already have no power out of school."

In the 2016–2017 school year, Ohio Ave received a fourth-grade transfer student who had seen his mother shoot another woman. While his mom was in jail, the boy's dad had taken custody of him, his first time raising children. The boy spiraled out of control, eventually stabbing a teacher at his previous school in the chest and hand with scissors. The teacher pressed criminal charges. The school requested a psychological evaluation, suspecting emotional disturbance, and transferred him to Ohio Ave.

"I was looking at this kid's records like, 'Oh my gosh!' The first couple of weeks I had to call security," Williams said. The boy would run out of the classroom without permission and curse at any adult around. But since he arrived, the boy had done a 180. "He used to have four to five incidents a day, and now he has one a month."

He loved the PAX game and worked with his team to try to win a prize. The school gave him four daily "passes" to leave the classroom when he was feeling overwhelmed, so he had control over when to walk out, but he had to plan and ration the passes. He used to burn through all four. Now he was down to one pass a day, and some days he didn't even need it.

"It really goes through my mind—how many kids are being identified as emotionally disturbed when in actuality it's not that they are having this long-term emotional disability but it's some kind of exposure to trauma and we're not taking the time to delve into the root cause and figure out what to do to support him?" she said.

As a child, Williams had gone to school with lots of kids who survived trauma. Her mom, a teacher, decided to bus Williams and her siblings to inner-city schools. Rather than walking five minutes to her neighborhood middle school, Williams took a twenty-five-minute bus ride to Champion Middle School in the center of the city. "She felt the teachers were stronger in the schools that were in the bad neighborhoods because they had to do more, they had to overcome more," she explained. "People said: 'You're picking the schools in the bad neighborhood?' It was more about programming for her."

Williams majored in biology in part because of the science focus she'd enjoyed in middle school, when she planned to become a doctor. But after earning her bachelor's, she changed her mind. Why go to school forever and end up in debt? She got a master's degree in elementary education and became a teacher. In 2012, seeking greater autonomy to make decisions that would impact more children, she made the leap to principal. "I love what I do. I love the school," she said. "I also advocate for principals and for people who supervise principals to understand the level of the work of the principal. You can't even describe it. It's nonstop."

During the school day, Williams likes to be in the hallways and classrooms, available to students and teachers who may need her. As a result, mountains of papers pile up on her desk. She told me: "The staff jokes, 'Your mountains are lower today,' or, 'It looks like the mountain is high.'" Williams does her own self-regulating through weekly visits with a counselor and stress management exercises, including breathing.

There's simply too much work to do in the day. Williams stays after school to complete paperwork and takes pride in her work. But whenever she has to choose between meeting the needs of the children in front of her and filling out forms, the kids win.

"You're going to have to decide what you're going to be known for and what you won't bend for. For me, it's this whole premise of the whole child. That's the thing that will take precedence over me doing budgetary stuff or a compliance notebook. I will say, you can't do everything and do it well," she said. "I'm a perfectionist. I really care about my job. I want to do well at everything; however, some things have to go to the wayside."

Before implementing PAX, the school used the red-green-yellow behavior charts that are so common in US classrooms. Each child has the three colors beside their name, with a clip to indicate the teacher's assessment of their behavior so far that day. In retrospect, Williams sees how that system actually exacerbates bad behavior. Children who are prone to outbursts flip out when they're moved down to yellow or red—especially since it's publicly visible to all their classmates.

"They do not want to be singled out for a negative," she said. Often these kids would just give up and stop trying to behave better. "Some kids couldn't get back from that. If they got red, they'd be, 'I'm done.'"

Ohio Ave began PAX in earnest with one dozen teachers trained in 2014–2015, and then the majority on board by the 2016–2017 school year. You can see the results in the drop in use of the time-out room. Teachers used to send students out all the time, and sometimes they'd stay out for hours. In 2013–2014, the school saw 355 time-outs for under an hour; that number fell 77 percent, to 83 time-outs, in 2016–2017. They experienced an even more dramatic drop in time-outs lasting more than an hour, which significantly impact instructional time. Those fell from 317 in the baseline year to 39 three years later—a whopping 88 percent decline.

"This means it's more time the child is in the classroom, they have strategies," Williams said. "They're still hearing the instruction that's going on, so they're able to get back on track or work on their work. If they go to the time-out room, they might take their work with them, but by the time they get back to the classroom they're already behind. The other kids are doing work. That sets the kid off again."

"Most of our kids are below grade level anyway—it's not like they're independent workers that can come back and get back on track," she said. "Before this method, they might say, 'Jeremy you're not in your seat.' It would escalate to more and take more time to resolve."

Davies felt skeptical when she first took the PAX training. The high-tech language and theoretical discussion bored her. *These kids are going to hate it,* she remembered thinking. She'd gotten into teaching to help students like herself: no matter how hard she tried, she'd always gotten Ds and Fs. She wanted to help nontraditional learners.

But as soon as Davies saw the on-site counselor, Kady Lacy, demonstrate a game with her kids, it clicked. Whenever Davies got stuck, she'd call Lacy and they'd work through the problem. Lacy came to Ohio Ave as part of Nationwide Children's Hospital's outreach to the community. The hospital wants to provide universal prevention to the most at-risk communities so that behavioral and mental health problems don't spiral out of control. Ultimately, untreated issues land children and adults alike in emergency rooms, where doctors can do little but patch them up. It's far more effective for professionals to work with at-risk families before problems get too big.

Nationwide Children's Hospital clinicians like Lacy receive full responsibility for individual schools: they see children for counseling and serve as a resource for each school's staff. Some Ohio school districts even train their bus drivers in trauma-informed practices so that they can intervene in problems without escalating kids' dysregulation. Each county's Alcohol, Drug, And Mental Health (ADAMH) board oversees the initiatives and gives grants to support programs such as PAX. Ohio's economy still hasn't recovered from the Great Recession: poverty remains rampant, and more than 50 percent of children in the state are considered economically disadvantaged. Ohio Ave Elementary qualifies as a high-poverty school. Some students are even homeless. Of the 331 total students, 86 percent are black, 7 percent are white, 5 percent are multiracial, and 2 percent are Hispanic.

"Being involved with the schools, this is an opportunity to get kids before they hit that school-to-prison pipeline. Our missions are to decrease the gap in the access to care and to remove non-academic barriers to academic success," said Kamilah Twymon, clinical coordinator for Nationwide's school-based services and community partnerships. "The schools recognize that sometimes kids bring a whole lot with them. Families, if they're at the beginning of this journey, it's very difficult to navigate the mental health system sometimes. Even if we can point them in the right direction, they're already dealing with a lot. It helps."

Twymon grew up on the west side of Columbus, raised by a vigilant single mom. The few times Twymon started drifting off the rails—cutting school, getting mouthy—her mom wrenched her back. Her mother would take time off from work to go to the school, and she would contact Twymon's friends' parents so they could all supervise their girls better. "My mom was on it every single time. It was more than punishment. It was discussions and learning opportunities," she said.

Twymon's three children—a sophomore in college and a junior and a freshman in high school—all went to Columbus city schools too, even after the family moved to the Pickerington suburb. "It's a combination of my personal values and having a personal stake and claim. I've always been an advocate for underprivileged and marginalized populations," she said. Immediately after getting her counseling license, she took a job keeping delinquent kids out of restrictive placement. She joined the Nationwide program hoping to catch the children earlier, to prevent some of the damage she saw in her clients. While her division doesn't make money for the hospital, she's proud of the money she knows is saved by interventions such as PAX—in lower utilization of Medicaid, fewer emergency department visits, less adult drug use, lower criminal involvement, and higher graduation rates.

PAX even qualifies as preventative care under grants given to address the opioid crisis.

〜〜

ON THE SURFACE, THE JACKSON family in rural Vermont may seem to have little in common with the teachers at Ohio Ave Elementary School. But I hope you now see how both life skills and social and emotional skills contribute to children's self-discipline—and how critical it is to build capability in both arenas. When children can take care of themselves and contribute to a household or community, they feel a sense of competence and purpose. This naturally lessens their impulse to act out. The more kids practice emotion management and impulse control, the better their self-control becomes, even for those kids without a trauma background.

Just as the PAX game builds students' self-discipline little by little, you can work gradually on developing these behavioral skills in your kids. Keep track of their development and age-appropriate goals. Invite them to participate in setting goals for themselves. Given how slow the process can be, it's important to continually remind children—and yourself—how much they're growing, whether in a handwritten journal, notes on your phone, or even a voice-recorded diary. Choose whatever method will help you quickly note where your kids are today—as a reference point for tomorrow.

Even though we aren't trying to control our children, we still hope to influence them. Unless we claim our role as our child's primary teacher of life skills and values, popular culture and peers will rush to fill the void. As you observe and listen to your kids more often, in keeping with the lessons of Chapter 7, you'll begin to identify skills and character traits that they could stand to strengthen. Tackle them one at a time. If your child struggles with keeping track of belongings, brainstorm together ways they can remember items when they leave school or a friend's house. If you notice that your child lacks empathy, begin modeling that quality in your conversations and mention it when you see them expressing even the smallest amount of empathy.

Capability is the final pillar in the Apprenticeship Model, and you will return to it over and over again as your children grow and tackle bigger challenges.

9

Limits and Routines

"THAT'S NOT FAIR!" MY ELEVEN-YEAR-OLD screamed at me. Maddie stormed from my parents' porch, where we'd been talking, and slammed the heavy oak and glass door leading into the house. Opened it. Slammed it. Opened it. Slammed it.

The house reverberated with the sounds of a tween thwarted. Soon her angry footsteps thudded in the direction of the living room. I took a deep breath as I felt the heat rising in my chest. My body itched to storm across the room and yell at her. Or maybe throw her bodily from the house. I took a deep breath of the cool breeze wafting across the porch. I struggled to be calm and firm. I reminded myself of everything I'd learned. *Her amygdala's activated. She probably has no access to the problem-solving, rational parts of her brain.*

This wasn't how I'd imagined the first day of summer vacation unfolding.

My children were done with camp for the season, and I'd cleared my work schedule for a couple of days so we could prepare at a leisurely pace for our family trip to California. Then I committed the parental crime of enforcing our family's screen rules. Just as with our chore chart and bedtime agreement, we created the screen time rules by consensus. Days before this explosion, I sat down with my nine- and eleven-year-old kids to rewrite the screen rules based on their suggestion that the daily limit be bumped from thirty minutes to forty-five minutes. It was summer, they argued, and I conceded the point. We were vacationing at my parents' lake house in Wisconsin while Brian worked back home, so the three of us drew up a fresh agreement to post on the wall. After the kids ate and cleaned up from breakfast, dressed and brushed their teeth, did ten minutes of math practice, and completed chores, they could enjoy forty-five minutes of screen time.

Usually the screen rules were a workable compromise between our kids' desire for some entertainment and our goal to include healthy activities as part of the day. But my daughter had violated the rules by picking up her iPad before she finished (or even started) her jobs for the day. When I caught her with the tablet in her room, she made a lame excuse. "I can't start the laundry until Ava brings me her clothes!" I expressed sympathy but didn't budge on banning her from screens for a day, which was our agreed-upon consequence.

This is the part of the Apprenticeship Model that skeptics sometimes fail to understand. Just because we tolerate a fair amount of chaos and include our kids' input in decisions, that doesn't mean there are no limits. Sure, we're more likely to respond to a yelling child with a hug than by banishing them to their room. Instead of ordering our children to do something, we give them information about the impact of their action (or inaction) on others. But when they violate an agreement we've set by consensus, we don't lift the consequence.

Because of our emphasis on honoring our kids' feelings and perspectives, when they are angry about a limit, boy, do they tell us! For the rest of the morning, my daughter grumbled and grumped about the house. First, she twisted around in the one squeaky chair until her sister complained. Then she came back to me with a renewed set of arguments against the screen time ban. Next she loudly complained that nobody cared about her.

My temper rose at each provocation. I tamped it down. Engaging would only prolong the conflict and distract her from experiencing the consequence of her actions—being banned from screens. "I care about you deeply, and I hope you decide to join me and your sister when we go to the library to check out guidebooks," I told her. I started packing up a lunch to take on our outing, with a sinking feeling inside that she would sulk away the entire, beautiful summer day.

Then a small miracle happened. She came trotting up to me with a neutral expression on her face. Not a scowl.

"Are you coming with us?" I asked, with a smile. She nodded. Before I knew it, she had talked her sister into joining my father on an errand and we two former combatants were companionably driving to the library. I wondered aloud: had she arranged this so the two of us could have time alone? "Yeah. I felt bad about this morning. I'm sorry," she said. I reached back and squeezed her hand.

This is what effective discipline can look like. Sticking to a limit doesn't always feel great or elicit a child's instant, sunny cooperation. But if I had yelled back when she exploded, it would've deepened our disconnection. If I had given her a time-out, she would've spent that time in her room plotting revenge on me. Instead, I had calmly cited the family rule. Nothing more. That had given her space to calm down and decide that she'd rather have a nice afternoon outing than sulk alone.

～～～

WHEN I STARTED THE RESEARCH that became this book, I imagined that with the right combination of encouraging language and developmentally appropriate strategies, my home life would become orderly and calm. But since I am raising children, not robots, I've had to accept that parenting is messy no matter what. Even after I'd internalized PEP principles intellectually, it took years for the language and mind-set to come naturally, especially in the midst of a conflict with the kids. I had to uproot some of my most closely held beliefs about parenting, and I relied on Brian and other like-minded parents for willpower to stay the course. It was painful to let the kids experience the full consequences of their choices—for instance, they missed cuddle time if they dawdled during bedtime—without twisting the knife with a snide comment or guilt-inducing look. Sometimes it took weeks to see even the slightest progress. At those times, I had to stick to my path based on faith alone.

I had to stop thinking that my goal was to say the perfect thing and make the right decision in every circumstance. So often the parenting advice industry tells us to be consistent above all. But we are all human. We have good days when we have bounteous patience to set a calm and firm limit with a disrespectful child. And then we have those bad days when we lose our cool. The bad days aren't cause for shame. They're an opportunity to model for our children how to apologize and make amends—or, if we can catch ourselves before we explode, a chance to model taking a five-minute break to cool down instead of reacting in anger.

Moreover, it's a lie that any parenting method works as long as you're consistent. Consistently berating or striking your child has been proven to cause long-lasting damage.

It's not easy to trust that kids will learn without pain or shame. When I first started relying on consequences instead of punishment, my tone of voice was often blaming and I sometimes rubbed in the lesson. Limits are arguably the toughest part of this parenting approach—as is often the case. You want to let the experience stand alone, so the child can learn from the consequences. That means having faith in the teaching.

Unfortunately, this also requires that we throw out some parenting tools that can feel satisfying—especially when we want to show the world we're a good parent. But there's no more shaming kids in public, and no more rescuing them from their mistakes, whether it's a forgotten school lunch or a now-regretted decision to sign up for the cheer team. This looks different when parenting a four-year-old as compared to a teenager, but the basic principle remains the same: give kids as much ownership as possible, with support, predictable routines, and agreed-upon consequences.

For example, a preschooler might not be able to come up with ideas for a smoother morning routine, but can choose whether they prefer to dress before breakfast or afterward. A ten-year-old, on the other hand, might be able to brainstorm an after-school schedule that includes independently getting a snack and doing homework before moving on to playtime. And a second-grader is old enough to sign an agreement that if Mom and Dad pay the soccer fees, they will participate in practices and games for the eight weeks of the season—even if they stop enjoying it after three weeks.

What is most important to remember is that it's okay for your kids to be upset. Sometimes it's those feelings of unhappiness or discomfort that prompt people to change. Certainly, your kids will develop resilience only by experiencing unpleasantness, not by being shielded from upset by you. When you're implementing a new approach like this, conflict may rise before it subsides, especially if you have older children.

How do you know if a consequence might actually be a punishment in disguise? Follow the "four Rs" rule. Consequences should be *related* to the behavior, *reasonable* in scope, *respectful* of the child, and *revealed* in advance. So if your child is having trouble remembering to put his bike away in the garage, you could brainstorm a consequence, such as losing the privilege of riding the bike for a week. It would be unrelated for the child to lose screen time. It would be unreasonable to lose the bike for three months. It would be disrespectful to yell at the child that they were irresponsible and call them names. And of course, you wouldn't want to announce that they were losing the bike for a week if you hadn't agreed on that consequence ahead of time. (See Jane Nelsen's *Positive Discipline* for more examples of the Rs.)

Don't worry about always needing a consequence for every problem behavior. You can brainstorm after the fact, because most likely the situation will occur again. Waiting for your chance doesn't mean you condone the behavior—you can tackle it at the next possible opportunity.

This chapter addresses limits in several of the most common areas of stress for parents: healthy eating, self-care, the morning routine, homework, chores, screen time, sibling fights, and taking responsibility for belongings, including lunch for school.

~~~

Four-year-old Alejandro and his seven-year-old sister, Mariana, tumbled through the front door of their family's Washington, DC, rowhouse, hair and clothes rumpled after the drive home from school. Alejandro wore belted baggy pants that pooled around his ankles, while Mariana sported leggings and a red T-shirt from her school, short-sleeved despite the December day.

Mariana made it as far as the stairway, which cuts through the front of the house, leading steeply upward. She crumpled into a lumpy ball of child, coughing and resting soft short curls on a rounded forearm. Her father, Colin, headed to the bathroom for a thermometer, which quickly confirmed what the parents suspected: Mariana had a fever.

"That's what I thought. All right. So much for my holiday party tomorrow," Camila said in a matter-of-fact tone.

"What party?" Colin asked.

"My work holiday party, during the day."

"I can probably swing by," he offered.

Alejandro was banging on a nearby cabinet, his face drawn into a knot of disgust at his father's offer of fruit for a snack. The door hung oddly; hinges askew, it didn't quite shut. Camila asked her husband to explore whether fiddling with a Phillips head screwdriver would fix it. As Colin moved in to look, Alejandro shifted back, scowl deepening.

"Would you like raspberries or blueberries?" Camila asked Alejandro, in Spanish.

He was having none of that. Why not gummy snacks?

"Because you didn't brush your teeth," Camila explained. Under the family agreement, when the children refused to brush their teeth at night, they couldn't eat sweets the following day.

"You know, the rocket ships and crackers," Alejandro asked, in English, acting as if Camila simply didn't understand his request.

"You can brush your teeth tonight and have sweets tomorrow. Today you must have fruit."

Alejandro responded by swatting at Camila's hips and legs with his arms.

"Why?" he wailed in Spanish. "No either!"

"Why don't you eat raspberries?" Camila suggested, setting off another round of wails and "No!" protests from Alejandro.

From her crumpled pose on the staircase, Mariana requested gummy penguins for her "sweet of the day." Each child could pick one sweet treat daily, as long as they were current on tooth brushing. Camila said yes, in Spanish.

Even worse than missing sweets is your sister getting sweets while you're banned.

"No, no," Alejandro cried piteously, at a higher pitch. He followed Camila as she walked into the kitchen. "I want a snack!"

Camila was having trouble finding Mariana's requested snack. "Did you pull out the gummy bear, penguin thingys?" she asked Colin. "They were in the car with the rest of the groceries, I believe."

Colin hadn't seen them.

Alejandro kicked the wall, surprising even himself, but then doubled down on the tantrum by throwing a pen. "I want something else for snack," he insisted, banging books, backpacks, pretty much anything at hand.

"We'll get you something," Colin said.

"I want something else for snack," Alejandro repeated, voice rising to a shriek of frustration. "This is not working out!"

The parents didn't try to stop the tantrum. That would've just escalated the situation, what Hoefle would call feeding the weeds. They continued with their after-school routine.

Colin spoke to Mariana in a calm voice. "Do you want to be on the steps or upstairs in bed? Is there a place you'd like to be?"

"I don't like this idea. This is not working out," Alejandro shouted. "Mama, I don't like this idea. I don't like it!"

Camila brushed by him as she strode out the door. "I'm going to check and see if I can find the gummies."

"I don't want it!" Alejandro continued in a piteous whine, then broke into full-fledged tears, crying. "Mama, Mama, Mama."

Camila returned from the car empty-handed. She later told me she'd gone outside not to search for the gummy snacks but to give herself space to calm down.

"Mama, Mama, Mama!" Alejandro said. "I don't want it!"

"Alejandro, Alejandro, calm down," Camila said in Spanish. "What don't you want?"

But Alejandro was beyond reasoning. He continued to wail "Mama, Mama" as he drifted around from entryway to kitchen and back again, finally retreating upstairs to his bedroom. Mariana was still coughing on the steps.

The parents discussed what to do for Mariana's fever, seemingly unfazed by the mutinous child wailing upstairs. Mariana relocated to the couch in the living room to rest. After barely a minute, Alejandro came back downstairs, calling for his mother. She plopped down on the steps beside him, rubbing his back and talking softly.

"What would you like for snack?" she asked. "Just blueberries, or raspberries too? Would you like cheese?"

Alejandro played with one of Camila's hoop earrings, deciding on raspberries.

"Only raspberries or something else?" she said.

"Something else."

"What do you want?"

"I want blueberries and then two raspberries," Alejandro said, completely calm now. "Like my sweet."

"He wants blueberries," she told Colin.

"Okay."

The afternoon continued smoothly as Alejandro went to wash his hands before preparing the snack with his mom. His parents had calmly enforced the limit, while tending to their other child and finding ways to regulate themselves when they got upset. That gave Alejandro space to calm down and accept the household rules about sweets. If they'd ramped up the discipline—when he swatted at Camila, for instance—it could easily have sparked a power struggle that wouldn't resolve for hours.

~~~

Everyone has bad parenting habits. Two of mine were shaming my kids in public and rescuing them from their mistakes. Both arose from my own idea of myself as a competent, nurturing mother. If my kids were rude in public, I'd correct them visibly so that everyone around us would see that I was a good mom. If they forgot a school lunch or left homework on the counter, I'd deliver it to them with a heart full of love before they noticed it was missing. I didn't see that I was preventing them from experiencing the discomfort that is so necessary for growth. An empty belly or self-conscious feeling would help motivate them to make a plan for remembering their belongings next time.

In retrospect, it seems crazy that I so often let short-term thinking and consequences override my long-term goal to help my children develop into responsible adults. But it's possible to abandon these bad habits, just as we expect our children to let go of theirs. Let your actions flow from the intention to support and guide your children in learning from the consequences of their actions. Don't worry about how they'll be perceived or how your parenting will be judged. Ignore that little voice in your head that catastrophizes based on today's behavior—have confidence that your kids will learn.

This discipline can feel invisible, because you're not directing or correcting children in public. They may show up for school with unkempt hair and missing a snack. The teacher and other parents don't see you at home chatting with the kids about how the day went and strategizing a better way to remember their snack. This private correction keeps the focus on learning without humiliating children in front of adults or their peers.

It simply takes time for experience to teach children the lessons they need to get along in life. From the outside, kids who are growing into their independence may not look as together as the children whose parents do everything for them or prod them into completing every step on a checklist. But over time, as your kids wrestle with the normal challenges of life—not with you and your stupid rules—they will increasingly take responsibility for their belongings, schedules, and actions. And your relationship with them won't experience the damage that nagging, blaming, or punishing can inflict.

Consequences may not look the way you imagine. You may not believe that your kids could really be learning if they endure consequences without crying or being visibly upset. The positive parenting guru Jane Nelsen—author of the *Positive Discipline* book and class series—addresses that objection: "Where did we ever get the crazy idea that in order to make children do better, first we have to make them feel worse?"

Kids may learn a different lesson than you imagine they will. They may find a short cut. Their choices may have side benefits you never imagined. When I stopped rescuing my children by delivering their forgotten lunches, they became expert at negotiating with their friends and classmates for portions of their lunches. I noticed that as my kids were packing their own lunches they often included more tuna packs, cookies, or chips than they could possibly eat themselves. It turned out that they were banking goodwill by sharing their treats with their lunchmates—in preparation for that day when they'd forget their lunch.

I had to accept this as a reasonable outcome. And in fact, which is more realistic for long-term success in life: trying to be perfect in anticipating every need you will have, or developing the interpersonal skills and relationships that will help you deal with the unexpected over the long term?

I saw this idea in action at a fair that our synagogue held to raise money for the preschool, when my kids were perhaps six and eight years old. Teenagers ran little carnival games, and there was a huge moon bounce and slide. I purchased $10 worth of tickets and gave half to each child. I watched as they blew through their tickets making little necklaces and jars of multicolored sand. Then they proceeded to the moon bounce, which cost three tickets. I knew that each of them had only one ticket left.

Aha! They would finally learn the lesson that they should've carefully planned their activities and used their math skills to figure out how many tickets would be needed for each one. I watched as they approached the volunteer ticket taker. But to my surprise, after a few words, they handed over one ticket each and bounded up the steps to the moon bounce.

When they finally piled out and retrieved their shoes, they walked over to me, their hair sweaty around their foreheads and their cheeks glowing.

"How did you get on the moon bounce?" I asked. "I thought you didn't have enough tickets."

"Oh, I asked the person, 'Would you be willing to take one ticket?'" Maddie told me nonchalantly. She took her coat from my hands and shrugged into it as we headed outside. I followed, stunned.

Your kids are more capable than you may imagine. They'll discover their own path in life, from small interactions to major choices. All they need is the freedom to experiment.

~~~

YOU'VE PROBABLY HEARD THE ADVICE to give choices to children, especially toddlers and preschoolers, when they start pushing back. Having choices gives your children some power in situations where they feel powerless. For example, at bedtime, ask your preschooler, "Would you like to brush teeth or read a book first?" When getting out the door in the morning, ask your toddler whether they'd like to hold Mommy's hand or carry the keys to the car. If they resist buckling into the car seat, ask if they'd like to be the "safety captain" who ensures that everyone is belted in before the car moves. Putting a child in charge of a task they've been resisting may be counterintuitive, but it's remarkable how often it works.

If giving them choices doesn't win your kids' cooperation, you may be only pretending to give them a choice—maybe you're actually giving them only options that get you what *you* want, not something they would choose. This hit home for me when I flew to Burlington to visit Hoefle's parenting class.

It was the second session of her six-week class. The parents seemed on board. They were listening closely to her explanation of how to encourage young children's independence. Give them information, she told them, not reminders. You want their brains working. Teach them one thing at a time, and let them practice.

"Allow them to be frustrated before you come in with your helpful comment like, 'How can we solve this?' Just pause in that frustration, so they learn they'll recover. Then offer one thing: 'What if you . . . ,'" she said. She moved around the room like a dancer, stretching and bending to give emphasis to her words.

"Slow the learning process down. We're always rushing. 'Come on. Get those shoes on,'" she said. "They should have time to sit down and put the shoe on and pull the tongue out and get the laces so. Just watch how quickly with young kids you go in to make it all neat and tidy. They'll keep you honest. They'll start doing things like this."

She put her hand off to the side, palm facing out, in the universal sign for "back off."

One mom asked for advice on handling her four-year-old son's reluctance to take baths or showers.

"So how do you get him in?" Hoefle asked.

"Oftentimes it's a bribe, for a TV show, or last week it was popcorn," the mom admitted. "I can't quite say, 'It's okay for you not to be clean for a week.' He just doesn't care."

"I don't care if he cares if he's clean. You care. The goal is to get him to take it, not to care," Hoefle said. "Your job is to mimic what will happen in the outside world so kids can make informed decisions.

"You can say things like, 'Listen, I can't force you to take a bath or shower. I have my reasons for why it's a good idea, but I'm not going to fight with you every night. Here's the thing: that's your choice. I have a choice too. To tell you the truth, you're a little ripe at the end of the day. I'm happy to read with you, if you sit there and I sit here.'"

She mimed sitting across the room from a child.

Most parents looked skeptical. One dad nodded.

"There are no such things as good or bad choices. There are things that move you towards what you want and away from what you want," Hoefle said. "In that moment the kid has to decide: *What do I want more, to be in a power struggle about the bath and the shower, or read on the lap of my mother? Huh. I want to snuggle next to my mom. So I have to give up this game.*"

She explained that a boy who takes a bath after being bribed has simply learned that he can get a treat if he stalls. He clearly doesn't have a fear of water. She warned the parents that they had to be patient and prepared for the child to choose what they didn't want for three, four, or five days in a row. The child might need to make the choice they didn't want several times before deciding that it wasn't working for him.

"This is going to happen a million times. You're going to have to allow your children to choose, and let them know you also have choice. So they don't feel pushed into doing what you want. It's really hard, but it works fast with kids," she said.

Say the issue is tooth brushing. You teach your child how to brush. You make sure they have the toothpaste they like and a toothbrush they picked out themselves. Now it's on them. Your only role is to decide whether to snuggle with them or, if they haven't brushed, read across the room from a distance.

One dad asked for clarification. "What you're describing, the result of your decision may not play out until later because you read later," he said.

That's right, Hoefle said. If you think through a plan and confirm that it's related to the issue, respectful, reasonable in scope, and revealed to the child in advance, just carry through in a matter-of-fact way. Don't threaten or lay out the scenario for them when they're about to make the "wrong" choice. Let it unfold.

"When do you spring that?" Lisa Rowley asked.

"I don't spring. The world doesn't spring. She's already told him nine thousand times. Really, everybody's supposed to take a bath," Hoefle said.

"Okay, I understand," Rowley said. "So she says, 'You don't need to,' but three hours later. . . . "

This was not what Hoefle wanted the class to do. Bending down to talk to the dad who commented earlier, she adopted a syrupy sweet tone of voice and pretended he was the kid.

"That's fine if you don't want to take a bath, but I'm not going to sit next to you later," she said. "It's like an invitation to a power struggle. The kid's like, 'Really?'" Her eyes grew wide.

"Now when you say, 'No, I told you I wasn't going to,' he says, 'Really, I'm going to crawl on top of you!'"

She mimed crawling on top of the dad. The class burst into laughter.

"Now she's going to come back to class and say it doesn't work!" Hoefle said.

Instead, the mom should be low-key, Hoefle explained, suggesting that she say, "'Love to. Gotta say, you're a little ripe.' Suddenly his brain goes, 'Oh yeah, it's bath night. I chose not to take a bath. This is the result of my choice. I'm still being read to, I'm just not being read to in the way I would like.' Now we have cooperation."

Again, the key is to alert your child to the consequence ahead of time, not in the heat of the moment. When bedtime rolls around, they may not remember that you're planning to read across the room from them, but after a couple of times experiencing this outcome, they will learn.

~~~

Nine-year-old Mariana Cullen swept the dirt from the wide front porch of her family's home. She spotted me and froze, blue plastic broom pressed against the dustpan. I gazed up at her, across a ten-foot-high flight of steps that climbed steeply from the sidewalk to the front door. Behind me, a Sunday morning soccer game began in the field across the street.

"Well, hello," I said to her. "Good morning."

Her mother, Camila, held a doormat she had brought outside to shake out. Mariana resumed sweeping.

"We had people over and the kids went under the porch, so we're just trying to sweep up a little bit of dirt," explained Camila. Her hair was pulled back from her face in a cloth hairband. I looked across the wide wooden slats of the front porch, imagining the hideout created underneath. Perfect for a gang of kids.

"So you went under the porch and then brought the dirt back up?" I asked Mariana. She nodded.

"It's filthy, but they love it," Camila said. "This whole area here. They take chairs and stuff down there. It's super, super dirty. It gets tracked in."

"We made mud balls yesterday," said Mariana, a beanpole with a lighter shade of her mom's short, curly locks. "It was so fun!"

"Oh. You made mud balls! I understand even better why it was so dirty," I said.

In the house, I accepted a coffee from Colin, who invited me to wait in the living room while they finished cleaning. As I walked back from the kitchen to the front hall, I caught a glimpse of six-year-old Alejandro, hanging on the interior staircase. As soon as he saw me, he bolted upstairs. Mariana wandered back into the house with a blue plastic water bottle swinging from her hand.

Camila came back in too, done with the porch. She explained that the unexpected cleaning had frustrated Alejandro because he usually did his chores quickly on weekend mornings and then got to use his iPad. He had declared that as soon as I arrived, he was going to hide.

True to his word, Alejandro couldn't be found in the bedroom, Camila's home office, the parents' bedroom, or even the attic playroom, where two lightweight pop-up castles dominated either corner, one pink and the other decorated with circus stripes. Camila seemed to know his hiding places and shook the thick curtains in every room, in search of his little body.

Finally, she discovered him in the living room, behind the couch, where Mariana sat. He slipped by and ran upstairs. Camila followed him. Soon, he was trailing her downstairs into the bathroom, where they wet a washcloth for him to use to scrub dirt from the doorknobs and handles. Later, she explained that he had offered to do only one, but in the end he cleaned both.

The cleaning done, the family next held a meeting in the living room, with visiting grandmother Rita. They each expressed gratitude for every other family member's actions and quickly reviewed the week's schedule. I stayed to chat with Camila and Colin while the kids and their grandmother went into the kitchen. After about twenty minutes, Camila checked on them and returned to report that Mariana had just made breakfast for herself and her brother.

I scurried into the kitchen to see Alejandro plopped onto a kitchen chair, scooping up fried eggs and toast with his fork. Mariana stood on her tippy toes to put a mug into the microwave.

"I heard you made breakfast," I said. "That looks good. Are those fried eggs?"

"Yes," she said. She started the microwave. "I like my milk with plain old 100 percent dark chocolate. It's from Nicaragua. My grandmother brought it."

She brought the warmed milk back to the kitchen table, where Alejandro already had a mug of chocolate milk. Both children idly stirred their mugs while they ate. Alejandro had a spoon in his mug, and Mariana stirred hers with a tiny metal whisk. We chatted about Girl Scouts and camping. After Alejandro wandered out of the room, Mariana walked to his side of the table.

"I'm going to mix up my little brother's now," she said. She stirred his chocolate milk with her whisk, then took a long sip. "This is good. Not bad."

She stirred a bit more and then announced: "Alejandro, your chocolate milk is ready!"

"Really?" he ran back in the room with a grin across his face.

~~~

HOMEWORK. I REALLY WISH IT had never been invented. Reams of evidence suggest that homework is useless for children younger than middle school. From the research on play, we know they're better off roaming the outdoors with siblings and friends, or exploring books, music, and art independently. So my first piece of advice is: don't worry too much about homework.

To be sure, most parents must deal with the fact that teachers expect children to complete homework. It helps kids to have a strong parent-school connection, so you don't want to undermine the teachers' authority.

Agree with your kids about some limits and routines for homework. When and where will it happen? How long should it take? What must be delayed until after homework is completed? (Hint: screen time.) Be open to trying out different routines to see what works best for your child. Some do better sitting straight down to homework after school. Others need some time to run around, since they've been sitting and focusing all day long.

Once you have your agreement, stick to it. Resist any commentary. Perhaps you agree that homework should take thirty minutes. (One good rule of thumb is ten minutes per grade of school.) Set a timer. The child can leave the homework table after it dings. This can help with dawdling. I know from my own experience as an adult that a task expands to fill the time allotted. Your children will soon learn that to finish everything, they need to be efficient and focused.

Advocate for your child at school. My family was lucky to have an elementary school principal who read the homework research and believed in the value of free play and connecting as a family after school. She encouraged her teachers to assign minimal homework.

In fourth grade, Ava ran into a roadblock with spelling words. Each week she received a list of twenty words and had to complete five different assignments as a way to memorize the words for the Friday quiz. She could write the words in different colors or make a crossword puzzle. She hated sitting down to do the writing, especially when the weather was beautiful. Some weeks she did only one of the assignments, despite all our insistence. The thing was: she got perfect scores on the quiz. Consistently.

Clearly, the additional assignments weren't needed for her to learn the words. She was resisting the burden of busy work with good reason. We sat down with her English teacher and came to an agreement that she'd study the words for ten minutes a day and turn in whatever writing she produced. Problem solved.

If your child seems to have too much homework, raise the issue with the teacher. Share the facts of what you've observed. For instance: "My child sits down at 5:00 p.m. to do homework and works straight until 6:00 p.m. Then they simply can't concentrate any further."

Ask for the teacher's help in solving the problem. Most educators will respond well to sincere outreach. Propose a trial of reduced homework for a few weeks. Teachers who see the quality of a child's schoolwork increase after such a trial period may be open to reduced quantity.

The main principle here is: homework is your child's responsibility. You shouldn't be correcting it, or hovering. It's a way for the teachers to assess where your child is in learning the curriculum. It's not a test of your own second-grade math skills. (Of course, you can be a resource if your child asks for some minimal guidance, or a check that he's on the right track.) That holds for the amount of homework assigned. If your child consistently can't finish the homework in a reasonable period of time, let the teachers know. Don't be a collaborator in the overwork culture rampant in our society.

This may seem like a radical position. But if you take charge of your child's homework in first grade, or third grade, or sixth grade, or tenth grade, when does it end? When does your child take over responsibility? The stakes may seem high, but they are lower when your children are still very young than at any time in the future. If you're in charge of homework through high school graduation, how will your child fare in college?

Hand over the reins now. Support your child in planning homework and setting up systems to keep track, and then let go. The sooner you make that transition, the better.

A friend of mine recently asked for advice because her kids felt so negative about homework. They did the minimal amount required, in a scrawl, and didn't seem to care that the teacher was disappointed or that their grades would suffer. "How do I fix their attitude?" she asked. I suggested that she use the tools in Chapters 6, 7, and 8 for connection and building capability: sharing the family values with respect to education, commenting on the kids' progress, and noting their interest in "nonschool" learning.

That being said, it's actually developmentally appropriate when children don't care about homework. Much homework *is* boring and useless. Many teachers don't really care either. Don't undermine your kids' accurate assessment by insisting that they should feel differently. They don't have to love it in order to accept the responsibility.

I came to this realization when Maddie was in third grade. As you know, I was a good girl, a typical A student who relished filling out worksheets with beautiful, round letters and neat columns of numbers. I took joy in dotting *i*'s and crossing *t*'s.

My children are just not wired this way.

Maddie's third-grade teacher convinced us that she was unmotivated and lazy, that she put in the minimal effort and achieved merely average academic results when her standardized test scores suggested that she was capable of much more. For months we emailed back and forth, puzzled over why Maddie was consistently falling short. She got in trouble for chatting in class, for reading a novel under her desk when she was supposed to be doing worksheets, for passing notes, for playing tricks on her best friend. I couldn't square these reports with the eagerly helpful and competent child we saw at home. So finally, at the suggestion of my sister-in-law, who was an elementary school teacher, Brian and I asked to observe the class.

What we saw shocked me. Unlike the classroom I remembered from third grade, children didn't sit in their desks for longer than thirty minutes. Nor did the teacher instruct the whole class at once: they were broken up into groups of about six students. During a two-hour "integrated learning block," each group switched activities every twenty or thirty minutes: they'd go from sitting around the teacher's desk for a small group lesson to sitting on the carpet to work with a partner on a learning game, to sitting at their own desks for independent work.

Aside from the one block of time when Maddie's group was working directly with the teacher, she was expected to maintain focus on an activity that the teacher didn't assess or evaluate. Many of the worksheets weren't turned in, and even if they were graded, it was simply with a check. No wonder Maddie found school boring and useless! No wonder her willpower to behave eroded when she saw the opportunity to chat with a friend or pull off a practical joke.

This experience was the turning point in my understanding of modern-day education—and my own children. I probably would've been fine in that classroom, because of the intrinsic joy I found in filling out worksheets. But for Maddie and Ava, three-quarters of their learning time felt like a waste.

After much debate and observation of other schools and classrooms, we eventually moved both kids to a private school with smaller class sizes and limited busy work. I know it is a privilege to be able to afford alternative education, but even for the three years that my kids remained in the public schools after my classroom visit, my mind-set had shifted. No longer did I think there was something wrong with them that had to be fixed immediately. When their academic results were mediocre, I saw that as a reflection of a bad fit between their temperament and the classroom environment. We all could take some steps to make it work and improve their ability to stay on task, but some pressure points would remain. I accepted that, and I stopped sending my kids the message—spoken or not—that there was something wrong with them.

Now that Maddie is in seventh grade, she finally cares about homework and how she does in school. Most days she arrives home already having finished some of her assignments during free periods, and after playing with the dog and roughhousing with her sister, she generally settles down to work.

Occasionally she moans or resists the after-school routine, but generally the trend is in the right direction. And when she struggles, the reason often turns out to be a learning problem—some math concept she didn't understand, or a project that was overwhelmingly big and required some support in breaking it down into steps. Our children will get there when they're ready, with our support, and we must be patient. Pushing them doesn't help—it merely cements their self-image as a bad or reluctant student.

In my experience, parents complain about homework battles with kids, but not quite as much as they do about screen time and sibling fights. I'll tackle those two topics next.

～～～

Alejandro sat glued to the screen of his iPad, manipulating the controls on a video game based on the animated film *Cars*. The beep of a timer sounded across the open-plan kitchen.

"Okay, my love, that was fifteen minutes," his mother, Camila, said, in Spanish, reminding him of their agreed-upon after-school screen time limit.

"No, no, it wasn't," responded Alejandro, a slight figure in baggy pants and an oversized yellow shirt from the Washington, DC, public school he attends. "I want to . . . "

"You want to. Do you want to help me? I'm going to start cleaning the veggies and making dinner."

"Yeah!" he replied, making no move to put away the iPad.

"Okay, Alejandro, I'm putting that away now," Camila said. She walked over to the table and reached a hand toward the device.

"No! I've almost finished this round."

"You have one minute, and then we need to put it away over there."

"What's that? Oh, now I know what happened. Everybody won. Mater is making a happy face," Alejandro said. "When I win, he's happy."

"Okay, enough," she said.

On a giant piece of slate that covered the kitchen wall, the family wrote shopping lists, problems to discuss, and ideas for family fun in chalk. Nearby, a laminated card for each child displayed crayoned images of every step in the morning routine (eat breakfast, brush teeth, backpack, shoes) and the after-school routine (homework, jobs, and free time). Before he sat down with his iPad, Alejandro had created his plan for the afternoon: doing his homework, cleaning the kitchen table of crumbs, and then, and only then, fifteen minutes of iPad time.

"Okay. Do you want to help me with dinner?" Camila asked.

"Yes."

"Let's go then. Let's see . . . " she turned to the kitchen. She looked at the food she'd set out on the counter earlier.

Finally, Alejandro turned off the iPad, his mind on food. "Hot dogs?" he asked in English, standing up to put away the device. He trotted to the sink to see what his mom was doing. Camila's calm insistence on the rules had paid off. She had resisted getting into a power struggle, while not backing down from the limit.

"No, no es hot dogs," Camila responded with a smile, in Spanish. "Do you want to use the knife and help chop? Sound good?"

"But I don't want to wash my hands," he said in Spanish.

"Did you wash them before when we were making snack?"

"Yes."

"You washed them? That's fine. They're clean."

Alejandro brought a bowl to the kitchen counter and pulled over a stool. Together, the pair began washing tomatoes for the evening's salad. Brussels sprouts, zucchini, and squash waited their turn.

～～

I'M GOING TO TELL YOU the best, guaranteed cure for sibling conflicts: have an only child.

If you've already given your child a sibling, it's too late. They will need to work out their own relationship. That's necessarily going to include verbal sparring and probably some physical tussles as well. This isn't a bad thing. Just as bear cubs and puppy dogs learn about limits and socialization through rough play, young children need this trial and error to figure out human relationships.

As you implement connection tools like special time, verbal encouragement, and regular appreciations, you will build a culture of warmth and bonding in your family. When you resist labeling your children, they'll feel less need to square off in opposite corners against one another. Gradually, sibling fights will lessen.

That said, you certainly can take additional steps to channel their energies in productive directions.

Most important, stay out of it as much as possible. Don't take sides. Don't get drawn into refereeing sibling disputes. As long as all your kids are older than toddlers and can defend themselves, you're needed only if there's blood or a broken bone. So often, they're fighting to get your attention. And if not, they may just be wrangling for fun.

I realized this one time when my children entered the kitchen, where I was cooking dinner, lunging at each other with light sabers and karate kicks. My temper rose. I really didn't need this on a busy weeknight. But just as I started to say something, one of them giggled. Realizing that their sparring was entertainment, I shooed them into another room and continued my dinner prep.

Focus on what you can do, like leaving the room or even popping in ear buds to listen to some calming music. If you do feel you need to intervene, put the children in the same boat—don't take one child's side. Trying to judge the situation will just encourage more rivalry.

Say things to your kids that give them information and may help them problem-solve, like: "I see two kids and one toy. That's a tough problem." If they continue fighting over the toy, you could always put it away, with a comment: "I see the toy is causing a problem, so I'll put it away for now. When you two have an agreement on playing with it together, I'll be happy to bring it back out again."

PEP founder Linda Jessup had a rule that any sibling fighting had to happen outside, no matter the weather. Children had a choice whether to fight outside or resolve disputes peacefully indoors. For a while, we followed this policy and nudged the children onto the lawn to work out their problems.

And of course, whenever you see them playing together cooperatively or appreciating each other, anchor that trait. Don't just smile to yourself and sneak out of the room to avoid disrupting the magic. Encourage the behavior and name it. That's how you will start to shift their own view of their relationship.

~~~

MY WHITE HAVANESE DARTED FORWARD, intent on a robin I hadn't even spotted at the side of our lawn. The bird took off toward a tree branch. I ran along with the dog, urging him across the grass. As my socks began to feel damp, I realized that the lawn was still soaked from a shower earlier.

"Let's go inside," I said. "I'll get you some food."

Buddy Bear scampered up the front steps. I stepped inside the house and looked at my watch. 7:43 a.m. The house was silent. I hung up the dog's leash and walked into the kitchen-den area of the house.

"Hi, Mom," said Ava, my ten-year-old. I was surprised to see her out of bed, where she'd been when I left to walk the dog. Ava's usually slow to rise. But she was already wearing shorts and a sweatshirt, not a bathrobe. Her long hair swung free of its typical ponytail.

My thirteen-year-old, Maddie, formed a lump in a chair by the window of the den. She smiled at something on her phone.

"There's no screens in the morning," I chided. I walked over to the trash can and tossed out the poop bag. I steeled myself.

"I guess we aren't going for bagels," I said, trying to keep my voice even. Before I left to walk the dog, I'd kissed each child awake with a reminder that in order to stop by our favorite bagel store, they'd need to be ready by 7:40 a.m., when I returned.

"I'm almost ready," Maddie yelped. She turned off her iPhone and stood up, stretching.

"I wish we could," I responded, keeping my voice level. I poured some leftover coffee into a mug and popped it into the microwave. Ava scooted around me to retrieve her croissant from the toaster oven.

"What the fuck!" Maddie shouted. I looked over and saw her face turning red, beneath hair still tousled from sleep. She clenched her fists. "Fucking Ava! Fucking . . . "

"We're definitely not going if there's cursing or violence," I said, invoking a basic agreement of our house. "I'm sorry you're disappointed, honey. Why don't you grab a croissant for the car?" *Firm and kind,* I thought to myself, *just keep moving through the morning routine.*

"A croissant isn't going to fill me up! I need a bagel. I'm going to sit in the stupid rehearsal for the musical all morning. I don't even have anything to do."

"I thought you were playing the bass."

"I only play on four songs and there's thirty-six other ones," she yelled, still standing in the middle of the den, legs planted and fists balled. "I can't even play the four songs. It's so boring. I'm not going to school. I'm just going to stay right here."

Don't pick up the rope, I told myself. *You'll just deepen her dysregulation if you argue.* I murmured something sympathetic and headed back to the front hall. Ava trotted after me, tucking her school iPad into her backpack. "Can you carry my sleeping bag to the car?" she asked. After school, she would be heading to a friend's sleepover birthday party.

"Why don't you make two trips to the car?" I suggested.

Maddie stormed past us in a cloud of curse words. She stomped up the stairs and opened her bedroom door with a fury. "It's all Ava's fault," she yelled.

"Please don't slam that door," I said, going back to the kitchen to retrieve my coffee from the microwave. I added stevia and milk and washed an apple for breakfast.

Slam. Slam. Crash. Thud.

Maddie thumped back downstairs and into the den. She snatched her phone from the chair. "Fucking phone! It's all your fault!" She stormed to the back of the house, where the kids' Legos littered our sunroom floor. "I'm throwing you away."

I tried to ignore the crashing and banging. I poured food into the dog's bowl. Ava quickly finished her croissant.

Maddie slumped back. Tears streamed down her face. She threw herself onto the couch, sobbing. "I'm so tired. I didn't get any sleep last night because Daddy was coughing."

"Oh, that's awful," I said.

I paused.

Should I give her a hug? Will she just push me away? At thirteen, her body had suddenly developed a new kind of density. She was as lean as ever, but somehow more solid. No longer a little kid.

"And now I've ruined everyone's morning!" she wailed.

I took six paces to the couch and perched beside her. I wrapped an arm around her shoulder and kissed her wet cheek. She turned her face to snuggle into my neck. I gave her a full hug. "You haven't ruined anyone's morning," I said. "It's only 7:57 a.m. There's hours left in my morning."

More sobs. I squeezed one last time and rose. "I know you're upset. I hope you decide to join us."

As I crossed the room, she croaked, "I'm coming. Please don't leave without me."

It was April. Since October we'd been working on the morning routine. It was the first year we drove both kids to middle school. I longed for the easy fallback that if they dawdled and missed the ride to school, they could walk themselves to the local elementary school. We finally settled on the agreement that the car would leave for school at 8:00 a.m., regardless of who was inside. Several times during this year, Ava had missed her ride and waited impatiently at home for a few hours until one of the adults—me or my parents—could drive her to school. Maddie had never missed the ride.

In the front hall, Ava slipped on her backpack. "I'll take your sleeping bag," I said.

By the time I came back inside for my coffee and gym bag, Maddie was buttering a croissant at the counter. I stood beside her.

"I'm sorry, Mom."

I put an arm around her shoulder and squeezed. "I accept your apology," I said. "I'm sorry that I wasn't back from the walk earlier."

I picked up my belongings and walked to the car. Later in the day, we would discuss the cursing, and Maddie would tidy up the table and stools she knocked over. She'd lose fifteen minutes of screen time, our agreed-upon consequence for using the phone before responsibilities.

We were back on track.

Part 3

Making It Stick

10

Modeling

IT'S NO SECRET THAT WE pass along our hang-ups to our kids. Even before I read the research about how children learn anxiety from their parents, I knew that some of my fears and foibles could be traced to my own mom and dad. That's okay. We all have our quirks and weak spots; it's what makes us human. The key is to understand yourself and your specific challenges and learn to manage them. To make the most of this book—to harness the lessons of neuroscience and behavioral science and follow in the successful path of Vicki Hoefle, Ross Greene, and the parents using PEP and PAX techniques—you must first deal with yourself.

My Achilles' heel was the quest for perfection, for the right answer. For most of my life, the answers to my burning questions were found within the pages of a book.

When I was pregnant, in 2003, I read *What to Expect When You're Expecting, The Girlfriend's Guide to Pregnancy,* and *The Mayo Clinic Guide to a Healthy Pregnancy.* I watched what I ate, took prenatal yoga, and even went to a prenatal swim class once a week. After the baby arrived, I went to a new moms support group and listened intently to everyone's stories, sifting through their trial and error for what would work with my child.

I was going to be perfect at this parenting thing.

As you probably know, it's not that simple. Our children surprise us from the moment they arrive as mewling bundles of joy— and sometimes before. If we're outgoing and gregarious, they may be cautious. If we're introverted and mellow, they may have the energy and propensity for chaos of a Tasmanian devil.

I had to let go of my goal of being perfect, doing parenting the right way, and planning for every contingency. I had to stop thinking that I would find some ultimate recipe for creating the perfect child and lock it in for life. Instead, I had to learn patience during the bumpy process of raising human beings.

Now my goal is working with my children to support them in defining and achieving their goals, as well as providing boundaries that articulate our family values and keep them safe. Rather than finding any one solution in the pages of a single book, I've gleaned many different ideas from different sources of information and tested them out in real life. I wake up every morning feeling optimistic that my kids and I will work together more cooperatively than we did the previous day, and when I encounter unexpected hurdles, I take a deep breath and tackle them. Every evening I go to sleep with the certain knowledge that I can try again tomorrow.

I agree with books like *The Gift of Failure* and *How to Raise an Adult*, which encourage parents to stop overparenting and just let their kids be. But I worry that parents will only read the headlines and take the message that that they should let their kids do whatever they want. Left to their own devices, many children would spend all day playing video games and eating junk food. My role as a parent is to help them discover their own passions within healthy limits, so they can leap into the world at age eighteen as capable, autonomous human beings who can control their impulses.

Our job is to help our kids understand their own internal roller coasters of emotions and stressors and to help them discover their unique tools to manage that ride. That's simply impossible unless we first get in touch with and learn to master our own turbulent internal landscape.

This hit me hard one day after school. My intense older child announced: "I've had a very stressful day. I can't handle this right now!" The chaos of snack and jostling with an energetic younger sister had pushed her over the edge.

But in her irritated voice, I heard an exact copy of my tone and the words that I would use with them. If they were too noisy, or I hadn't gotten enough sleep, I would feel on edge and jittery and dys-regulated. But rather than taking responsibility for bringing myself back under control, I would blame the circumstance or—worse—blame my own children. I had to learn to own whatever moods and feelings washed over me and to model self-regulation if my kids were going to learn to do the same. I realized that in deciding to become a parent, I had lost the luxury of reacting with immature outrage when my feelings or pride get hurt. From then on, I made an effort to say things like, "I'm feeling stressed. I need to take a five-minute walk to calm down."

Perfection and rigidity were holding me back as a parent. Every parent has different baggage. Maybe you're managing an anxiety or mood disorder. In their lifetime, about 29 percent of US adults experience an anxiety disorder, 25 percent deal with an impulse control disorder, 21 percent have a mood disorder, and 15 percent abuse substances, according to government data.

Those without a diagnosis have plenty of room for improvement too. Perhaps, like Camila Cullen, your children stir hot rage in your chest that is far out of proportion to whatever offense they committed. Or you experience any raised voice or complaint as a major problem. You may have grown up in a family where negative emotions weren't allowed, much less discussed.

If you haven't already, take some time to look at any dysfunctional ways of communicating or interpersonal habits of your own. Learn to govern them and develop strategies for minimizing their impact on your kids. The same holds for our goals regarding our kids' screen use. Before imposing limits on them, we must look at how we're modeling technology and begin making any changes needed in our own screen habits.

Every parent's approach will look different. Some take a few deep breaths and center themselves before responding to the situation in a constructive way. Others go for a hard run when they feel anger start to creep up their neck, or take the dog for a walk in the woods. Before shouting a warning, others are able to suppress that instinct long enough to gauge whether their child is doing something truly danger-ous or whether their fear is unfounded. Your children are observing you every second of the day—behave in the way you hope they will behave themselves when they're raising your grandchildren.

For many parents, a big part of this transformation is understanding how many of our impulses are driven by the worry about "what people will think." Notice and question your scripts for what a good parent does or how children should act. Letting go of these narratives may resolve some of the conflict in your home.

After nine chapters focusing on children's behavior, this chapter will give us a chance to talk about adult actions. I'll share the story of my own attempt to release the dream of perfection, as well as one mom's story of managing her own anxiety and depression so that her children don't inherit her struggles. Throughout the chapter you'll see how modeling impacts kids and the value of taking the time to understand yourself and learn new approaches to life.

~~~

A ROUGH-HEWN WOODEN SIGN LABELED THIS WAY marked the path to the Mountain Cloud Zen Center in the arid foothills of the Sangre de Cristo Mountains outside Santa Fe. Walking around the bend in the trail, I spotted the zendo, nestled between thick junipers and piñon pine trees that provided a shock of green against the rocky desert landscape. The adobe building boasted the vita beams typical of Southwestern architecture; they ended in a skinny triangle you might see crowning a Japanese temple.

I followed the blond heads of Sam and Francesca McMeekin. The two children ran up the steps into the zendo. Walking beside me, their mom, Shannon McMeekin, explained the Family Sangha, a community in which parents and children gather briefly and then part to separate mindfulness meditation sessions. A lean, blond woman with a warm smile, Shannon wore slate-blue leggings and a striped fleece over a pink T-shirt. We walked through the golden-brown doors of the zendo. We left our shoes in cubbies, then stepped into the central hall, lined with windows through which the brilliant spring sunshine flooded. At the far end of a room that seemed all golden wood and light, a small bronze statue of the Buddha faced us.

The ten adults and eight children began to settle down, climbing onto the knee-high wooden platform, called a tan, running around the walls. They sat cross-legged. Some knelt atop dark brown cushions. The room quieted. I claimed a seat.

By the entrance, the children jostled for spaces beside their friends. Seven-year-old Sam was juggling a stuffed aardvark and a jar filled with viscous liquid and sparkles. The jar slipped from his hands and the top flew off. Thud. A mixture of glycerine and soap began seeping onto the dark packed mud floor of the zendo.

"Mom, Sam's thing just exploded all over the floor!" called Frankie, age ten.

"What?" Shannon looked over from her meditation cushion, feeling a flush rise on her cheeks, her throat tighten, and her heart race. She took a breath through her nose and exhaled slowly through pursed lips, what she calls a straw breath, to calm her physiological response.

"Oh, Shannon, that's not okay for the floor," said Teri, an older woman with close-cropped gray hair.

"It just fell!" Sam wailed.

"I know, I know, I know, I know," Shannon responded, walking over to her son. "Get the cap and we're going to clean it up."

Sam grabbed the cap and handed it to Shannon. She retrieved a rag from the nearby bathroom and knelt. She scooped up the gloopy mixture. Sam had wanted to share the jar, a mindfulness tool he had made—the swirling glitter representing stresses in his mind—with his friends at the Sangha. Shannon took in another deep breath, reminding herself simply to acknowledge the feelings of anxiety and embarrassment that washed over her, to notice the self-critical inner monologue that said she should've glued the cap shut, and to calmly shift into problem-solving.

"We're going to share a song now," said the leader, moving on with the afternoon's program. Shannon rubbed at the glitter on the zendo floor. Her mentor, Kate Reynolds, seated in the middle of the room, began the song.

Since the 1960s, when enthusiasts brought the Eastern practice of meditation to the United States, a variety of schools have flourished: Vipassana or mindfulness, Zen, Shambhala, Dzogchen, Tibetan, mantra, Qi gong, Tai chi, Transcendental, and even yoga, which includes similar elements.

The common thread is a regular practice of sitting quietly and bringing the mind's attention to a single focus. The goal is to fully inhabit the present moment, without dwelling on the past or planning for the future. There are many possible focus points: your breathing, a word, a teacher's voice, the physical sensations in your body, a sound, or your steps in walking meditation. As your mind naturally wanders, you gently bring it back to the object of meditation. This practice helps develop mental discipline.

Through regular meditation, your mind develops flexibility and strength that can be applied to any daily challenge. Because of your regular practice, you can instantly return to that place of calm when you need to approach a crisis rationally.

I grew interested in mindfulness meditation fifteen years ago because of the evidence that it improves well-being and combats insomnia, anxiety, and depression. Not to mention the studies suggesting that the brains of people who regularly meditate over many years develop greater capacity to learn and process information.

I tried online audio and in-person meditation groups, but I kept falling asleep. Whenever I sat down to meditate, my mind would wander and before long my chin would drop to my chest. I'd snap up my head with a little snore, embarrassed at my lack of focus. Finally, I gave up.

Years later, when my children started struggling with big emotions, I took another pass at meditation. Books and blogs and other moms raved about how the practice helped their little ones manage anger and frustration. I jumped on board, trying out meditation CDs and little picture books. My children refused to cooperate. They declared that meditation was boring and useless.

I used the child meditation techniques on the nervous kids on the neighborhood summer swim team, as I lined them up for their events. I taught them to breathe in the scent from an imaginary flower and to release their breath as if they were blowing through a soapy wand to create bubbles. They loved it. But my own children resisted. How could I open their minds to this breakthrough solution?

My desperation led me to Santa Fe and Shannon McMeekin.

~~~

SHANNON FIRST FOUND MEDITATION WHEN life had ripped her open.

It was 2006. After a turbulent childhood shaped by her father's untreated bipolar disorder and the related boom and bust of family fortunes, she finally felt optimistic about the future. She and her husband,

Nicholas, were expecting their first child and building a healthy life together in Santa Fe, a laid-back city that values wellness. It was a welcome change from the East Coast intensity of Shannon's teens and twenties, when she'd wrestled with anxiety and depression. She'd run herself ragged working in film production in New York City and keeping up with club life. A friend suggested that she visit Santa Fe for a summer housesitting gig. She came, met Nicholas, and never left. Her parents even moved west to be near their future grandchild, buying a house up the road. Her dad was the healthiest that she'd ever seen him; working as a volunteer firefighter, he apparently was stable. She finally felt connected to her father, whose mental health issues kept them from being close during her childhood.

Then he died, following an unexpected stroke. She found herself sandwiched between her mother's grief, her own loss, and the struggle of caring for Frankie, a fussy baby, which led to attachment problems.

"When he died suddenly and shockingly, I couldn't believe our story just ends here. It just broke my heart. It was such a loss," she told me a few days after the Family Sangha. We were sitting on the sagging couch in her office at the Sky Center, the nonprofit where she's a family therapist helping schools and families with suicide prevention and other mental health challenges.

"It became really clear to me that the fact I didn't have any spiritual practices, it made it so hard for me to cope with his death. I didn't know what I believed. I didn't know where he went. I was so lost without any kind of [spiritual] community. I had nowhere to put my grief. It was the hardest, hardest time," she said. She glanced down at the tinfoil-wrapped cheese sandwich on her lap, blinking away tears.

A weekly prenatal yoga class had comforted her. "Yoga was a huge anchor for me to feel peaceful and be able to sit with my emotions. I think of it as mindful movement. Yoga enabled me to get in touch with my body and my breath," she said. After Frankie arrived, Shannon continued practicing yoga at home. She left her job as an art gallery director. Instead, she worked from home part-time on graphic design and event planning projects, while parenting Frankie and a baby boy, Sam, who arrived in 2009.

Shannon's favorite part of yoga was the final pose, shavasana, lying in stillness on her back. When Sam was about a year old, she signed up for Kate Reynolds's mindful parenting class. It clicked. For the first time, she felt connected to both her body and her mind. Mindfulness helped her manage her oppressive feelings and thoughts. Her lifelong struggle with anxiety and depression took a turn. She learned to notice the rush of emotions washing over her and to simply acknowledge them rather than try to fight them.

Mindfulness even led her to a new career. She earned a master's in social work, became a family therapist, and began leading mindfulness groups in schools through the Sky Center. And mindfulness got her through a thyroid cancer diagnosis in the fall of 2010, followed by a complete thyroidectomy. Not to mention a year of seesawing emotions until a second endocrinologist got her on the right dose of hormones.

"It's been such an amazing coping mechanism for me," Shannon said. That's not to say she's cured—while she's now cancer-free, maintaining good mental health will always be a focus of her life. "As much as I try to put the stamp of 'healed' on myself from my childhood, I can't separate my mindfulness practice, my choices, my new career, from the impact my dad and his mental illness had on my life."

But instead of seeing anxiety as a shameful or unwanted aspect of herself, Shannon reframes it as a superpower that helps her. Her hypervigilance helps her read situations early and size up people accurately. She's more aware and can make better decisions. She manages the negatives and tries to appreciate the positives. For her, mindful parenting means pausing the instinctual reaction she might have to a child's behavior or comment and then intentionally choosing her response, instead of reacting with anger or irritation or criticism. That pause might be as simple as one deep breath before responding, or as controlled as waiting until the next day to address something after everyone cools down.

Families pass along mental illness like an unwanted heirloom. It's rarely pure genetics; more often mental illness arises from a combination of biology and environment. Anxiety in particular is high; remember from Chapter 2 that almost one-third of children now receive an anxiety diagnosis. An anxiety disorder can appear in many forms: feeling on edge, being irritable, tiring easily, or having trouble sleeping or concentrating. The bottom line is excessive, uncontrollable worry that prevents normal functioning at work, in school, or in relationships.

Frankie grew from a colicky baby into a clingy toddler and then a volatile young child. The smallest incident would spark an epic tantrum, which seemed to scare Frankie as much as it alarmed her parents. "She would say things like: 'Help me, Mommy, I'm not okay. I need help,'" Shannon recalled. Shannon recognized such feelings from her own childhood. "Because I grew up in a state of constant crisis, my body got trained to be vigilant. I always had this sense that something was threatening."

Shannon responded by teaching Frankie mindfulness. Having learned to hold her anxiety close and accept it as part of herself, she encouraged Frankie to understand and discuss her own feelings. When Frankie was eight, they watched the animated movie *Inside Out,* which depicts a tween girl's personified emotions as she navigates her family's move to San Francisco and a new school. As much as the characters of Joy, Sadness, Anger, Fear, and Disgust resonated with Frankie, they didn't seem quite adequate. Many mother-daughter chats followed.

"Frankie said: 'I have more feelings like that in my body,'" Shannon recalled. "I said, 'Yes, in our family, we have more feelings. We have a history and we have to understand them.'"

Shannon experiences anxiety as heat. It spreads, physically, over a triangle connecting her sternum, belly button, and heart, topped by a column of tightness running up her throat. She encourages Frankie to recognize the bodily experience of a panic attack in order to understand it. They also both write in journals and find that naming, recording, and acknowledging anxiety helps tame it.

"When I was about nine," Shannon said, "riding on a bike down the road to my house, I have a vivid memory of the mailbox, the leaves on trees, and the sky. I realized I have a voice inside my head that's always talking to me. Then I noticed myself noticing that voice. I thought, *Who is this voice?* The journaling helped me to always have that voice and witness to my life."

Shannon models a calm response to feelings of anxiety for her kids. She's aware that she could easily have followed the same life path as her father, who abused drugs and alcohol and never was able to create a stable home for his children. "In college, I turned to marijuana as a coping mechanism, and it really worked," she said. "I'm worried about adolescence and what it will mean for Frankie. Will she take the first sip of beer and realize, 'This works, this dulls the anxiety.' I hope if we have this ongoing closeness, that won't happen."

~~~

IN AVA'S FIRST-GRADE YEAR, MY husband and I suggested that she check out the introductory meeting of the beginning orchestra at a nearby music school. She eagerly picked out the violin when the instructors let the children try a violin, a viola, and a cello. She loved going to her orchestra rehearsals, a jumble of musically inclined children that perfectly suited my little extrovert. To my delight, she also willingly went along to weekly, one-on-one violin lessons with a teacher in our neighborhood.

This was a welcome change from her older sister, who grudgingly took piano for a couple of years. Every practice became a battle. Every lesson brought gentle chiding from her teacher. We finally accepted defeat and let her quit. Perhaps the instrument didn't suit her temperament, I thought. Unlike band or orchestra, piano students don't have a regular social gathering as part of rehearsal or performance.

I took the lack of struggle before Ava's violin lessons as evidence that our newfound parenting strategies had given us the perfect recipe for instilling a love of learning. Our daughter was intrinsically motivated to learn a challenging skill! I came back down to earth the day she and I were walking hand in hand away from the lesson and she said, plaintively, "Why can't I just get the Jolly Rancher without having to go to the lesson?" I hadn't even noticed that she was collecting this weekly treat from her teacher.

When children who experience the Apprenticeship Model of parenting at home go out into the "real world," they very well may enjoy the Jolly Rancher they get after a violin lesson, or the class pizza party earned for weeks of good behavior. This isn't a problem. Those experiences can serve as the focus of a thoughtful discussion about why home is different than school, and the values we hope our children will internalize.

What if your kids are shamed, scolded, and punished in school or activities run by old-school adults—the kind of behavior that Chapter 3 taught us can provoke our kids' fight-or-flight response? The trusting relationships they have with their primary caregivers should inoculate them against lasting harm from these encounters. After all, many adults can point to teachers who served as negative mentors, giving an enduring example of how not to treat another human being. These experiences also help our kids develop resilience as they see that they can survive harsh treatment, and perhaps even learn something.

It's tempting to want to share new techniques that are working with your friends. Although you certainly can recommend this book, and I hope you do, it's always tricky giving unsolicited advice to teachers or other parents in hopes of modifying their behavior. One idea: use the same strategies you use with children. Connect with them, notice their strengths, and express empathy for the challenges they face. At that point, they might be more open to input, especially if you first ask permission to give advice. A gentle question can often be more thought-provoking than a sentence that begins: "You should . . ."

If any suggestion or model in this book doesn't resonate with you, leave it aside for now. If sticker charts or other incentive systems seem to be working, don't worry about it for the time being. Adapt the ideas in this book to your own style. The parenting language that I use is often mild and tentative. I might say, "I noticed you were . . . ," to describe an episode of misbehavior and encourage a problem-solving conversation, as Ross Greene does. Or instead of commanding a child, I'll use the phrase I learned in PEP, "Would you be willing to . . . ," as the preface to a request, whether to help load the dishwasher or pick up backpacks.

Parents who come to my workshops sometimes bristle at phrases like these and view them as weak. I encourage them to try out more collaborative and neutral language before rejecting it, but I also recognize that the Apprenticeship Model can and should look different based on your personality, your child's needs and skills, and your family's cultural background. The way kids in Baltimore and Columbus form bonds with parents and adults will differ from parent-child connections in Washington, DC, Santa Fe, Maine, and other communities described in this book.

I wouldn't expect African American or Latino families, or those in other parts of the country, to act the same as my Asian-Jewish-white household firmly entrenched in the mid-Atlantic. My family is demonstrative and silly, which may not feel right to you, depending on your personality and style. But while the language may differ, the fundamentals of mutual respect, open-minded listening, and a focus on problem-solving are vital to reaping the benefits.

We may need to reject some of our cultural and family background to embrace the Apprenticeship Model. I have a history of authoritarian parenting on both my father's Episcopalian side and my mother's Chinese side. Yet I believe I can keep the enriching parts of my heritage while shedding those traditions that will undermine mental health in the children being raised today.

Immigrant parents' success at teaching their children to value hard work and education can be compatible with respect and collaboration. Parenting is not a race to age eighteen, with an Ivy League acceptance letter being the prize and American parents trying to mimic our counterparts in China, France, Denmark, or whichever other country produced the highest test scores or happiness survey results this year. Media firestorms that erupt over the latest formula for academic, artistic, or athletic success represent another temptation to competitive parenting that we must resist as we let our children define success for themselves, not based on our wishes.

My hope is that as individual families and communities begin to move in the direction of this kind of parenting, a critical mass of Apprenticeship Model adherents develops who can shift how our society views discipline—and how we view success. It's not enough to protect the children in our own homes from anxiety, dependence, and other ills. We want them to go into the world to find spouses, friends, and coworkers who are also resilient, independent, and capable. That's only possible with widespread change.

Nobody should expect to be a "perfect" parent who never slips into doling out punishments or rewards in a weak moment. Rather than sink into self-criticism, think of your lapses as learning opportunities for everyone, and models for your children of how to recover from a mistake. Every day you have hundreds of interactions with your children. When one doesn't go the way you want, never fear. You will soon have a chance for a do-over.

~~~

BACK IN THE ZENDO, AFTER Shannon cleaned up Sam's mess, the children left the parents for separate meditation sessions. I followed the kids, eager to observe techniques I could bring home to my family.

We sat on the floor of the dining room in a rough circle. Two older Buddhists gave instructions to eight squirmy, farty, giggling children. The women's voices held that edge of controlled fury and exasperation that I knew well from my own life.

I felt nothing but sympathy.

We all introduced ourselves to the group. Sam drew out his first name in three syllables, to the delight of the other kids, who burst into giggles. Iggy and Hadley, classmates of Sam's in first grade, were especially vocal in appreciating his humor.

"I don't know if you could hear him because you were laughing," Teri, the leader, enunciated crisply, in an overly sweet tone. "Will you say it again please?"

"Sam."

After everyone finished their introductions, Teri attempted to make the squiggly oval of bodies into more of a circle.

"Now listen, Iggy, could you move back a little bit so we're more complete," she said, only to react in horror a second later when Sam scooted back also, disrupting the line of children's bodies. "Sam, no, no."

More giggles.

"Betty, I would like Iggy to come over here," she said to her partner.

"Can I be in the corner of the room where all the bad kids go?" Iggy asked.

"No, this is not a silly time. I want you over here please, not next to Sam," she said.

Teri managed to ring a meditation bell, and the children listened to the echo in relative silence, broken only by giggles and the muffled sound of siblings hitting each other. Iggy squirmed on his belly and scooted back to be fully under the table in the dining room.

Teri attempted to read a book called *Master of Mindfulness,* punctuating her reading with injunctions and threats. The children stayed silent for perhaps a half-minute at a time before farting and giggling.

"Betty, you need to take him away if he can't sit still," Teri said. "You need to calm down," she told Sam.

A bit later, the children began singing softly, interrupting the reading.

"Let's be a little bit more respectful. That's important," said Betty.

"Hadley, do you think you could be still for two minutes?" Teri asked in exasperation.

"Maybe," the little girl replied.

"Well, try!"

After about ten minutes, Teri took the five older children, including Frankie, into a small separate room—almost a large closet—and I went with them. We sat silently without much distraction and actually meditated. Teri read a few more books, and then the big and little kids were reunited for more mindfulness exercises, including a walking meditation. Although it didn't go off perfectly, the walking meditation won the most cooperation from the little kids that afternoon.

Whenever Sam and his first-grade friends were present, their mischievous energy disrupted the group. Mercifully, our time together ended, and the children were reunited with their parents in the meditation hall for announcements and a brief good-bye.

I lingered to chat with Kate Reynolds, a tall woman with a wide-open smile and shoulder-length brown hair that looked like it had been blond when she was a child. In a rich, deep voice, she told me about her dharma talk to the parents, which I missed while observing the kids.

"The culture we live in, that we're just steeped in now, is like a fast-moving river. There's just so much momentum in it. It's so easy to lose sight of what really matters for the sake of getting through the tremendous to-do list of every day," she said as we settled, cross-legged, in the now-empty room. "Mindfulness and meditation is an opportunity, in river language, to pull into an eddy and rest and reset. It's not hard. There's eddies available everywhere, unlike most rivers. Anywhere you want one, there's a space to pull out and connect with what really matters, what you really think, what you really want."

Like Shannon, Kate found meditation at a crisis point in her life. Her daughter was four, and her high-energy son was one. Parenting was harder than she had ever imagined. "I really did not think I was going to survive parenting. I was, like, just desperate," she said, recalling her frequent comment at the time: "I really love my kids, but I'm not particularly fond of parenting."

She was a family therapist trained in dialectical behavior therapy (DBT), an intensive treatment developed for people with suicidal thoughts and borderline personality disorder. One-quarter of the DBT curriculum centers on mindfulness, the teachings that attracted her the most. Driving by a Buddhist center one day, she spotted signs saying DHARMA FOR KIDS and MEDITATION FOR PARENTS and wheeled her car around to the parking lot. That's how she discovered a meditation teacher who led her into starting her own parenting meditation class. "My life sort of took off from there," she said.

Now a meditation teacher herself, she finds that regular immersion in mindfulness practice helps her to parent the way she wants. "It's absolutely necessary for me to teach to keep my shit together," she told me with a laugh. "If I am not anchored to it, it's so easy to become automatic and distracted and controlling, and then I'm my mother. I'm my mother's mother, and her mother, and that family of origin is coming out of me. Not that that was all bad, but it's not what I want."

Thinking of the kids' experience at the Family Sangha, I commented on how hard it is for young children to quiet their minds and meditate. "What have you found works, especially with the kids who maybe need it most?" I asked her.

"What they need the most, they need the grownups to know how to do it," Kate said. "It's so tempting to want to deliver something to kids that we are not willing to do ourselves. Most important is people in their lives that are aware of it and attempting it themselves, and then modeling it for kids."

~~~

EARLIER IN THE DAY OF the Family Sanga, we dropped off Frankie for lacrosse with some other tween girls. Nicholas, Shannon, Sam, and I took our bikes to a nearby trail that ran alongside the railroad tracks. After a short ride, we headed back to Nicholas's truck.

"Sammer, slow down," Shannon said as we neared a busy intersection. She put a firm hand on the shoulder of his bright yellow fleece. "Don't go too close." The four of us pulled up and stood with our bikes at the beginning of the crosswalk.

After an interminable wait, the light signaled that we could cross. Nicholas led the way, with Sam zooming eagerly behind. Shannon and I could see them approaching a side street that we'd all need to cross. The road contained no moving cars.

"Stop!" Shannon called, from half a block away. But Sam kept going, slowing with the slight uphill incline, until he reached the street. Nicholas was already across, standing astride his bike as he watched his son's progress.

"Okay, Sam, go!" Nicholas said. Sam pumped down on the pedal just as a black SUV rounded the corner and headed toward him.

"Stop, Sam!" Shannon shrieked, pushing her bike into motion to catch up with her son. Her whole body was tense and rigid, with no sign of straw breathing or mindfulness.

By now, Sam had biked halfway across the street, but he was moving slowly since he had no momentum.

"Come on, Sam," Nicholas encouraged him.

"Nicholas, mixed messages," Shannon called.

The SUV moved slowly, but surely, toward the little figure on a bike. Sam paused, unsure.

"Keep going," Nicholas said. The driver of the SUV brought the car to a halt and waved him across.

Sam resumed forward movement, reaching his dad on the sidewalk. As Shannon approached, she saw that she knew the SUV driver, and they chatted briefly as Nicholas put the bikes in the truck. Inside the truck, Sam said: "That was scary."

"Nicholas, that was really mixed messages," Shannon chided. Later, she confessed to me that she and her husband would've had words if I hadn't been in the car with them. To me, Sam never seemed in real danger of being hit. I could understand Shannon's concern, but felt it was anxiety driving the protective hand on his shoulder and her instruction to stop biking.

The incident came up later at a family dinner with Grandma Lois.

"I almost got hit by a car at the end," Sam said. "I was scared."

"He was almost hit by the car?" Frankie responded. She looked up from a plate of chicken stew and rice, eyes wide.

"I was driving and Daddy said cross and the car was coming."

"I was telling him to stop and Daddy was telling him to go, so poor Sam was caught in the middle," Shannon explained.

"I was braking and just rolling," Sam said.

"And then I knew the driver," Shannon interjected, and the conversation turned to how she knew the SUV driver.

"Dad, do you want to bike now?" Sam said. Clearly, the experience hadn't diminished his enthusiasm. Nicholas finished up his meal, and the two headed into the mild New Mexico evening for a ride at dusk.

I helped clear plates to the sink. I felt reassured. Even this family, committed to meditation, still struggles with in-the-moment mindfulness. A thought popped into my head: could my failure at meditation, which for years I had seen as a dead end, possibly be the beginning of success? I resolved to download some meditation apps that Shannon recommended and give it another try. I wouldn't worry about my kids refusing to sit down to meditate with me. If I could become more calm and regulated, they would at least benefit from the modeling I provided.

<hr />

AT MY KIDS' ELEMENTARY SCHOOL, Halloween is a huge deal. The kids coordinate costumes and some dress in group costumes, like different-colored crayons or characters in a fairy tale or movie. One year a friend of mine asked for advice: her daughter and some friends were planning a group costume, but another girl had complained to her mom about being excluded. My friend was worried that her daughter, Tasha, was a bystander in letting the other girl—her onetime best friend—be left out.

The girls were already eleven years old, I said, and needed to work these issues out themselves. I suggested that my friend have an open conversation with Tasha about how the excluded girl would feel, without passing judgment or giving advice. In the end, Tasha might learn more from going along with the scenario and then feeling bad about the outcome, as opposed to having the mothers intervene. If Tasha felt no remorse, her mom would have learned that she needed to strengthen empathy in her tween.

My friend realized—as I continually do—that a significant part of her reaction to the scenario was fear of how the other moms in our community would judge Tasha—and by extension her mother—for her behavior. It is often hard, but we should try our best to lay down this burden. Kids are up against enough challenges without also having to serve as validation for their parents' child-rearing skills.

I'm stable enough to handle the possibility that my neighbors think I'm making bad parenting choices, because I know in my heart that those choices are right for my children. Even if I later change my mind about how to handle something with regard to my kids, the path I took to get there was valuable.

There are many things you cannot change: technology, competitive schooling, the structure of modern institutions. You can take small steps to insulate yourself from anxiety-provoking conversations about kids' accomplishments, or to keep family life and mealtimes device-free. But ultimately, you're stuck in this era. It may help to acknowledge that even if portable electronics and omnipresent media pose challenges, they also open opportunities for our kids' generation. Indeed, for all the stress and anxiety that suffused the childhoods of young Millennials like my twenty-five-year-old stepdaughter, many of them are growing into creative, open-minded, social justice–oriented young adults.

If the situation you're in makes you wonder if you're "doing it wrong," focus on the common threads in the Apprenticeship Model: strong adult-child connections, communication that uncovers the underlying causes of misbehavior, and training kids in cognitive, social and emotional, and essential life skills. We saw those three elements in Vicki Hoefle's students in Vermont, the educators trained by Ross Greene in Maine, the classrooms playing the PAX game in Maryland and Columbus, and the PEP families of the Washington, DC, area. Remember the lessons of Chapter 3: empathy will help your children's brains make the neural connections necessary for self-regulation, and they can't learn or solve problems in the midst of an emotional outburst.

Even if you shift your parenting just slightly in the direction you want to head, you're improving your children's world. Celebrate those small changes and the resulting improvement in your family life. Don't look for immediate proof that your discipline style is working. You may not see it until interactions go more smoothly a few days or weeks later.

We are the only parents our children have, so we must find the courage to be our best selves—and to forgive ourselves when we fall short. It's worth the effort.

11

Create Lasting Change

THE GONZALEZ-MCCOY HOUSE SOUNDED LIKE the site of a World Wrestling match.

Thud. Shriek. Aaak!

Chloe Pearson, six, and Jesse Temchine, four, jumped from the third step of the staircase leading upstairs and landed in the hallway between the den and the dining room. They scrambled back up the stairs to jump down again. From the second floor, I could hear the distant screams and thumps of two nine-year-olds, Sawyer Pearson and Milo McCoy, and two eight-year-olds, Mariana Cullen and Rosa McCoy, engaged in who-knows-what violent pastime.

But no adults jumped up to intervene. The four couples chatted with each other about politics and Ayurvedic diets while they prepared curry cauliflower and pesto, Brussels sprouts, rice, and steak for this multifamily dinner party. A couple of dads started a fire in the den. Host Andy McCoy grilled on the patio, and the moms bustled around the kitchen and set the dining room table. Everyone was dressed casually but nice—in dark jeans, sweaters, and collared shirts.

From the beginning of the evening until the door closed on the last guest, all the adults displayed a high tolerance for loud and rough child play. They deftly redirected kids who were over the line, whether their own children or a friend's, without yelling or scolding or lecturing. They tolerated chatter about "chicken doodle butt" and farts, while spotting potential meltdowns over Pokémon card trades and gently heading them off. Other than that, the eight kids—ages four to nine—were pretty much independent, roaming the three floors of the house at will.

All the parents were graduates of the PEP parenting curriculum. Andy and his wife, Ana Gonzalez, signed up for PEP 1 and coincidentally found that Jesse's parents, Ben Temchine and Mikaela Seligman, were in the same class. Meanwhile, Camila and Colin were taking PEP 1 with me and Brian as their leaders. The four couples asked to be assigned to the same PEP 2 class, which Eric and Nicole Pearson joined after having different instructors in the first class. PEP 1 and PEP 2 each usually comprise eight weekly meetings.

Colin started encouraging other families at the kids' school to check out PEP. As the room parent, he shared books and audio resources that he felt were useful. The parents I met said that being together reinforces the firm and kind strategies they learned and helps them stay on the paths they've charted that are different from what they experienced in the families in which they grew up.

"We love our friends. We cherish them dearly, and we really try to support them," Andy told me. He grew up with an authoritarian father whom he loves but whose parenting he doesn't want to emulate. "It's a huge support network for the parents in terms of how they support their kids and all of us guys raised wrong. We just want to do things better."

〜〜〜

FOR DECADES, PERHAPS CENTURIES, HUMAN beings have tried to figure out what keeps us stuck in dysfunctional habits and how to effectively change behavior. Whether it's weight loss, smoking cessation, or alcohol abstinence, researchers have found that social support not only increases the odds of successful behavior change but also makes people more likely to stick with their new behaviors for good. One study found that people lost more weight when meeting in a group to discuss strategies and set goals than when they met one-on-one with a counselor. Moreover, participants who formed buddy groups to continue after the end of the program were more likely to maintain their weight loss. These findings underlie the success of programs from Weight Watchers to Alcoholics Anonymous, all of which build on positive feedback from peers and the optimism about your own future that comes from seeing others successfully overcome challenges similar to your own.

Possibly the hardest part of successfully changing your parenting is sticking with it in a world that is busy and judgmental. When Maddie decided in third grade that she didn't need to brush her thick, long hair before pulling it into a tangled ponytail, a chorus of objections rose in my throat. I could just imagine the judgment from other parents and her teachers. But I stopped myself from insisting—she deserved to have autonomy over her own body at least. The more freedom I gave her in areas like this, the more willing she became to cooperate with morning and evening routines and to help around the house.

As a buffer against that critical world, create your own community of support. Invite other parents to meet and discuss these ideas. You can use this book—or any of the books and other resources listed in the pages that follow—as the basis for a conversation. Get support from a tribe of like-minded parents, even if it means creating your own group. One reason Brian and I continue to volunteer as PEP leaders is to stay immersed in these ideas. It makes it harder to stray from the parenting path we've chosen in those moments when we're tired or low on willpower. Writing this book truly kept me honest, as I often found myself writing about strategies that I put into action hours later.

Don't expect that you'll finish this book and leap into wholesale change. One review of seventy-seven parent education programs found that the most successful ones involved parents practicing their new skills with their children over the course of many weeks. (Successful programs also focused on increasing positive parent-child interactions and teaching emotional communication skills.) Expect that it will take time to adopt these new habits. All the educators who implemented the models in this book received training and practiced with supervisors and peers while learning the new skills.

As PEP founder Linda Jessup put it to the group of parents in her PEP 3 class, learning to parent in a new way is "very much like potty training. First you just make a big mess, and it just feels normal, and you don't even know you wet your diaper.

"Then you begin to recognize you're wetting yourself. At that point, it's too late to be proactive, but it's the next step in learning to be potty-trained. The third step is you recognize the feeling that you have to go to the bathroom and you begin to head for the bathroom, and at first you often don't allow enough time, so you still make a mess, but you're progressing and are ahead of the game. It's very much the same with these well-established patterns. First we make a mess, but even being able to recognize it is a start. Then to be able to recognize it sooner and take action to not go down that path."

One of my favorite tools for parents trying on a new style is the "mumble and walk away" technique described in Chapter 7. Perhaps your child says something oppositional, and you feel the heat of anger flare up inside you. You open your mouth—and remember you've decided not to yell. But you don't know what to do instead. Give yourself breathing room to figure out your next steps. Pretend you hear a distant phone buzzing or that you left a pot on the stove. Mumble an excuse and exit the room quickly. Do whatever it takes to avoid falling into your old angry habits.

When I was a brand-new mom, I loved comparing notes in the mom-and-baby support group I attended weekly at a local birthing center. We shared tips for nursing, sleeping, and dealing with know-it-all relatives. But as my kids grew, I found comparisons with other people's kids to be less useful. In fact, they sometimes fed my worst impulses.

Your children need to experiment, fail, and try again to find their path through life. So do you. Pay attention to whether certain friends or family members make you feel more competitive or anxious. Notice anything else that triggers unhelpful parenting behaviors in you. Maybe social media drives these impulses. Once you figure out your danger areas, limit your exposure.

Don't feel you need to convince naysayers that your parenting choices are right for your child. You know that they are. You may want to come up with some inoffensive answers to their arguments in support of reward-punishment parenting. If they say, "It worked for me," or, "I turned out okay," you could mildly comment that times are different now, or that your kids have different needs. Or just smile and nod.

~~~

WHEN MADDIE WAS IN FOURTH grade, I started leading PEP parenting classes. I was heady with my new insight about the right way to parent and quick to diagnose instances of bad parenting around me. I had all the answers. Then, to my horror, Maddie's fourth-grade teacher, Jaclyn Chernak Sandler, introduced a behavior-tracking app called Class Dojo. Sandler awarded each child Class Dojo points for desired behavior, like being on task or participating, and deducted points for unwanted actions, like missing homework. People in the positive parenting camp view Class Dojo as the spawn of the devil: a cold, manipulative way to control kids' behavior that undermines intrinsic motivation. It's like the PAX game seen through a funhouse mirror. Instead of behavior parameters set by the whole class in the context of a fun group activity, the teachers define good and bad unilaterally and single out children on an individual basis.

Unfortunately for me, my daughter didn't read the research. She loved Class Dojo. She spent ages customizing her avatar, a cartoon monster with choices of color, hairstyle, and body parts. She eagerly checked her ranking, exulting at a green positive behavior point and despairing when she earned a red negative point. Over the course of the year I saw her often discouraged when she dipped into the red, but it didn't dim her enthusiasm for the technology—or for Sandler, who became her favorite elementary school teacher. Maddie even asked us to set up a family Class Dojo so that the kids could earn points for doing chores, being loving, and the like.

Although I am not likely to recommend Class Dojo or begin rewarding behavior with prizes, this experience helps me keep the reward-punishment debate in perspective.

Fourth grade was filled with learning and excitement for my daughter because Sandler focused on the three pillars of the Apprenticeship Model: nurturing relationship, communicating, and building skills, within a structure of clear limits and routines. My daughter felt her teacher's caring and interest every day and could always confide in her about a problem. She grew academically and in behavioral skills because of the mix of challenge with support. These pieces outweighed what research tells us is the negative aspect of reward-based behavior modification schemes.

The episode also helped me check both my judgment of other people's parenting and my envy of their perfectly behaved children. For one thing, we don't know what goes on behind closed doors. And for another, every parent creates a unique relationship with their children, shaped by the kids' temperament, interests, and skills. As tempting as it may be to wish away our child's negative qualities, they are here to stay. Rather, we should do our best to work with our child, view them in a positive light, and accept the hand we've been dealt. My kids may be more hyperactive than I was, and our dinner table more chaotic than my childhood mealtimes, but at least my kids will be more physically fit and will explore more diverse interests than I did in my youth.

Taking this view is known as a strength-based approach to parenting. Rather than fretting about our child's differences—whether from temperament, skill level, or brain function—we can look for the positive side. A child with ADHD may grow up to be a creative genius or dynamic leader. The mixed martial arts champ and inspirational speaker Scott Sonnon—whose parents ignored doctors' advice to institutionalize him because of his learning disabilities—says that doctors delivering a diagnosis of dyslexia should tell parents, "Congratulations! Your child is one hundred times more likely to become a millionaire entrepreneur."

If we parents can't envision a successful future for our children, they'll be forced to find it on their own. This is a lonelier way to grow up, and a less effective way to parent—we're supposed to enable our children to pursue their dreams, not limit them.

As we strive to imagine our kids' future, it's difficult not to look across the fence to our friends and neighbors. Comparing my children to other children used to send a pang of fear or regret through my chest, as I wondered: *Should I have been doing Kumon with my kids every day after school?* or, *Why isn't my daughter trying out for the soccer academy?* Competitive parenting is responsible for many bad parenting choices, and we should all develop ways to keep it at bay.

Connecting with a group of like-minded parents is a good start—we can take turns reminding each other that our children thrive on independence and autonomy and that their worth isn't defined by their grades or extracurricular triumphs. The PEP community serves that role for me and Brian, as does our neighborhood, where kids often play spontaneously in each other's yards.

I tell my children that their job until age eighteen is to figure out who they are, what fuels their passion, and how they will contribute their unique skills to the world. My role is to support them in sorting that out, not to impose my own choices on them. As skilled as my daughter is with a soccer ball, I'm not going to force her to continue to play just because she's talented and it may look good on her college application.

We can exercise our good judgment without being judgmental. When I see another parent sternly bossing around their children in public, my heart breaks a little. But I also remind myself that I don't know the full story of that family. I can use the experience to inform how I want to parent without concluding that that parent is good or bad, or right or wrong.

Parenting in this way means consciously breaking with the norms in the culture around us. My mother sometimes wonders if we're pampering our children by incorporating their opinions into our household routines. "The rest of the world won't cater to them," she argues.

But I see it as giving them a deep well of encouragement from which to draw strength to face the world. The Apprenticeship Model develops their self-advocacy and negotiating skills, as well as giving them a chance to live with the decisions they make. They are building the responsibility, perseverance, and flexibility of mind that will serve them well for success in adulthood. Children are remarkably adept at code-switching. They know just how far they can push their mother versus their father, versus their grandparents, versus their teachers, and they adjust their behavior accordingly.

~~~

Vicki Hoefle ground to a halt halfway through her second-session curriculum the evening I visited Burlington. The parents kept bringing up scenarios for her to solve. When is screen time a privilege that goes along with a responsibility (good) and when is it a bribe (bad)? How should they handle a child who lingers over dinnertime? The mom in the green raincoat raised her hand.

"Now what?" Hoefle said with mock impatience.

"We had an incident this weekend where my son had a playdate. They did something naughty," the mom said.

"What did they do?"

"They wrote all over a door in markers."

"At your house?"

"Yes."

"How old are they?" Hoefle asked.

"Four."

"What are you doing with markers where everybody can get them?"

"My six-year-old left them out and I didn't realize they were there."

"So they wrote on the door and that's naughty because . . . "

"If you would write on paper or places other than your walls and doors," the mom responded with a chuckle.

"But is it naughty? Do you think he was doing it to be bad?"

"I think he knows the difference between right and wrong," she said.

"Okay. I just wanted to check. So what did you do?" Hoefle said.

"I had a talk with him," she said.

The room exploded with laughter. They'd already gotten that Hoefle thinks parents talk and lecture too often. They were already forming a community.

"So what's the problem? In one sentence, what's the problem?"

The mom was stumped. She stuttered a bit.

"Failure to manage markers," offered another mom.

"What's the problem that you're solving in that moment?" Hoefle pressed.

Green raincoat was still at a loss.

"That's what's tripping you up," Hoefle said.

"How to repair the door," suggested a pregnant mom.

"Yes! The problem is the door has markers on it. You're trying to make the kid the problem," Hoefle said.

"So make him clean the door?" green raincoat asked.

"Make him? Well, you could try. Good luck with that."

More chuckles.

Instead, Hoefle suggested, the mother could ask her four-year-old, "'So you wrote on the doors. How did that start?' I want to know what got him excited, so I can give him good information. 'Uh huh. What did you think would happen when we saw the door?' I always smile when I say that because then they think, *Maybe I'm not going to get in trouble.*"

She continued with the mock conversation between the mom and child after she discovered the marks on the door.

"Actually, I didn't know."

"Okay, that's good information, you didn't know. If you had to guess, now, what might happen, what would you guess?"

"No TV?"

"Nope," Hoefle said, voicing the mom's response in the mock conversation.

"I don't know."

"'The door has to get cleaned,' the mom will explain. 'So how do you do that?' I lead them right in. I already know where the path is. I'm just moving them to the idea that of course the door is going to get cleaned and would they like to use the Brillo pads? 'Do you know where they are? No? Would you like me to go into the kitchen with you?'"

The room fell completely silent as the parents processed these ideas.

"Truthfully, I don't care about the door," Hoefle said. "I could give two craps about the door. If my kid was diagnosed with an illness, I can tell you I wouldn't care about the door or the markers on the door. I have to put that in perspective all the time. Is this something that's going to get me cranked up? No way in hell. It's a learning opportunity.

"My house is not on the market. I don't have a realtor coming to show it. What do I want to teach my child? That people make mistakes. This is an opportunity to take responsibility for that mistake, to learn to think before you do things, which is a lifelong skill, and then to make amends. That's it. Same thing a million times."

She encouraged the class to slow the whole process down, to engage their children's brains in solving the problem and planning the next steps. It's not magic, but just a matter of parents keeping their cool and understanding that the problem isn't that the child did something bad.

"The problem is: there's markers on the door. Now we can get him involved. But not if we say he's the problem. Then we have to fix him. There's nothing wrong with him. He made a mistake," she said.

~~~

MIKAELA SELIGMAN, FORTY-SEVEN, WAS HOLDING forth about politics, leaning her shoulder against the pale green wall of the dining room.

Her four-year-old son, Jesse, barreled into the room and thumped up against her side. With tangled, shoulder-length brown hair, wide eyes, and an oversized striped sweater, he resembled a character from Mercer Mayer's Little Critter books. He began punching her thigh, urgently.

"Jesse," said her husband, Ben Temchine, forty-two, a dark-bearded man wearing a lumberjack-style shirt under his bulky sweater. "Can you come over and tell me what you want and I'll get it, so Mom can finish what she was saying? I noticed because you're hitting her."

Jesse trundled across the room to his dad, who squatted down to listen.

"Is there dessert?" he asked.

"There is dessert," Ben replied. "As soon as I see it, I'll come and get you."

Jesse seemed placated and was about to leave when his dad asked: "Can you check every now and then on the fire? Is it small or is it still big?"

With purpose, Jesse zipped into the den, then returned to report: "It's still big."

"Will you check every now and then?" Ben asked, standing back up in conversation with the rest of the parents. Jesse nodded and returned to the den where two six-year-olds, Alejandro and Chloe, were practicing gymnastics.

"I have to check on the fire that it's still big. I can't let it get small," he announced.

The older kids made encouraging faces. He plopped down to watch their gyrations. Chloe's mom, Nicole, watched also. Chloe paused as Jesse scooted his rear toward the wall, giving her space for a cartwheel.

I noticed Ben's skill in managing Jesse's undue attention by listening to his concern, assuring him it would be addressed, and smoothly giving him a positive way to contribute by asking him to check on the fire. I could almost see Jesse stand taller as he shouldered the responsibility.

Chloe took a running start and completed a cartwheel.

"Your legs were straight up," Nicole remarked, after applauding and giving Chloe a double thumbs-up. That was PEP-approved specific feedback describing her daughter's pose, as opposed to the empty-calorie praise of a generic "good job."

"Alexia is so good," Chloe said, referring to a classmate.

"Yeah, she doesn't give up," her mom said.

Chloe's bottom lip curled into a tiny pout as she imagined her distant rival.

"Keep going, keep practicing," Nicole encouraged her.

Chloe explained to her mom that she'd try another cartwheel later, in a room with no carpet.

"I'm going to go upstairs," she announced.

But first, she needed to know the status of brownies. Once she was assured on that score, she raced up the stairs.

In another setting, without the support of this group of like-minded friends, Ben might have noticed judgmental eyes on him while dealing with Jesse's hitting. Nicole might not have felt free to watch rambunctious children with an eye to connecting rather than curbing their energy. Certainly, the children's active play wouldn't have been tolerated by just any group of friends. This community's tacit acceptance made it easier for parents to connect, communicate, and build their children's capability, all while everyone shared an enjoyable Saturday night.

~~~

AVA APPEARED AT THE DOOR of my bathroom. I put down the blow dryer. This was odd. My sleep-loving child wearing shorts, sweatshirt, and backpack at 7:30 a.m. She even looked as if she'd brushed her teeth.

"I'm ready," she chirped. "Can we go to Dunkin' Donuts?"

It was nearly the end of the school year for Ava, ten, and Maddie, thirteen. The previous evening I had promised to take the kids to Dunkin' Donuts before school as a special treat. We could go as long as everyone was 100 percent ready at 7:40 a.m., so we'd arrive at school on time at 8:15 a.m. We'd established that timeline through a family agreement at the beginning of the year.

"Sure! Check on your sister to see if she's ready," I responded. Better finish up the hair quickly.

Ava reappeared shortly, a sour look on her face.

"She's still in bed."

"Well," I said, "maybe you can hurry her along."

This was another first. Usually Maddie's the one on top of her game, up and dressed early. Ava disappeared.

She returned with a wail. "She says she doesn't want to go!"

Uh oh.

As you know by now, my children can throw epic tantrums. They kick furniture and doors. They knock over objects. Even at ten and thirteen, a mood could sweep over them that touched everyone in the house. It felt like an emotional tornado, perhaps especially because puberty was coming closer for both of them.

"Mom, can you please take me to Dunkin' and we'll grab takeout and come back to get Maddie?"

I considered the request. It wasn't unreasonable. I could finish dressing for my work conference after I dropped the kids off. I'd already walked the dog.

But would that be rescuing Ava? I thought back to Vicki Hoefle's injunction that every child should face a challenge every day in order to learn courage and become capable. Surely she would tell me to let Ava experience her disappointment and rise to the challenge of managing her emotions and figuring out an alternative breakfast plan. She'd also remind me to be fair to myself, by not putting extra stress on my busy workday. *I'll stay connected to her,* I resolved, *even while saying no.*

"I'm sorry, honey, we agreed on 7:40, and she's nowhere near ready. I can understand you being disappointed. I bet you can find something downstairs to eat," I responded. I braced myself for high winds.

"That's not fair!" she shouted. "I was ready on time, and I won't get to go because she's not ready."

"I can really understand you being upset," I replied, keeping my voice warm and empathetic. "It's frustrating when you take care of your responsibilities but you can't move ahead in the day because of someone else's choices. Sometimes that's part of being a family."

She stomped away. I picked up the flat iron, trying to ignore the sounds coming from the other room. *Thump. Crash.* I finished my hair and walked into the bedroom.

Ava was lying on my bed, her face crumpled and tears on her round cheeks. There was no obvious property damage.

"There's nothing in the house to eat! I'm hungry and it's all Maddie's fault!"

I sat beside her and put a hand on her leg. I resisted arguing about the state of our pantry: Brian had gone shopping a few days earlier and bought eggs, toast, cereal, and plenty of fruit. I ignored that Ava was blaming someone else for the condition of her stomach.

I suggested a few food options. All were rejected.

"What about blueberry muffins? I think we have some muffin mix, and there's just enough time for you to cook," I said.

She jumped up to look in the pantry. I headed down the hall to find Maddie still in bed. Her stomach hurt. I gave her a hug and suggested a few remedies. When I walked downstairs, Ava was in tears again.

"There's no blueberry muffin mix! Only lemon poppy. I like the artificial blueberries," she complained.

I sympathized and expressed confidence that she could figure out breakfast. I gave her a little space while I fixed my coffee and apple slices. Suddenly, to my surprise, she decided that lemon poppy was acceptable. But she wondered aloud if we would have time. She decided to make mini-muffins so they'd bake quicker.

"Mom, will you help me?" she asked.

Even with tears still on her cheeks, she was beaming. I preheated the oven. She read the instructions on the package and assembled the ingredients efficiently. We worked together companionably. She insisted on taking the lead—she likes to mix up the dough and spoon it into the muffin tins.

"I'm not giving any to Maddie," she announced.

"Even though she's made breakfast for you so many times?"

"The last time she made breakfast she said she was never going to do it again because I didn't say thank you," she said. "She even said 'keys' to me like I was a little kid. It was so condescending." (Remember in Chapter 8, I described our family code word "keys" as a reminder to use good manners.)

Another test of my resolve. Of course I want my children to be generous with each other. But it has to come from within. I can't force it. I can only model generosity.

"Well, it's certainly your choice since you made these muffins," I said. "But I wonder what will happen the next time she bakes something and you want a taste."

Ava bustled around. No response. I let her ponder.

Maddie slumped into the kitchen. I gave her a hug and inquired about the stomach. Still tender but better. She took some fruit because she didn't think she could eat anything else. Except maybe a muffin.

"You can't have any," Ava said.

I braced myself.

"Oh, that's too bad," Maddie responded, with a hangdog look. Playing for sympathy.

I bit my tongue. I grabbed the rest of my belongings and headed to the car. Ava started to pack up the muffins to eat on the ride to school. Maddie had left the room, so I leaned over and whispered: "Do you think you might want to bring an extra muffin in case you change your mind and let Maddie have one?"

She nodded.

I pulled the car to the front of the house and listened to NPR while waiting for the girls. Ava came out first. Cheerful and bursting with pride. I felt so relieved that I had resisted the many impulses I had to interfere with her opportunities to learn that morning. She'd managed to hit the trifecta: emotional regulation, problem-solving, and moral decision-making.

Then Maddie emerged from the house with a muffin in her hand. *Uh oh. Did she steal it when Ava wasn't looking?*

I turned to look at my youngest child in the backseat. "Why does Maddie have a muffin?" I asked.

"I gave it to her. But just one," she responded.

~~~

AT THE END OF THE night, the Cullen parents and the other adults gathered by the fire, talking about parenting and politics, water skiing and food. Before I even noticed that Eric had slipped out of the room, he was standing in the hallway with Sawyer and Chloe.

"Sawyer, Chloe, do you want to say good-night?" asked Eric. The kids smiled their thanks at Ana and Chris.

"You're going skiing tomorrow?" Camila asked.

"Yeah. We're going skiing," Sawyer replied.

"All right, let's go," Eric whispered, and the kids looked around for their coats.

How did that happen? I wondered to myself, annoyed that I didn't notice the expert parenting moves Eric and Nicole must have deployed to pry their kids away from the Pokémon TV show upstairs. Then again, perhaps the kids were motivated to leave because they wanted to be well rested for their fun outing the next day.

Eric dashed upstairs to look for a missing sock, while Ana reassured the group that nobody else needed to hurry to leave.

"My kids will put themselves to sleep if they need to. They're like, 'Oh, we're tired, good-night,'" she said.

"Thank you for having us," said Eric, returning from the upstairs level with socks and shoes in hand.

Everyone gave kisses and hugs good-bye.

"Thank you for hosting us," Nicole said.

Chloe waited in bare feet as her parents said good-bye.

"Chloe's patiently waiting," Ben observed. Specific praise again.

The Young-Pearson family walked out the door and into a mild February night. Ana watched from the window as they headed toward their car on Park Road, a windy, single-lane street that—while residential—is the primary route from the hip Mount Pleasant neighborhood into tony Cleveland Park.

"I love how Nicole's carrying Chloe's shoes," she said. "Chloe just lost her shoes. But she doesn't care."

"Who?" Camila asked.

"Chloe. She's shoeless, but now Eric is carrying her," Ana explained.

"Nothing wrong with shoeless. There's no glass," Colin said.

The conversation continued about favorite bookstores and restaurants, about the kids' after-school routines.

And then twenty minutes later, the same thing happened again. I looked up to see Camila standing with Alejandro and Mariana, obediently putting on their coats with absolutely zero argument. Even a flurry of excitement over a red wine spill didn't distract them from leaving. Camila stood calmly with a bag slung over her shoulder as the children tied their own shoes.

"We'll see you. Ciao," she said.

"Ciao," Ana responded.

"Mariana, buenas noches," said Colin, who was staying to help with cleanup from the party.

"Y Papa?" Alejandro asked his mom.

"Papa has to help with the carpet," Camila explained.

"Gracias, Camila, gracias, Alejandro. Buenas noches," Andy said.

And then, without a murmur of protest, the Cullen children left the party. This was quite a change from the hellions described in

Chapter 1, and so different from the end of many multifamily parties, when sugared-up kids refuse to leave because they've been out of control for hours.

~~~

I'VE FOUND MY OWN COMMUNITY through PEP leaders and students and through my neighborhood friends who accept my approach just as I accept their choices for their own children. Even the same philosophy looks different in different homes, after all.

I hope everyone understands that writing a parenting book doesn't make me an expert on what's the best strategy for any given child. Truly, only the people in a relationship can fully understand its dynamics. Not only are you the person capable of the most insight into your child's needs, you are the one who can best fill them.

That said, it's not enough to raise our own kids so that they grow up to be resilient, capable adults. They also need peers, spouses, and coworkers who aren't crippled by anxiety, depression, and self-doubt. Our whole society needs to embrace the Apprenticeship Model. For that to happen, we need social support.

You can start by finding or creating your tribe, such as an online or local parenting group, a book club, a religious community, or a discussion group. If you live in a neighborhood without other kids, look for ways to create some of the opportunities for spontaneous, kid-directed play of past generations, without putting children at risk. Maybe a babysitting coop or a regular playgroup can bring you and your family closer to where you want to be. You'd be surprised how quickly one family becoming more unscheduled can free up an entire community to disarm in the competitive parenting arms race.

Expect to run into stumbling blocks as your children grow or your life changes. And I realize that some of the advice in this book may seem impossible for you to implement. How can you supervise homework if you're at work until 6:00 p.m. while your child is in after-care? How can you get a teenager who barely speaks to you to do chores and agree to restrictions on screen time? Feel free to start small, taking the steps that seem to lead to the easiest changes. Open your mind to possibilities. Question those notions that you accept as truth, such as: *I can't take away my child's phone when every other kid in the grade has access to screens at night.* You never know how many other parents will jump on board once you're brave enough to take a stand. Your child may even welcome the limits.

Make a list of your big takeaways from this book, your moments of epiphany. I'm guessing that they're slightly different for each reader. We all come to parenting with our own expectations, baggage, and individual temperaments. Some of the behavior I tolerate may be way beyond your comfort zone. Some of the lines that I draw may seem unnecessary to you. You are the expert on your own child.

Refer to that list when you get discouraged. It will help you remember why you started on this path of changing entrenched behavior and forging a new parenting style in your home. For me, the list includes those character traits I want my children to embody at ages eighteen and twenty-five—I need to keep focused on the long-term goals. Our children will never learn self-discipline if we're always controlling their behavior.

Start another list—a list of all the victories you experience along the way. Maybe it's a power-hungry child backing down from an argument. Or your toddler agreeing to put on their seat belt in the car. Or something as profound as bedtime without argument or bribery, and a peaceful adult hour while the children get themselves to sleep. Our kids change so quickly, and it can be easy to take their new cooperative behavior in stride and focus on new emerging problems. Remind yourself of how far you all have come by celebrating the small wins.

On a Friday night early last summer, I went to our neighborhood pool for the weekly parent happy hour and pep rally for our community swim team. Two friends and I were chatting on the pool deck, near the chairs and picnic tables where most adults congregate. The chatter of kids finishing their pasta dinners and noises from the pool created a low din around us.

Two boys started bouncing a tennis ball against the wall and leaping to catch it, barely five feet from us. I didn't take much notice until my friend growled in their direction: "That ball better not hit me!"

I realized their rough play could easily hurt one of the parents or young children standing in that area. I recognized one of the boys, from the swim team. I'd often given him an encouraging word or asked about his hobbies when lining him up for the races—my favorite volunteer job on the team.

"Hey, Daniel," I said, taking a step nearer. "Nice reflexes. You caught that one when I was sure it was going into the pool."

He paused the game and looked at me with the neutral, not-quite-hostile look that many tween boys have perfected.

"I'm concerned that you might hit one of the parents or little kids in this area. Would you be willing to take the play over to the grassy area by the basketball courts?" I asked with a smile.

He grunted his assent and sprinted off with his playmate to the spot I'd suggested. Nothing miraculous, but quite a change from how the boys his age had ignored me on the school playground eight years earlier. Because I had a connection with him, communicated clearly, and expressed faith in his capability, I won cooperation in a way that I couldn't have before I started this journey.

We often expect that we should be able to solve any troublesome parenting issue by taking a series of actions that will lead to prompt resolution. Certainly, there are some behaviors—like running into a car-filled street or biting another child—that we can't live with for the time it takes to reach a solution. We must act unilaterally to protect our child or even our own sanity. But other concerns, like teaching healthy eating or table manners, deserve time for the child to learn—and for you to see whether your approach is working. Give yourself that breathing room.

If you take only one insight from this book, I hope it's this one: childish misbehavior isn't an emergency situation or a sign of something gone wrong, but simply a natural part of growing up. Pause and respond with intention to your child's behavior. Getting out of reactive mode will improve your connection to your kid, give you a chance to communicate better, and offer your child the space to build their capability for whatever the situation is, without you swooping in. That mind-set shift in itself is a huge step forward that strengthens all three pillars of the Apprenticeship Model.

In sailing, you cannot head straight to your destination. You must harness the power of the wind against your sails in order to chart a course that slants across the direct line to your goal, at as small an angle as possible. When that puff of air runs out, you switch sides, tilting the other side of your boat toward your target. You continue "tacking," switching back and forth, as you head toward your goal at an angle. The boat takes a zigzag path as you come ever closer to your objective.

Sometimes the wind dies and you drift along, seeming to make no progress. If you get impatient and try to point the boat more squarely toward your destination, your sails will flap and you will grind to a halt.

Parenting is similar. There simply is no shortcut to the long process of children learning from life, with your loving guidance. As much as we'd like to extract the hard-won knowledge in our brain and implant it into theirs, they must experience life for themselves. They must draw their own conclusions.

Our job is to cheer them on when they succeed, and catch them when they fall. And to pray for a strong offshore breeze that will speed the sailboat along.

Age-Appropriate Jobs

The household jobs listed here are categorized by the age when typical children can master them. Start small and plan to work alongside your child at least until age eight. Most important: invite your children to learn a job, don't force them.

Toddlers (Two to Three Years Old)

- Dust areas within reach
- Fill a pet's food and water bowls
- Put dirty laundry in the hamper
- Help a parent sweep or clean up spills
- Pick up and put away toys
- Shred lettuce for salad or help mix ingredients together

Many children this age can also manage to:

- Make their bed, with help
- Put out clean towels and toilet paper, with help
- Spray and wipe windows and counters, with help

Preschoolers (Four to Five Years Old)

- All the jobs on the previous list
- Set the table
- Help a parent chop and prepare food
- Bring belongings in from the car
- Help carry in groceries
- Empty trash cans

- Water indoor plants
- Clean grit from sink
- Match socks and sort laundry
- Clean floors with a broom, light vacuum, or dry mop
- Spray and wipe windows and counters, with help
- Pour cereal, butter bread, and make other no-cook meals

Young School Age (Six to Eight Years Old)

- Everything on the previous lists
- Take out the trash
- Unload dishwasher and put away dishes
- Clean the inside of the car
- Help put away groceries
- Vacuum or wet mop the whole room
- Fold laundry and put away, with help
- Spray and wipe shower stall or bathtub
- Spray and wipe outside of toilet; scrub the bowl
- Help rake leaves or shovel snow
- Help take a pet for a walk or change a dirty cage/tank
- Fix snacks and pack lunch for school
- Write thank-you notes or the family's weekly schedule (if you have a calendar on display)
- Chop food with a sharp knife and cook simple meals on the stove (think mac-and-cheese or scrambled eggs)

Tweens (Nine to Twelve Years Old)

- All the jobs on the previous lists, with minimal supervision
- Help wash the car
- Operate the washer and dryer
- Rinse dishes and load dishwasher
- Clean the kitchen counters and sink
- Clean mirrors and the entire bathroom
- Cook simple meals, like fried eggs or pasta bake

Teens (Thirteen to Eighteen Years Old)

- All the jobs on the previous lists, independently
- Mow the lawn
- Supervise a younger child
- Change lightbulbs and the vacuum bag
- Plan and cook an easy family dinner
- Go grocery shopping and run other family errands
- Learn to maintain a car, bike, and household appliances

Top Takeaways and Resources

This book is a work of narrative journalism, not a parenting manual. For hands-on advice in implementing the Apprenticeship Model, please see www.katherinerlewis.com or consult the resources that follow.

Self-Regulation

Our impulse to protect children from any harm can undermine their mental health, because taking a risk or experiencing a setback helps them learn self-regulation.

Children don't need additional motivation to behave, they need skills. Instead of rewards and punishment, parents should provide training and a model of self-regulation.

Screen for factors impacting behavior: overscheduling, lack of sleep or outdoor play, electronics overload, poor diet, or an undiagnosed learning, attention, or mood disorder.

Our role isn't to make sure our kids do everything right, it's to give them increasing independence and responsibility, while teaching them skills they need to succeed and being their emotional support when they fail. Stop thinking: *What reward or punishment will make them behave?* Instead, think: *What skill do they need?*

Connection

Empathy and physical touch help any human self-regulate. It's more powerful when it comes from a parent or other close relative.

Adults can help babies learn executive function, emotional regulation, and cognitive skills in five simple steps: the Boston Basics. For more, see http://boston.thebasics.org/.

Connect through special one-on-one time, verbal encouragement, weekly family fun, doing household work together, and specific appreciations of a child's contributions or interests, rather than broad praise. When a child is upset, connect before you correct.

For more tools, see http://pepparent.org, *Parenting with Courage and Uncommon Sense* by Linda Jessup and Emory Luce Baldwin, and *Positive Discipline* by Jane Nelsen.

Communication

Ask questions to stimulate kids' critical thinking, not to solve the problem for them. Talk less and listen more. Don't assume you know what's wrong; get the child's input. Speak with the respect you'd offer a friend. Give information, not orders. Develop nonverbal signals and agree in advance on whether and how to remind kids of responsibilities.

When learning a new communication style, consider the "mumble and walk away" technique. Say no as rarely as possible. Use "when-then" or positive phrasing instead. Or Vicki Hoefle's "convince me" technique.

Don't label children. Describe their behavior and anchor positive traits you notice. Specific verbal feedback will encourage a child, whereas broad or over-the-top praise may actually discourage the behavior you want, as seen in Carol Dweck's research.

Ross Greene's model involves active listening; finding a solution the adult and child can agree upon; and systematically tackling problem areas one by one. For more detail, see www.livesinthebalance.org or Greene's books, most recently *Raising Human Beings*.

Capability

Focus less on academic, sports, and arts performance and more on emotion management, executive function, and life skills. It helps children's mental health to contribute to the family, school, or community.

Vicki Hoefle's books give a structure for systematically building children's skills. Start with small and manageable chores, keep it fun, and work alongside young children.

Help children learn what helps them self-regulate, whether a quiet corner, physical exertion, a fidget or stress ball, conversation, a hug, or another tool. The PAX Good Behavior Game builds students' social-emotional skills without taking up classroom time. For more information, see https://paxis.org/.

Unwanted behaviors are "weeds" that grow when watered with attention. Ignore them. Highlight desired behaviors instead.

Limits, Routines, and Modeling

Consequences should be set by mutual agreement and be respectful, reasonable, revealed in advance, and related to the unwanted behavior or action. Let experience teach the lesson. There's no need to chastise the child or rescue them from being upset.

It's okay for adults to have bad days or struggle with self-regulation ourselves. Stop worrying about what the world around you thinks of your parenting. Learn what you need to model healthy stress management, conflict resolution, respectful communication, and use of technology. Be open to outcomes that are different than you imagined—but may still be acceptable. Expect learning to take time.

Put a child in charge of a task they've been resisting or pick the most difficult kid to help. Homework is kids' responsibility. Advocate for them—or help them self-advocate—if teachers assign too much. View screen time as a privilege that accompanies responsibilities. Stay out of sibling conflict as much as possible, and never take sides.

Find or build support networks of like-minded adults. Be patient as you implement new tools. Focus on solving problems, not fixing your kids.

Acknowledgments

MY UNDERSTANDING OF CHILDREN'S BEHAVIOR rests on decades of hard work and breakthroughs by psychologists, researchers, and educators who have devoted their careers to this important topic. I'm particularly grateful to my teachers at the Parent Encouragement Program, who first provoked me to question my long-held assumptions about parenting and relationships, including Patti Cancellier, Sue Clark, Marlene Goldstein, Linda Jessup, Lynne Marks, and Kerry Mayorga.

I am forever indebted to my agent, Richard Pine, for believing in this project—and that books can change people's lives. I feel so fortunate that my manuscript landed in the sure hands of my editor, Benjamin Adams, who shared my vision for this book and provided invaluable editing and narrative guidance. Thank you to Eliza Rothstein, Lyndsey Blessing, and the whole team at Inkwell Management for their advocacy and contributions to this project. I extend thanks to everyone at PublicAffairs and Hachette Book Group for lending their talents to bring this book into the world, including Lindsay Fradkoff, Pete Garceau, Jaime Leifer, Peter Osnos, Clive Priddle, Melissa Raymond, and Melissa Veronesi.

This book only exists because Monika Bauerlin took a chance on my pitch for a magazine article. My deepest thanks to Monika and her colleagues at *Mother Jones,* notably Mike Mechanic and Marianne Szegedy-Maszak, for seeing the story's potential and for shaping and presenting it so expertly. Sections of Chapter 7 first appeared in *Mother Jones* magazine as "The End of Punishment."

My humble gratitude to Ross Greene, Nina D'Aran, Leigh Robinson, and the Central School teachers and parents who opened their doors for me to observe before I even had an assignment—and for their patience with years of follow-up and fact-checking. A huge thank-you to Vicki Hoefle, Dennis Embry, Olympia Williams, Brandy Davies, and their Ohio Ave ES colleagues; Kady Ermisch, Melissa Rothblatt, and Nationwide Children's Hospital; and Nadia Nieves, Joel Yang, Nim Tottenham, and Ronald Ferguson for their generosity with their time, expertise, and willingness to let me tag along as they worked. I offer my deep appreciation to every parent who shared with me their personal experiences, disappointments, and hopes for their children.

As an independent journalist bereft of a newsroom, I depended on the feedback and encouragement of thoughtful readers of both the proposal and the manuscript: Jamila Bey, Jon Birger, Patti Cancellier, Rayenne Chen, Tina Hsu, Brian Lewis, Samantha Merrill, Diane Leach Putnick, Bruce Reynolds, Chris Reynolds, Yoke San Lee Reynolds, Kim Roosevelt, Matthew Skinner, Miranda Spivak, and Laura Vanderkam, who is the best accountability buddy possible. I also drew courage and inspiration from my writing family:

- The National Gallery of Art group, especially Mei Fong, Mary Kane, Christine Koubek, Christy Lyons, Tammy Lytle, Chuck McCutcheon, John McQuaid, Susan Milligan, Amy Rogers Nazarov, and Bara Vaida.
- The talented artist and writers with whom I've shared creative space in residencies at the Carey Institute, Poynter, Ragdale (Fabdale Session 7!), and the Virginia Center for the Creative Arts, especially John Copenhaver, Kristina Marie Darling, Alyss Dixon, Rasha Elass, Alexandria Marzano-Lesnevich, Kenneth R. Rosen, Sarah Shourd, Chandra Thomas Whitfield, and Clare Wu.
- The generous DC-area writing community, with special thanks to Jenny J. Chen, Tyrese Coleman, Vanessa Mallory Kotz, Stephanie Mencimer, Emily Paulsen, Brigid Schulte, and my Newhouse colleagues.
- The Asian American Journalists Association, particularly my longtime friends Mei-Ling Hopgood, Cheryl Lu-Lien Tan, and Doris Truong.

So many people contributed advice, a timely introduction, or hard-won experience. They are too many to name, but include Trudi Benford, Lara Heimert, Pauline Hubert, Jennifer Margulis, Seth

Mnookin, Amanda Morin, and Tiffany Sun. I feel so fortunate to count Joanne Bamberger, Linda Fibich, and Eric Pianin among my mentors; they provided counsel on thorny issues, offered me opportunities, and wrote an embarrassing number of recommendation letters! Thank you to Samantha Goldstein for the hours of research support and to Laura VanDruff for Spanish-to-English translation. My dear mom friends—you know who you are—thank you for always being there to share a laugh, tissue, or text of support throughout this parenting adventure. To all those who helped in ways small or big, please know I am truly appreciative.

The Virginia Center for the Creative Arts, Ragdale Foundation, and Logan Nonfiction Program at the Carey Institute for Global Good provided invaluable time, space, and creative community while I was writing this book. Thank you for supporting writers and artists.

I am enormously grateful to my family for their unwavering support and enthusiasm for this six-year-long project. In particular, thank you for the perspective and feedback shared by Michelle Ng, Sophia Colón Roosevelt, Kim Roosevelt, Priscilla Roosevelt, Anne Skinner, and Matt Skinner. Thank you for your continual interest and encouragement, Herbert, Barbara, Joanna, and Eric Lewis. And to the sister I'd been hoping to get, Donna Lewis, thank you for the empathy, cheerleading, and mutual unconditional love, and for immortalizing me in the funny pages.

Mom and Dad, you are always in my corner. Thank you for the line editing, child care, and carpool help both planned and last-minute, and most of all, for your unshakable confidence in my eventual success when the road ahead seemed impossible. I couldn't ask for a better brother and friend than Chris Reynolds. Your passion for ideas and your belief in the value of mine carried me through many tough spots—and then you pushed me to a higher level.

My children are both the inspiration for this work and eager participants. Ava, Maddie, and Samantha, you each have changed me for the better as a mother and a human being. Thank you for filling my days with joy, challenge, silliness, and unexpected richness.

The forever love of my life, Brian, cheerfully took over parenting and household duties for week after week while I struggled with words. Thank you for the gift of your time and energy, and for being my true partner in life, family, and the journey to understanding.

Selected Bibliography

Chapter 1: Introduction

Statistics on parents' time with children are taken from a Pew Research Center analysis of American Time Use Survey data by Juliana Menasce Horowitz, Kim Parker, Nikki Graf, and Gretchen Livingston, "Americans Widely Support Paid Family and Medical Leave, but Differ over Specific Policies," March 23, 2017, www.pewsocialtrends.org/2017/03/23/americans-widely-support-paid-family-and-medical-leave-but-differ-over-specific-policies/.

Data on the drop in discipline problems were found on the Maine Juvenile Justice Advisory Group website, www.maine.gov/corrections/jjag.

Chapter 2: An Epidemic of Misbehavior

Description of research from email correspondence with Elena Smirnova and her translation of Elena O. Smirnova and Olga V. Gudareva, "Igra i Proizvol'nost u Sovremennykh Doshkol'nikov" ("Play and Intentionality in Modern Preschoolers"), *Voprosy Psikhologii* 1 (2004): 91–103.

Elena Bodrova, Carrie Germeroth, and Deborah J. Leong, "Play and Self-regulation: Lessons from Vygotsky," *American Journal of Play* 6, no. 1 (2013): 111.

Jean M. Twenge, "Time Period and Birth Cohort Differences in Depressive Symptoms in the US, 1982–2013," *Social Indicators Research* 121, no. 2 (2015): 437–454.

Jean M. Twenge, *iGen: Why Today's Super-Connected Kids Are Growing Up Less Rebellious, More Tolerant, Less Happy—and Completely Unprepared for Adulthood—and What That Means for the Rest of Us* (New York: Simon & Schuster/Atria Books, 2017).

Yalda T. Uhls, Minas Michikyan, Jordan Morris, Debra Garcia, Gary W. Small, Eleni Zgourou, and Patricia M. Greenfield, "Five Days at Outdoor Education Camp Without Screens Improves Preteen Skills with Nonverbal Emotion Cues," *Computers in Human Behavior* 39 (2014): 387–392.

Ethan Kross, Philippe Verduyn, Emre Demiralp, Jiyoung Park, David Seungjae Lee, Natalie Lin, Holly Shablack, John Jonides, and Oscar Ybarra, "Facebook Use Predicts Declines in Subjective Well-being in Young Adults," *PloS One* 8, no. 8 (2013): e69841.

Dimitri Christakis, "Media and Children," TEDxRainier, posted to You-Tube on December 28, 2011, https://www.youtube.com/watch?v =BoT7qH_uVNo.

Pooja S. Tandon, Chuan Zhou, Paula Lozano, and Dimitri A. Christakis, "Preschoolers' Total Daily Screen Time at Home and by Type of Child Care," *Journal of Pediatrics* 158, no. 2 (2011): 297–300.

For American Academy of Pediatrics report on kids and digital media, see Yolanda (Linda) Reid Chassiakos, Jenny Radesky, Dimitri Christakis, Megan A. Moreno, and Corinn Cross, "Children and Adolescents and Digital Media," *Pediatrics* 138, no. 5 (2016): e20162593.

Dimitri A. Christakis, Frederick J. Zimmerman, David L. DiGiuseppe, and Carolyn A. McCarty, "Early Television Exposure and Subsequent Attentional Problems in Children," *Pediatrics* 113, no. 4 (2004): 708–713.

Trina Hinkley, Vera Verbestel, Wolfgang Ahrens, Lauren Lissner, Dénes Molnár, Luis A. Moreno, Iris Pigeot, et al., "Early Childhood Electronic Media Use as a Predictor of Poorer Well-being: A Prospective Cohort Study," *JAMA Pediatrics* 168, no. 5 (2014): 485–492.

D. A. Christakis, J. S. B. Ramirez, and J. M. Ramirez, "Overstimulation of Newborn Mice Leads to Behavioral Differences and Deficits in Cognitive Performance," *Scientific Reports* 2 (2012): 546.

Victoria J. Rideout, Ulla G. Foehr, and Donald F. Roberts, "Generation M^2: Media in the Lives of 8- to 18-Year-Olds," A Kaiser Family Foundation Study (Menlo Park, CA: The Henry J. Kaiser Family Foundation, January 2010).

Kathleen Ries Merikangas, Jian-ping He, Marcy Burstein, Sonja A. Swanson, Shelli Avenevoli, Lihong Cui, Corina Benjet, Katholiki Georgiades, and Joel Swendsen, "Lifetime Prevalence of Mental Disorders in US Adolescents: Results from the National Comorbidity Survey Replication–Adolescent Supplement (NCS-A)," *Journal of the American Academy of Child and Adolescent Psychiatry* 49, no. 10 (2010): 980–989.

Peter LaFreniere, "Evolutionary Functions of Social Play: Life Histories, Sex Differences, and Emotion Regulation," *American Journal of Play* 3, no. 4 (2011): 464–488.

Sergio Pellis and Vivien Pellis, *The Playful Brain: Venturing to the Limits of Neuroscience* (London: Oneworld Publications, 2013).

Peter Gray, *Free to Learn: Why Unleashing the Instinct to Play Will Make Our Children Happier, More Self-Reliant, and Better Students for Life* (New York: Basic Books, 2015).

Jane E. Barker, Andrei D. Semenov, Laura Michaelson, Lindsay S. Provan, Hannah R. Snyder, and Yuko Munakata, "Less-Structured Time in Children's Daily Lives Predicts Self-Directed Executive Functioning," *Frontiers in Psychology* 5 (2014).

Roberta M. Golinkoff and Kathy Hirsh-Pasek, *Becoming Brilliant: What Science Tells Us About Raising Successful Children* (Washington, DC: American Psychological Association, 2016).

Sandra L. Hofferth and John F. Sandberg, "Changes in American Children's Time, 1981–1997," in *Children at the Millennium: Where Have We Come From? Where Are We Going?*, vol. 6, edited by Timothy Owens and Sandra L. Hofferth (Oxford: Elsevier Science/JAI, 2001), 193–229.

Sandra L. Hofferth, "Changes in American Children's Time: 1997 to 2003," *Electronic International Journal of Time Use Research* 6, no. 1 (2009): 26.

"America's Tutor Boom: By the Numbers," *The Week,* October 13, 2011, http://theweek.com/articles/481041/americas-tutor-boom-by-numbers.

Liz Moyer, "Tutoring Kids: The Pressure Is On," *Wall Street Journal,* The Juggle Blog, October 13, 2011.

Richie Poulton, Terrie E. Moffitt, and Phil A. Silva, "The Dunedin Multidisciplinary Health and Development Study: Overview of the First 40 Years, with an Eye to the Future," *Social Psychiatry and Psychiatric Epidemiology* 50, no. 5 (2015): 679–693.

Richie Poulton, Simon Davies, Ross G. Menzies, John D. Langley, and Phil A. Silva, "Evidence for a Non-Associative Model of the Acquisition of a Fear of Heights," *Behaviour Research and Therapy* 36, no. 5 (1998): 537–544.

Richie Poulton, Ross G. Menzies, Michelle G. Craske, John D. Langley, and Phil A. Silva, "Water Trauma and Swimming Experiences Up to Age 9 and Fear of Water at Age 18: A Longitudinal Study," *Behaviour Research and Therapy* 37, no. 1 (1999): 39–48.

Richie Poulton, Barry J. Milne, Michelle G. Craske, and Ross G. Menzies, "A Longitudinal Study of the Etiology of Separation Anxiety," *Behaviour Research and Therapy* 39, no. 12 (2001): 1395–1410.

Chapter 3: The Brain and Discipline

Joseph Ledoux, *Synaptic Self: How Our Brains Become Who We Are* (New York: Viking Adult, 2002).

Joseph Ledoux, *The Emotional Brain: The Mysterious Underpinnings of Emotional Life* (New York: Simon & Schuster, 1996).

Daniel J. Siegel and Tina Payne Bryson, *The Whole-Brain Child: 12 Revolutionary Strategies to Nurture Your Child's Developing Mind* (New York: Delacorte Press, 2011).

Harry T. Chugani, Michael E. Behen, Otto Muzik, Csaba Juhász, Ferenc Nagy, and Diane C. Chugani, "Local Brain Functional Activity Following Early Deprivation: A Study of Postinstitutionalized Romanian Orphans," *Neuroimage* 14, no. 6 (2001): 1290–1301.

Vincent J. Felitti, Robert F. Anda, Dale Nordenberg, David F. Williamson, Alison M. Spitz, Valerie Edwards, Mary P. Koss, and James S. Marks, "Relationship of Childhood Abuse and Household Dysfunction to Many of the Leading Causes of Death in Adults: The Adverse

Childhood Experiences (ACE) Study," *American Journal of Preventive Medicine* 14, no. 4 (1998): 245–258.

Other resources that are helpful for understanding the ACE study include: Centers for Disease Control and Prevention (CDC), "Adverse Childhood Experiences (ACEs)," www.cdc.gov/violenceprevention /acestudy/; and ACES Too High News, "ACEs Science 101: ACEs Science FAQs," https://acestoohigh.com/aces-101/.

Nadine Burke Harris, "How Childhood Trauma Affects Health Across a Lifetime," Ted talk video, posted to YouTube September 2014, https:// www.ted.com/talks/nadine_burke_harris_how_childhood_trauma _affects_health_across_a_lifetime/transcript?language=en.

Gershoff, Elizabeth Thompson Gershoff, "Corporal Punishment by Parents and Associated Child Behaviors and Experiences: A Meta-analytic and Theoretical Review," *Psychological Bulletin* 128, no. 4 (2002): 539.

Ming-Te Wang and Sarah Kenny, "Longitudinal Links Between Fathers' and Mothers' Harsh Verbal Discipline and Adolescents' Conduct Problems and Depressive Symptoms," *Child Development* 85, no. 3 (2014): 908–923.

James A. Coan, Hillary S. Schaefer, and Richard J. Davidson, "Lending a Hand: Social Regulation of the Neural Response to Threat," *Psychological Science* 17, no. 12 (2006): 1032–1039.

George W. Brown, G. Morris Carstairs, and Gillian Topping, "Post-hospital Adjustment of Chronic Mental Patients," *The Lancet* 272, no. 7048 (1958): 685–689.

Jill M. Hooley, "Expressed Emotion and Relapse of Psychopathology," *Annual Review of Clinical Psychology* 3 (2007): 329–352.

Criticism and the Course of Mental Disorders," in *Social Neuroscience: Brain, Mind, and Society,* edited by Russell K. Schutt, Larry J. Seidman, and Matcheri S. Keshavan (Cambridge, MA: Harvard University Press, 2015).

Jill M. Hooley and John D. Teasdale, "Predictors of Relapse in Unipolar Depressives: Expressed Emotion, Marital Distress, and Perceived Criticism," *Journal of Abnormal Psychology* 98, no. 3 (1989): 229.

Jill M. Hooley, Staci A. Gruber, Laurie A. Scott, Jordan B. Hiller, and Deborah A. Yurgelun-Todd, "Activation in Dorsolateral Prefrontal Cortex in Response to Maternal Criticism and Praise in Recovered Depressed and Healthy Control Participants," *Biological Psychiatry* 57, no. 7 (2005): 809–812.

Jill M. Hooley, Greg Siegle, and Staci A. Gruber, "Affective and Neural Reactivity to Criticism in Individuals High and Low on Perceived Criticism," *PLoS One* 7, no. 9 (2012): e44412.

Jill M. Hooley and David J. Miklowitz, "Perceived Criticism in the Treatment of a High-Risk Adolescent," *Journal of Clinical Psychology* 73, no. 5 (2017): 570–578.

Jill M. Hooley, Staci A. Gruber, Holly A. Parker, Julien Guillaumot, Jadwiga Rogowska, and Deborah A. Yurgelun-Todd, "Cortico-Limbic

Response to Personally Challenging Emotional Stimuli After Complete Recovery from Depression," *Psychiatry Research: Neuroimaging* 171, no. 2 (2009): 106–119.

Olivia L. Conner, Greg J. Siegle, Ashley M. McFarland, Jennifer S. Silk, Cecile D. Ladouceur, Ronald E. Dahl, James A. Coan, and Neal D. Ryan, "Mom—It Helps When You're Right Here! Attenuation of Neural Stress Markers in Anxious Youths Whose Caregivers Are Present During fMRI," *PloS One* 7, no. 12 (2012): e50680.

Edward L. Deci, Nancy H. Spiegel, Richard M. Ryan, Richard Koestner, and Manette Kauffman, "Effects of Performance Standards on Teaching Styles: Behavior of Controlling Teachers," *Journal of Educational Psychology* 74, no. 6 (1982): 852.

Edward L. Deci, John Nezlek, and Louise Sheinman, "Characteristics of the Rewarder and Intrinsic Motivation of the Rewardee," *Journal of Personality and Social Psychology* 40, no. 1 (1981): 1.

Edward L. Deci, Allan J. Schwartz, Louise Sheinman, and Richard M. Ryan, "An Instrument to Assess Adults' Orientations Toward Control Versus Autonomy with Children: Reflections on Intrinsic Motivation and Perceived Competence," *Journal of Educational Psychology* 73, no. 5 (1981): 642.

Kathleen E. Anderson, Hugh Lytton, and David M. Romney, "Mothers' Interactions with Normal and Conduct-Disordered Boys: Who Affects Whom?" *Developmental Psychology* 22, no. 5 (1986): 604.

Chapter 4: The Old Methods Don't Work

Hesiod, *Works and Days,* 174, translation available at http://www.perseus .tufts.edu/hopper/text?doc=hes.+wd+180.

Julie Bort, Aviva Pflock, and Devra Renner, *Mommy Guilt: Learn to Worry Less, Focus on What Matters Most, and Raise Happier Kids* (New York: American Management Association/AMACOM Books, 2005).

Judith Warner, *Perfect Madness: Motherhood in the Age of Anxiety* (New York: Riverhead Books, 2005).

Diana Baumrind, "Effects of Authoritative Parental Control on Child Behavior," *Child Development* (1966): 887–907.

Avidan Milevsky, Melissa Schlechter, Sarah Netter, and Danielle Keehn, "Maternal and Paternal Parenting Styles in Adolescents: Associations with Self-Esteem, Depression, and Life-Satisfaction," *Journal of Child and Family Studies* 16, no. 1 (2007): 39–47.

Koen Luyckx, Elizabeth A. Tildesley, Bart Soenens, Judy A. Andrews, Sarah E. Hampson, Missy Peterson, and Bart Duriez, "Parenting and Trajectories of Children's Maladaptive Behaviors: A 12-Year Prospective Community Study," *Journal of Clinical Child and Adolescent Psychology* 40, no. 3 (2011): 468–478.

Laurence Steinberg, Susie D. Lamborn, Sanford M. Dornbusch, and Nancy Darling, "Impact of Parenting Practices on Adolescent Achievement:

Authoritative Parenting, School Involvement, and Encouragement to Succeed," *Child Development* 63, no. 5 (1992): 1266–1281.

The data on working mothers come from the Bureau of Labor Statistics and a Pew Research Center analysis of American Time Use Survey data.

For a description of the University of Michigan's Panel Study of Income Dynamics, see the PSID website at https://psidonline.isr.umich.edu /Studies.aspx.

Melissa A. Milkie, Kei M. Nomaguchi, and Kathleen E. Denny, "Does the Amount of Time Mothers Spend with Children or Adolescents Matter?" *Journal of Marriage and Family* 77, no. 2 (2015): 355–372.

Carol S. Dweck, *Mindset: The New Psychology of Success* (New York: Random House, 2006).

Angela Duckworth, *Grit: The Power of Passion and Perseverance* (New York: Scribner, 2016).

Daniel H. Pink, *Drive: The Surprising Truth About What Motivates Us* (New York: Riverhead Books, 2009).

Nadine M. Lambert, Jonathan Sandoval, and Dana Sassone, "Prevalence of Hyperactivity in Elementary School Children as a Function of Social System Definers," *American Journal of Orthopsychiatry* 48, no. 3 (1978): 446.

Patricia N. Pastor, Cynthia A. Reuben, Catherine R. Duran, and LaJeana D. Hawkins, "Association Between Diagnosed ADHD and Selected Characteristics Among Children Aged 4–17 Years: United States, 2011–2013," NCHS Data Brief 201 (Hyattsville, MD: National Center for Health Statistics, May 2015).

Jeffrey P. Brosco and Anna Bona, "Changes in Academic Demands and Attention-Deficit/Hyperactivity Disorder in Young Children," *JAMA Pediatrics* 170, no. 4 (2016): 396–397.

Harris Cooper, Jorgianne Civey Robinson, and Erika A. Patall, "Does Homework Improve Academic Achievement? A Synthesis of Research, 1987–2003," *Review of Educational Research* 76, no. 1 (2006): 1–62.

Chapter 5: The Way Forward

Vicki Hoefle, *Duct Tape Parenting: A Less Is More Approach to Raising Respectful, Responsible, and Resilient Kids* (New York: Routledge, 2012).

The data on sleep are from National Sleep Foundation, "National Sleep Foundation 2014 Sleep in America Poll Finds Children Sleep Better When Parents Establish Rules, Limit Technology, and Set a Good Example," March 3, 2014, https://sleepfoundation.org/media-center /press-release/national-sleep-foundation-2014-sleep-america-poll-finds -children-sleep.

Candice A. Alfano and Amanda L. Gamble, "The Role of Sleep in Childhood Psychiatric Disorders," *Child and Youth Care Forum* 38, no. 6 (2009): 327–340.

Natalie D. Riediger, Rgia A. Othman, Miyoung Suh, and Mohammed H. Moghadasian, "A Systemic Review of the Roles of n-3 Fatty Acids in

Health and Disease," *Journal of the American Dietetic Association* 109, no. 4 (2009): 668–679.

Lisa M. Bodnar and Katherine L. Wisner, "Nutrition and Depression: Implications for Improving Mental Health Among Childbearing-Aged Women," *Biological Psychiatry* 58, no. 9 (2005): 679–685.

Edward L. Deci, Richard Koestner, and Richard M. Ryan, "A Meta-analytic Review of Experiments Examining the Effects of Extrinsic Rewards on Intrinsic Motivation," *Psychological Bulletin* 125, no. 6 (1999): 627–668.

Edward L. Deci, "Effects of Externally Mediated Rewards on Intrinsic Motivation," *Journal of Personality and Social Psychology* 18, no. 1 (1971): 105–115.

Richard M. Ryan, "Control and Information in the Intrapersonal Sphere: An Extension of Cognitive Evaluation Theory," *Journal of Personality and Social Psychology* 43, no. 3 (1982): 450–461.

Rudolf Dreikurs, with Vicki Stolz, *Children: The Challenge: The Classic Work on Improving Parent-Child Relations—Intelligent, Humane, and Eminently Practical* (New York: Plume 1991).

Betty Lou Bettner and Amy Lew, *Raising Kids Who Can: Use Good Judgment, Assume Responsibility, Communicate, Effectively Respect Self and Others, Co-operate, Develop Self-esteem, and Enjoy Life* (Media, PA: Connexions Press, 1990).

Chapter 6: Connection

Myron A. Hofer, "Hidden Regulators in Attachment, Separation, and Loss," *Monographs of the Society for Research in Child Development* 59, nos. 2–3 (1994): 192–207.

Myron A. Hofer, "Maternal Separation Affects Infant Rats' Behavior," *Behavioral Biology* 9, no. 5 (1973): 629–633.

Danya Glaser, "Child Abuse and Neglect and the Brain: A Review." *Journal of Child Psychology and Psychiatry and Allied Disciplines* 41, no. 1 (2000): 97–116.

Betty Hart and Todd R. Risley, "The Early Catastrophe: The 30 Million Word Gap by Age 3," *American Educator* 27, no. 1 (2003): 4–9.

Public high school graduation rates are taken from National Center for Education Statistics, "Public High School Graduate Rates," updated April 2017, https://nces.ed.gov/programs/coe/indicator_coi.asp.

The statistics on the achievement gap are from The Achievement Gap Initiative at Harvard University, "Facts on Achievement Gaps," http://www.agi.harvard.edu/projects/FactsonAchievementGaps.pdf.

Chapter 7: Communication

Ross W. Greene, *The Explosive Child: A New Approach for Understanding and Parenting Easily Frustrated, Chronically Inflexible Children* (New York: HarperCollins, 1998).

Ross W. Greene, *Lost at School: Why Our Kids with Behavioral Challenges Are Falling Through the Cracks and How We Can Help Them* (New York: Scribner, 2008).

Shaun Ho, Sara Konrath, Stephanie Brown, and James E. Swain, "Empathy and Stress Related Neural Responses in Maternal Decision Making," *Frontiers in Neuroscience* 8 (2014).

Sara H. Konrath, William J. Chopik, Courtney K. Hsing, and Ed O'Brien, "Changes in Adult Attachment Styles in American College Students over Time: A Meta-analysis," *Personality and Social Psychology Review* 18, no. 4 (2014): 326–348.

Thomas H. Ollendick, Ross W. Greene, Kristin E. Austin, Maria G. Fraire, Thorhildur Halldorsdottir, Kristy Benoit Allen, Matthew A. Jarrett, et al., "Parent Management Training and Collaborative and Proactive Solutions: A Randomized Control Trial for Oppositional Youth," *Journal of Clinical Child and Adolescent Psychology* 45, no. 5 (2016): 591–604.

Chapter 8: Capability

Heidi R. Riggio, Ann Marie Valenzuela, and Dana A. Weiser, "Household Responsibilities in the Family of Origin: Relations with Self-efficacy in Young Adulthood," *Personality and Individual Differences* 48, no. 5 (2010): 568–573.

Marty Rossman, "Involving Children in Household Tasks: Is It Worth the Effort?" University of Minnesota, College of Education and Human Development, September 2002, http://ww1.prweb.com/prfiles /2014/02/22/11608927/children-with-chores-at-home-University-of -Minnesota.pdf.

Suicide and self-harm data are taken from CDC, National Center for Injury Prevention and Control, "Injury Prevention and Control: Welcome to WISQARS™," www.cdc.gov/injury/wisqars (accessed August 17, 2017).

Rashelle J. Musci, Catherine P. Bradshaw, Brion Maher, George R. Uhl, Sheppard G. Kellam, and Nicholas S. Ialongo, "Reducing Aggression and Impulsivity Through School-Based Prevention Programs: A Gene by Intervention Interaction," *Prevention Science* 15, no. 6 (2014): 831–840.

Depeng Jiang, Rob Santos, Teresa Mayer, and Leanne Boyd, "Latent Transition Analysis for Program Evaluation with Multivariate Longitudinal Outcomes," in *Quantitative Psychology Research,* edited by L. A. van der Ark, D. M. Bolt, W.-C. Wang, J. A. Douglas, and M. Wiberg, proceedings of the 80th annual meeting of the Psychometric Society, Beijing, 2015 (Springer International Publishing, 2016), 377–388.

Kenneth A. Dodge and Nicki R. Crick, "Social Information-Processing Bases of Aggressive Behavior in Children," *Personality and Social Psychology Bulletin* 16, no. 1 (1990): 8–22.

Chapter 9: Limits and Routines

Jane Nelsen, *Positive Discipline: The Classic Guide to Helping Children Develop Self-Discipline, Responsibility, Cooperation, and Problem-Solving Skills* (New York: Ballantine, 2006).

Sara Bennett and Nancy Kalish, *The Case Against Homework: How Homework Is Hurting Our Children and What We Can Do About It* (New York: Crown Publishers, 2006).

Alfie Kohn, *The Homework Myth: Why Our Kids Get Too Much of a Bad Thing* (Cambridge, MA: Da Capo Press, 2006).

Emory Luce Baldwin and Linda E. Jessup, *Parenting with Courage and Uncommon Sense,* 3rd ed. (CreateSpace Independent Publishing Platform, 2015).

Chapter 10: Modeling

Julie Lythcott-Haims, *How to Raise an Adult: Break Free of the Overparenting Trap and Prepare Your Kid for Success* (New York: Henry Holt and Co., 2015).

Jessica Lahey, *The Gift of Failure: How the Best Parents Learn to Let Go So Their Children Can Succeed* (New York: HarperCollins, 2015).

Ronald C. Kessler, Patricia A. Berglund, Olga Demler, Robert Jin, Kathleen R. Merikangas, and Ellen E. Walters, "Lifetime Prevalence and Age-of-Onset Distributions of DSM-IV Disorders in the National Comorbidity Survey Replication (NCS-R)," *Archives of General Psychiatry* 62, no. 6 (June 2005): 593–602.

Mental health prevalence data are taken from National Institute of Mental Health (NIMH), "Questions and Answers About the National Comorbidity Survey Replication (NCSR) Study," www.nimh.nih.gov /health/topics/ncsr-study/questions-and-answers-about-the-national -comorbidity-survey-replication-ncsr-study.shtml.

Research results on meditation benefits are available at National Center for Complementary and Integrative Health, "Meditation: In Depth," https://nccih.nih.gov/health/meditation/overview.htm.

Kevin W. Chen, Christine C. Berger, Eric Manheimer, et al., "Meditative Therapies for Reducing Anxiety: A Systematic Review and Meta-analysis of Randomized Controlled Trials," *Depression and Anxiety* 29, no. 7 (2012): 545–562.

Madhav Goyal, Sonal Singh, Erica M. S. Sibinga, et al., "Meditation Programs for Psychological Stress and Well-being: A Systematic Review and Meta-analysis," *JAMA Internal Medicine* 174, no. 3 (2014): 357–368.

Jason C. Ong, Rachel Manber, Zindel Segal, et al., "A Randomized Controlled Trial of Mindfulness Meditation for Chronic Insomnia," *Sleep* 37, no. 9 (2014): 1553–1563.

Chapter 11: Create Lasting Change

Charles Duhigg, *The Power of Habit: Why We Do What We Do in Life and Business* (New York: Random House, 2012).

Jennifer Wyatt Kaminski, Linda Anne Valle, Jill H. Filene, and Cynthia L. Boyle, "A Meta-analytic Review of Components Associated with Parent Training Program Effectiveness," *Journal of Abnormal Child Psychology* 36, no. 4 (2008): 567–589.

Index

KATHERINE REYNOLDS LEWIS is an award-winning journalist and certified parent educator who regularly writes for *The Atlantic, Fortune, USA Today*'s magazine group, the *Washington Post, and Working Mother* magazine. Her byline has also appeared in *Bloomberg Businessweek, MSN Money, Money,* the *New York Times, Parade, Slate,* and the *Washington Post Magazine.* She has received fellowships from the Carey Institute for Global Good, the National Press Foundation, the Poynter Institute, and the University of Maryland's Casey Journalism Center. Residencies include Le Moulin à Nef, Ragdale, and the Virginia Center for the Creative Arts. Previously, she worked as a national correspondent for Newhouse News Service and Bloomberg News, after graduating cum laude from Harvard University with a physics degree. She lives in the Washington, DC, area with her husband and their three children. For more information, visit www .KatherineRLewis.com.

PublicAffairs is a publishing house founded in 1997. It is a tribute to the standards, values, and flair of three persons who have served as mentors to countless reporters, writers, editors, and book people of all kinds, including me.

I. F. STONE, proprietor of *I. F. Stone's Weekly*, combined a commitment to the First Amendment with entrepreneurial zeal and reporting skill and became one of the great independent journalists in American history. At the age of eighty, Izzy published *The Trial of Socrates*, which was a national bestseller. He wrote the book after he taught himself ancient Greek.

BENJAMIN C. BRADLEE was for nearly thirty years the charismatic editorial leader of *The Washington Post*. It was Ben who gave the *Post* the range and courage to pursue such historic issues as Watergate. He supported his reporters with a tenacity that made them fearless and it is no accident that so many became authors of influential, best-selling books.

ROBERT L. BERNSTEIN, the chief executive of Random House for more than a quarter century, guided one of the nation's premier publishing houses. Bob was personally responsible for many books of political dissent and argument that challenged tyranny around the globe. He is also the founder and longtime chair of Human Rights Watch, one of the most respected human rights organizations in the world.

. . .

For fifty years, the banner of Public Affairs Press was carried by its owner Morris B. Schnapper, who published Gandhi, Nasser, Toynbee, Truman, and about 1,500 other authors. In 1983, Schnapper was described by *The Washington Post* as "a redoubtable gadfly." His legacy will endure in the books to come.

Peter Osnos, *Founder*